CW00617661

Theology after the Birth of God

Radical Theologies

Radical Theologies is a call for transformational theologies that break out of traditional locations and approaches. The rhizomic ethos of radical theologies enable the series to engage with an ever-expanding radical expression and critique of theologies that have entered or seek to enter the public sphere, arising from the continued turn to religion and especially radical theology in politics, social sciences, philosophy, theory, cultural, and literary studies. The post-theistic theology both driving and arising from these intersections is the focus of this series.

Series Editors

Mike Grimshaw is associate professor of Sociology at Canterbury University in New Zealand.

Michael Zbaraschuk is lecturer at the University of Washington, Tacoma, and visiting assistant professor at Pacific Lutheran University.

Joshua Ramey is visiting assistant professor at Haverford College.

Religion, Politics, and the Earth: The New Materialism
By Clayton Crockett and Jeffrey W. Robbins

The Apocalyptic Trinity
By Thomas J. J. Altizer

Foucault/Paul: Subjects of Power
By Sophie Fuggle

A Non-Philosophical Theory of Nature: Ecologies of Thought
By Anthony Paul Smith

On Philosophy as a Spiritual Exercise: A Symposium
By Philip Goodchild

The Counter-Narratives of Radical Theology and Rock 'n' Roll: Songs of Fear and Trembling
Edited by Michael Grimshaw

Theology after the Birth of God: Atheist Conceptions in Cognition and Culture
By F. LeRon Shults

THEOLOGY AFTER THE BIRTH OF GOD

ATHEIST CONCEPTIONS IN COGNITION AND CULTURE

F. LeRon Shults

palgrave
macmillan

First published in 2014 by
PALGRAVE MACMILLAN®
in the United States—a division of St. Martin's Press LLC,
175 Fifth Avenue, New York, NY 10010.

Where this book is distributed in the UK, Europe and the rest of the world,
this is by Palgrave Macmillan, a division of Macmillan Publishers Limited,
registered in England, company number 785998, of Houndmills,
Basingstoke, Hampshire RG21 6XS.

Palgrave Macmillan is the global academic imprint of the above companies
and has companies and representatives throughout the world.

Palgrave® and Macmillan® are registered trademarks in the United States,
the United Kingdom, Europe and other countries.

ISBN 978-1-349-47336-6   ISBN 978-1-137-35803-5 (eBook)
DOI 10.1057/9781137358035

Library of Congress Cataloging-in-Publication Data

Shults, F. LeRon.
    Theology after the birth of God : Atheist conceptions in
cognition and culture / F. LeRon Shults.
        pages cm
    Includes bibliographical references and index.
    1. Religion—Philosophy. 2. God. 3. Gods. 4. Theology.
    5. Atheism. I. Title.

BL51.S5246 2014
211—dc23   2014002190

A catalogue record of the book is available from the British Library.

Design by Newgen Knowledge Works (P) Ltd., Chennai, India.

First edition: August 2014

10 9 8 7 6 5 4 3 2 1

For Wesley J. Wildman

Contents

Illustrations

Series Preface

Radical Theologies encompasses the intersections of constructive theology, secular theology, death of god theologies, political theologies, continental thought, and contemporary culture.

For too long, radical theology has been wandering in the wilderness, while other forms of theological discourse have been pontificating to increasingly smaller audiences. However, there has been a cross-disciplinary rediscovery and turn to radical theologies as locations from which to engage with the multiplicities of twenty-first–century society, wherein the radical voice is also increasingly a theologically engaged voice with the recovery and rediscovery of radical theology as that which speaks the critique of "truth to power".

Radical Theologies reintroduces radical theological discourse into the public eye, debate, and discussion by covering the engagement of radical theology with culture, society, literature, politics, philosophy, and the discipline of religion.

Providing an outlet for those writing and thinking at the intersections of these areas with radical theology, *Radical Theologies* expresses an interdisciplinary engagement and approach that was being undertaken without a current series to situate itself within. This series, the first dedicated to radical theology, is also dedicated to redefining the very terms of theology as a concept and practice.

Just as rhizomic thought engages with multiplicities and counters dualistic and prescriptive approaches, this series offers a timely outlet for an expanding field of "breakout" radical theologies that seek to redefine the very terms of theology. This includes work on and about the so-labeled death of god theologies and theologians who emerged in the 1960s and those who follow in their wake. Other radical theologies emerge from what can be termed underground theologies and also a/theological foundations. All share the aim and expression of breaking out of walls previously ideologically invisible.

Chapter 1

The gods Are Born—and We Have Borne Them

Crazy people are often difficult to ignore, especially when they are yelling provocative things like "God is dead" in the midst of a busy marketplace. The madman in Nietzsche's famous aphorism, however, despite the intensity of his message and style of delivery, was met with relative indifference. When they heard him crying out that he was looking for God, some of the nonbelievers paused long enough to tease him: Has God lost his way like a child? Is he afraid of us? Has he emigrated? The madman jumped into their midst, piercing them with his eyes. "Where is God?" he cried; "I'll tell you! God is dead! God remains dead! And we have killed him...We are all his murderers. But how did we do this? How were we able to drink up the sea? Who gave us the sponge to wipe away the entire horizon?...Are we not continually falling? And backwards, sidewards, forwards, in all directions? Is there still an up and a down? Aren't we straying as though through an infinite nothing?" The crowd just looked at him—a bit disconcerted, but silent. Smashing his lantern on the ground, the madman sighed: "I come too early...my time is not yet."[1]

No doubt many readers will have jumped past the quotations in the first paragraph, skipping ahead to this one to see if it offers anything more interesting. We've all heard this before. Claims about the death of God are deathly boring. Depending on whether or not one is an active participant within a religious in-group, such proclamations seem either obviously wrong or wrongly obvious. The message that "God is dead" gets surprisingly little traction in our mental and social worlds. It lacks sex appeal. For reasons we will explore in detail below, the idea of divine *genitality* is much more interesting—and disturbing—than the idea of divine *mortality*. Insights from a wide variety of scientific disciplines are converging to help explain how gods are conceived within human minds and nurtured within human groups as a result of naturally evolved, hypersensitive cognitive and coalitional tendencies that produce perceptual errors and cultivate out-group antagonism. The theoretical and practical relevance of this message will make it much more difficult to ignore.

Nietzsche also portrays the madman as bursting into churches and singing *requiem aeternam deo* (grant God eternal rest). Even there, among the believers, he is met relatively calmly and politely ushered out. Business—and church—carry on as usual. For the most part, the academic discipline of theology has also carried on as usual. Like many other modern masters of suspicion, as well as the "new atheists," Nietzsche goes out of his way to criticize the problematic assumptions and deleterious consequences of monotheism, especially the slave morality of the Christian religion. Yet, theologians bound to such coalitions have found it surprisingly easy to immunize themselves from such challenges. Even within the academy and the public sphere, they go on appealing to the authoritative revelations of the supernatural agents putatively engaged in the religious rituals of their own groups. A growing number of scholars within other disciplines, as well as policy makers within pluralistic contexts, find this so annoying that they are tempted to ban theology from the marketplace of ideas.

This temptation is especially strong for atheists, and understandably so. However, I will argue for a different sort of atheistic strategy as well as a different atheistic message—both of which emerge out of philosophical reflection on empirical findings and theoretical developments within the biocultural study of religion. All of this will require a reconceptualization of religion, theology, and atheism. In the sense in which I will use the term, *religion* has characterized small-scale human groups for at least the past sixty thousand years. *Theology*, on the other hand, only emerged during the first millennium BCE within socioecological niches that required new ways of adapting to the increased psychological and political pressures of life in more heavily populated, complex literate states.

A specific conception of "God"—an infinite person with an eternal plan for human groups—has played a central role in the (re)production of the major religious traditions that trace their roots to the West Asian axial age. However, as many reflective individuals within and around those traditions have repeatedly pointed out, albeit for different reasons and with varying degrees of intensity, this idea is simply unbearable. Nevertheless, like the members of the religious coalitions they serve, most theologians, grinning or not, have continued trying to bear it.

Why Is Nietzsche's Madman So Easy to Ignore?

God seems to have survived his death without much difficulty. Why do religious people find it so easy to dismiss the idea that "God is dead"? The problem was not that the madman had come too early. No, if his goal was to disrupt people's reliance on supernatural agents to make sense of the world and act sensibly in society, as they stray "as though through an infinite nothing," he had the wrong message. Had the madman read carefully through the last couple of decades of scientific literature in the biocultural study of religion, he would proclaim instead that *the gods are born—and we have borne them!* As we will see, this message opens up a new way of conceiving *atheism* as a positive force, rather than merely as a negative reaction to (mono)theism. In fact, one of the negative implications of the latter, often taken as "gospel" by members of religious coalitions, is that humans can *not* adequately interpret the natural world or appropriately inscribe the social world without help from imagined disembodied intentional forces. *Atheism*, on the other hand, is conceived as an affirmation: yes, we can. Or, at least, we can live trying.

But why is it so difficult to engender atheism? The reasons why most people seem impervious to objections to the notion of a personal God who cares for their own group can be clarified by a set of hypotheses that have emerged within and across disciplines such as evolutionary biology, cognitive science, neuropsychology, archaeology, cultural anthropology, behavioral ecology, political economics, and comparative religion. Theoretical insights from these (and many other) fields, which contribute to what I will call the *biocultural* study of religion, are converging to support the claim that supernatural agent conceptions are naturally reproduced in human thought as a result of evolved *cognitive* mechanisms that hyperactively detect agency when confronted with ambiguous phenomena and, once conceived, are culturally nurtured as a result of evolved *coalitional* mechanisms that hyperactively protect in-group cohesion. These tendencies are part of our phylogenetic and cultural heritage.

In other words, gods are easily "born" in human minds and "borne" in human cultures today because contemporary *Homo sapiens* share a suite of perceptual and affiliational dispositions that were naturally selected in early ancestral environments where the survival advantage went to hominids who were able to quickly detect relevant agents such as predators, prey, protectors, and partners in the *natural* milieu, and who lived in groups whose cohesion was adequately protected by attachment and surveillance systems that discouraged defecting, cheating, and freeloading in the *social* milieu. In chapter 2, I will return to these two sorts of theogonic (god-bearing) mechanisms, which I call *anthropomorphic promiscuity* and *sociographic prudery*, and outline the ways in which they reciprocally reinforce each other in the ongoing reproduction of gods in groups. As we will see, these evolved defaults aided human survival in a variety of ways, solidifying personal identity and enforcing social order. However, this is also true of other tendencies that seem to come to us "naturally," such as racism, sexism, and classism. Such biases may have helped bind selves and societies together for millennia, but this does not mean that we have to hold onto these old habits as we continue adapting within (and altering) our rapidly changing late modern environments.

Of course, the original message of Nietzsche's madman has not been completely ignored. Some conservative Christian theologians reacted by appealing to classical apologetic proofs (God cannot be dead because his existence must be thought) or to contemporary spiritual experiences (God cannot be dead because his presence is actually felt). Some liberal theologians tried to incorporate the madman's proclamation directly into their doctrinal constructions: the death of God *is* thinkable, but only as a moment of divine "self-emptying" disclosed in the cross of (a now resurrected) Christ. Thomas Altizer, whose *Apocalyptic Trinity* was an earlier volume in the Radical Theologies series in which the present book appears, has been a central player in the "secular" theology movement since the 1960s. In *The Gospel of Christian Atheism*, he argued that it was through the "self-annihilation" of the "originally transcendent" God, who became "fully and totally" incarnate in Christ, that humans now "truly know this divine process of negativity."[2]

Insights from the biocultural sciences of religion can help us understand why this "death of God" movement died out so quickly, leaving room for a whole host of "post-secular" proposals for faith in a "weak" biblical God who suffers with his people.[3] For reasons we will examine in the following chapters, the latter sort of proposal is more easily embraced within local religious communities than the former. Assertions about the alleged moribundity of God are so maximally counterintuitive that they do not even distract people from their practical work in the marketplace, much less disrupt their ecclesiastical rituals. The role played by gods in the shared imagination of religious groups makes their death (nearly) unthinkable. The radical theology I advocate here is not another search for an "authentic" version of Christianity—or any other religious coalition whose cohesion depends on the revelation of (and ritual engagement with) supernatural agents. On the contrary, I will argue that after the discovery of the "birth of God," theology can now follow a radically atheist trajectory that has long been suppressed within it.

For reasons I hope to make clear, the challenges and opportunities faced by *postpartum* theology will be very different than those of *postmortem* theology. The critiques of religion (and theology) that have emerged out of the biocultural sciences are significantly different than those leveled by Nietzsche, Feuerbach, Marx, Freud, and other twentieth-century skeptics. They are not simply newer versions of classical *projection* critiques, which have been surprisingly easy for religious people to dodge. The various scientific models we will explore in the following chapters could more properly be called *detection/protection* theories of religion. They unveil the very mechanisms that have enabled the religious evasion of complaints about anxiety-based projections.

Human beings evolved to detect other agents and to protect their own groups, but the integration and intensification of these hypersensitive tendencies led to the mistaken detection and violent protection of supernatural agent coalitions. The instincts behind these theories are not wholly new. At one point, Nietzsche himself suggested that what led to belief in "another world" among early humans "was *not* a drive or need, but an *error* in the interpretation of certain natural events, an embarrassing lapse of the intellect."[4] Decades earlier, Feuerbach had criticized the Christian religion not only for its anxious projection of a transcendent divine father figure, but also for its limitation of the allegedly universal love of God to a particular group.[5] What the combined insights of the biocultural study of religion provide, however, are *empirically based* scientific theories that explain the *actual mechanisms* that lead to the *generation* of religious conceptions in human cognition and to their *reproduction* in human cultures.

Bearing gods in Cognition and Culture

It should be clear enough by now that my use of the term *bearing* is meant to do double duty, indicating the way in which gods are both *born* in human cognition (due to an overactive detection of agency) and *borne* in human cultures (due to an overactive protection of coalitions). The concept of *gods*, however, calls for further clarification. In common parlance, the term "god" usually evokes images of (male) Greek deities, Buddhist devas, or even the "God" of the Abrahamic monotheisms. Among scholars operating within the biocultural study of religion, however, it is a common practice to use the label "gods" as a shorthand way of referring to all kinds of culturally postulated discarnate entities, including animal spirits, ancestor ghosts, angels, bodhisattvas, and jinn, as well as more powerful divine beings like Zeus, Yahweh, or Vishnu. For the sake of this multidisciplinary dialogue, I will follow this practice, using the terms *god* and *supernatural agent* interchangeably as designations for any putative disembodied (or contingently embodied) force that is attributed intentionality (or related person-like qualities) and imaginatively engaged in ways that bear on the normative judgments of a human coalition.

Supernatural agents multiply like rabbits in the human Imaginarium, reproducing rapidly in fertile cognitive fields cultivated by participation in religious rituals. But only some of these god conceptions have been domesticated and bred across generations: those that are imaginatively engaged in ways that reinforce cooperation and commitment in human groups. For reasons we will explore in detail below, the reproductive success of this sort of supernatural agent within (some) *Homo sapiens* coalitions during the Upper Paleolithic provided a survival advantage to the individuals within them. Eventually some of these small, "god-bearing" groups moved out of Africa and into the Levant. Their genetic offspring outcompeted all other hominid species and spread across the continent into Asia and Europe, and eventually into Australia and the Americas. Their descendants—all living humans—share a phylogenetic inheritance, reinforced by millennia of social entrainment practices, that predisposes them to keep on bearing gods.

Making sense of these complex phenomena, which are shaped by the *reciprocal* interaction of cognitive *and* cultural dynamics, requires the integration of insights from a wide variety of perspectives. Some scholars within the social sciences and humanities looking over the disciplinary wall at scientists in fields like evolutionary psychology have worried about a rigid biological reductionism that would render their own fields irrelevant. Some cognitive scientists looking back over the wall have worried about a relativist social constructivism that does not take their own fields seriously. One still finds these extreme positions in some circles, but, as the suspicion on both sides has begun to subside, new conceptual space is being created and explored using new experimental methods that embrace explanatory pluralism.[6] Biology and culture, genes and memes, brains and groups are so entangled in mutual resolving evolutionary processes that they can only be explained together.

My use of the phrase "biocultural study of religion" is not intended to blur the appropriate lines between distinct research communities, or to demarcate a new singular academic field or discipline. Given the astonishing fruitfulness of the open integration and overlapping application of these diverse theories and research methods to religious phenomena, trying to set such boundaries would be counterproductive. We might think of it as a "field," but the metaphor should be construed not in geographical but in physical terms: a dynamic force field of interconnected and open explanatory events. If we think of it as a "discipline," the focus should not be on deciding its departmental location but on disciplining ourselves to remain interconnected and open during every event of explanation. The theoretical and empirical literature that creates and fills this multi-disciplinary conceptual space is rapidly expanding.[7] In the following chapters, I will introduce and explicate a heuristic framework, based on a reconstruction and integration of some key concepts derived from this research, which I hope will help to unveil the mechanisms that continue to reproduce supernatural agents in contemporary minds and cultures.

Divine reproduction has always been a popular theme within religious mythology. When couched in the context of such world-founding narratives, the idea of the birth of gods (or the birthing of goddesses) has not been that difficult for most people to accept. Insofar as we conceive supernatural agents in our own image, they naturally fit into our intuitive familial categories. It is not at all surprising to hear that they (like us) are already spawned and always spawning. Their behavior in such stories, however, is often quite surprising. In Hesiod's *Theogony,* for example, Gaia is angered by Uranus's treatment of their children (the Titans), and so gives a sickle to her youngest son, Chronos, who castrates his father and throws his testicles into the sea (from which various divinities emerge). Chronos now controlled the cosmos, but a prophecy foretold that one of his own children would destroy him. And so he devoured each of his children (the gods) soon after his wife Rhea gave birth to them. However, Rhea tricked Chronos into swallowing a stone instead of his youngest son, Zeus, who escaped and eventually did overthrow his father.

Stories about the bearing of gods do not always involve castration and cannibalism—at least not explicitly. One of the core narratives in the Christian religion is the birth of the baby Jesus in a Bethlehem manger. While most religious practitioners intuitively find such ideas compelling, many reflective theologians find them troubling. If Jesus really was the Son of God, truly divine like his eternal Father, and if Mary was his temporal mother, then it would seem to follow that she was the bearer of God (*theotokos*). On the other hand, if Jesus did not have a human father, as many Christians came to believe within a few decades after his death, then how could he be truly human? This sort of question proliferated and fueled the major Christological debates in the patristic period and beyond. Can the finite bear the Infinite? How could the body of the heavenly (risen) Christ be truly present in the earthly (unleavened) bread consumed at mass? How and why did the Holy Spirit inseminate the body of *this* unwed Jewish girl? The doctrinal inventions of the real presence of Christ in the Eucharist and of the virgin conception of Jesus in Mary are not so thinly veiled expressions of cannibalistic and castration themes found in other theogonies.

My interest here, however, is not in the details of any particular myth, but in unveiling the cognitive and coalitional forces that generate and sustain *all kinds* of theogonies. I am using this latter term not in the narrow sense of popular literary accounts of the genesis of the gods, as in Hesiod's portrayal of the swallowing of divine offspring and the mutilation of titanic genitals, but more broadly as a way of referring to any narrative imaginative engagement that reinforces god-conceptions within a particular religious coalition. My concern is not with debates over whether Mary, for example, can be considered *theotokos* (the God-bearer), but with the sense in which our species as a whole can be considered *Homo deiparensis* (god-bearing hominids).

Religious conceptions can become a heavy burden in human life, bearing down on us in ways that are psychologically and politically painful. *Must* we continue to bear them? The message that the gods are born(e) in the mental and social space of human life has the potential to accomplish what the proclamation of the "death of God" could not. It may help us learn to let the gods go so that we can learn to live together—on our own. As we will see, the monotheistic idea of God is becoming increasingly unbearable—philosophically, psychologically, and politically. We need a new way of dealing with religious conceptions.

Conceiving Religion

How should we conceive of *religion*? Like the phenomena it is often used to describe, this pregnant—all too pregnant—concept engenders enormous controversy. Some scholars have argued that the term ought to be secluded from polite academic society. Does the baggage borne so long by the Western concept of "religion" mean that we should set it aside? Such questions are important not only to scholars concerned about academic compliance to hotly contested disciplinary definitions, but also to those whose alliance to a particular tradition or defiance against all such traditions compels them to join the increasingly polemical public discourse about the value of "religion" in human life. Clearly articulating a conceptual apparatus that can guide such conversations is an important and ongoing task, one that I will begin to take up in the next chapter.

However, it is equally important to ask what religion *conceives* and how it goes on reproducing itself. Where do "religions" come from? How—and what—do they reproduce? What engenders religiosity, and how is it nurtured? In the following chapters, I will suggest an answer to all of these questions: *shared imaginative engagement with axiologically relevant supernatural agents.* Axiology is the study of value (*axios*), which, at least in the pragmatic philosophical tradition, can include discourse about the dynamics of and criteria for intellectual and aesthetic as well as ethical engagements.[8] All natural human agents—including atheists—imaginatively engage one another in ongoing processes of evaluating and being evaluated, processes that interact at multiple levels (biological, psychological, political, etc.). Religion, however, involves imaginative interactions with *supernatural* agents, whose axiological relevance for a particular group is constituted and regulated by its members' shared belief in manifestations—and shared practice in manipulations—of those agents.

Scholars within the humanities and social sciences are often wary of theoretical conceptions of religion because of the way in which they have sometimes functioned under the constraints of essentialism and colonialism. The former refers to the way in which terms can be utilized as though they represent unchanging ideas that are actualized more or less fully in particular cases. The latter refers to the way in which essentialist terms that are (supposedly) fully actualized in one in-group are taken as the basis for evaluating out-groups, authorizing or condoning force to make "them" assimilate to (or keep away from) "us." Categorizing specific persons into generic groups has indeed too often contributed to our anxious attempts to "colonize" others based on preconceived "essentialist" notions of race, class, or gender. All sorts of terms can be, and have been, used in this way (Western, civilized, rational, etc.). During the nineteenth and early twentieth centuries, the term "religion" was in fact utilized in this way, provincially defined by Christian scholars who saw their own as the "consummate" religion, the final step on a long path that had begun with "primitive" forms of animism. After the historicist, contextual, and linguistic turn(s) in the philosophy of science, most scholars of religion today work hard to distance themselves from such narrow conceptions.[9]

One strategy is to use extremely broad definitions of religion such as "concern about issues of ultimate importance" or "awe-filled response to the universe." These conceptions are usually offered in the context of arguments about whether it is possible to be a naturalist (or a secularist) and still value "religion." For the purposes of our philosophical reflection on the relation between theology, atheism, and religion, however, such definitions are too broad to pick out anything empirically relevant or conceptually interesting. Many members of communities normally considered "religious"—whether aboriginal tribesmen or evangelical Christians—have no time for (or interest in) reflecting on ultimacy and wondering at the cosmos. On the other hand, many atheists are passionate about exploring issues of ultimate importance and are fascinated by the physical universe, which they find awesome indeed. In their evaluations of the order of nature and society, however, atheists are most definitely *not* involved in shared imaginative engagement with the supernatural agents of a particular coalition. As we will see, leaving these aspects out of discussions of "religiosity" is also problematic because it leaves hidden the ongoing activation of mechanisms that continue to reinforce the violent protection of in-groups based on the mistaken detection of coalition-favoring gods.

In the context of this book, I will use the term "religion" to indicate this emergent, complex set of integrated features that has in fact been discovered in all known cultures: shared imaginative engagement with axiologically relevant supernatural agents. This terminological strategy is not intended as a general solution to a general methodological problem. It serves a particular function: addressing the problem of conceiving religion—in both senses—in the context of a reconstructive analysis of empirical findings within the biocultural sciences and an exploration of their theoretical and practical implications for the discipline of theology and the future of atheism. This is not the only way to conceive of religion, but all "religions" may be conceived in this way. This is not all that religions produce, but everywhere it is produced I will call it "religion." This strategy is also both antiessentialist and anticolonialist. It provides the conceptual tools for understanding—and a pragmatic impetus for dissolving—the evolved cognitive and coalitional forces that intensify abstract idealizations and group conflicts.

Theologians have traditionally operated within intellectual workshops sponsored by specific religious coalitions, within which they offer reflections on divine revelation and guidance on ritual practices. Many scientists and philosophers assume that this is all theology does and all that it can do. In dialogue with the biocultural study of religion, however, theologians can rediscover and renew a critical and creative practice that has long been suppressed by or domesticated within religious groups. I will argue that this ancient discipline, if appropriately reconstructed, can play an important role in liberating us from God-conceptions, freeing up energy for wholly *naturalist* interpretations and creatively *secularist* inscriptions of our shared worlds.

Atheist Conceptions after the Birth of "God"

Nietzsche's madman could assume that those at work in the marketplace and at worship in the churches already knew whom he had in mind when he announced the death of *God*. But how was this particular idea of a supernatural agent conceived—and why has it stuck around? The term "God" has a wide semantic range, so wide that one even finds it used by scientists who are committed atheists, as when Stephen Hawking described the quest for a unified theory of physical cosmology as a search for the "mind of God."[10] In his early work, even Nietzsche had used the term to indicate the "artist's meaning (and hidden meaning) behind all that happens—a 'God,' if you will, but certainly only an utterly unscrupulous and amoral artist-God who frees himself from the dire pressure of fullness and *over-fullness*, from *suffering* the oppositions packed within him"[11] Many philosophers and theologians use the word "God" as a placeholder for that which in some sense conditions all finite entities or events, the absolute infinite, or "ground of being," without attributing it any human-like and coalition-favoring features. The word is also occasionally used to refer to the highest (male) supernatural agent within a religious tradition, such as Brahman or even Buddha.

The most common sense in which the term "God" is used, however, is to designate the Deity imaginatively engaged by coalitions affiliated with the Abrahamic traditions of Judaism, Christianity, and Islam. People today who argue about whether (or simply assume that) God is dead are usually members of societies that have been deeply shaped by these monotheistic religions. Acknowledging the diversification and syncretism that continue to characterize and modify religious practices around the world, for the sake of conceptual analysis, scholars of comparative religion still distinguish between the traditions that trace their origins to developments during the first millennium BCE in East Asia (Confucianism, Daoism), South Asia (Hinduism, Buddhism), and West Asia (Judaism, Christianity, Islam).[12] Karl Jaspers was the first to use the phrase "axial age" to indicate the revolutionary phase of human history that lasted from approximately 800 BCE to 200 BCE and significantly altered the psychological and political landscape of human life across the most densely populated areas of the globe. Research on this important era has escalated in recent years and, although scholars debate dates and details, it is still considered a key turning point (axis) in civilizational transformation.[13]

In the wake of the West Asian axial age, a new sort of religious conception was born(e) within the doctrinal formulations of the major monotheistic traditions. God was portrayed as the infinite personal Creator of all finite reality, an all-knowing and all-powerful disembodied intentional Force. In order to avoid confusion with other usages of the term "God," and for other analytic reasons to be explained below, I will designate this idea as GOD (with small capitals). It was the attempt to conceptualize infinity as *intentional,* or to represent the intentionality of the coalition's most important supernatural agent as *infinite,* that led to the birth of GOD. One of the tasks of this book is to explain how this religious conception was engendered, and why it continues to be borne despite the philosophical, psychological, and political problems it produces.

However, the main focus of my project, as the title suggests, is the discipline of theology, which has played a central role in bearing GOD. As we will see in chapter 3, this academic field has been bombarded by attacks from scientists in the biocultural study of religion. Instead of avoiding or defending against such attacks, I want to intensify the critical gaze upon theology; the glaring light of these sciences can help us more clearly see (and so finally be able to separate) two very different trajectories within this discipline. The main purpose of my project, as the subtitle suggests, is the liberation of an atheist trajectory that has been bound up within this field of inquiry, a reflective and innovative force that was also conceived during the axial age. The idea that humans can understand nature and arrange society without the help of the gods was only rarely borne in antiquity, but it was in fact born (e.g., in the schools of Epicurus, Cārvāka, and Zhuangzi). As the concept of GOD has become increasingly unbearable over the centuries, however, the plausibility and feasibility of atheist conceptions have grown, eventually contributing to the emergence of naturalism and secularism.

What does this have to do with theology? I propose a reconceptualization of this field of inquiry as *the construction and critique of hypotheses about the existential conditions for axiological engagement.* Most theological hypotheses have indeed been religious. That is to say, they have appealed to supernatural agents taken as axiologically relevant within the shared imagination of the monotheistic traditions to which theologians have been traditionally bound. Although a variety of finite gods play a role in the evaluative practices of such groups (e.g., angels, demons, saints, jinn, etc.), it is GOD who allegedly determines the conditions for the very existence of all finite axiological engagement. Ideas about limited, changing gods (of a certain sort) are easily reproduced within minds and groups, but the arrival of—and the attempt to nurture—the idea of an unlimited, unchangeable GOD exerted unimaginable mental and social pressure on human life.

There have always been voices within these religious traditions that have resisted this concept of GOD, challenging its theoretical coherence, practical consequences, and affective constraints. For a variety of reasons, many intellectuals, activists, and mystics within monotheistic religions have pushed back against notions of an anthropomorphic (male) Deity who exercises absolute control over the inscription of every psyche and polis. For the most part, however, these voices have been silenced or domesticated, pulled back into the biocultural gravitational field created by the integration of evolved theogonic mechanisms. Theology emerged within the socioecological niche we call the axial age, playing an important adaptive role in helping to hold together expanding empires and to promote an expansive individualism. Today we live in a very different niche, with new global challenges—and new opportunities. I hope to show how the discovery of the birth of GOD *within religion* can contribute to the liberation of an atheistic trajectory *within theology*, disclosing and releasing the generative power *within atheism*.

The key question is whether theology (in the sense defined above) can be emancipated—like the other sciences—from religion. During the high Middle Ages, theology was considered the "queen" of the sciences. As the explanatory power of the other sciences grew in early modernity, she was slowly nudged off the throne. Today, her place in the academic court is dubious, at best. She gets very few invitations (to mix metaphors slightly) in the interdisciplinary dating game. It is not hard to understand why. It is no fun dating someone who keeps talking about an invisible father figure (or heavenly big brother), whom she believes is always watching. But what if theology could wean itself from its reliance on the sustenance of religious groups and its habit of nurturing gods? If theology can learn to stop coddling religious conceptions, and instead generate critical and creative hypotheses about the conditions for axiological engagement that do not appeal to supernatural agents, it can serve a useful function in the ongoing conversation about religious reproduction. After all, the erstwhile queen knows what a royal pain it can be to bear and care for the gods.

Having "the Talk" about Religious Reproduction

Where do babies come from? Why do parents keep them around? Even though they may embarrass or annoy some of the adults to which they are directed, these are quite natural questions for children to ask. As the oldest of six, I had five rather obvious opportunities to pose them—and I learned over time that it was best to curb my curiosity about human reproduction in certain contexts. For scientists who research human cultures—past and present—the sudden arrival of (and provision of care to) infants comes as no surprise. Archaeologists do not need to dig around for answers to such questions as they uncover artifacts at historic (or prehistoric) sites. Anthropologists do not need to include interview questions on these themes to make sense of the replenishing of the living populations they investigate.

Scholars who study human societies do indeed refine their hypotheses as they try to develop ever more plausible interpretations of the distinctive patterns of kinship structure, courting and mating rituals, pregnancy and birthing practices, and neonatal health-care policies of specific communities. However, if an earlier civilization was composed of anatomically modern humans, then historians can reasonably assume that infants appeared within the population as a result of the same basic procedures that produce them today, when... well, you know. If the members of a contemporary collective are *Homo sapiens*, then sociologists can appropriately surmise that they naturally reproduce and care for their offspring in the same general way—and for the same basic reasons—that the rest of us do.

As a result of a convergence of theoretical proposals based on empirical findings within a wide variety of disciplines that meet in the "field" of the biocultural study of religion, scientists are now gaining a similar level of confidence about the processes by which conceptions of supernatural agents arise and are tended to within the imaginative intercourse of human groups. Like natural human offspring, different supernatural progeny have different features and are treated differently across religious families of origin. Nevertheless, they are all (re)produced by the same basic cognitive and coalitional mechanisms. Participating in sexual and religious reproduction comes relatively easily for most people in all known human societies. Why? Because these activities are motivated by naturally evolved tendencies that are part of our shared phylogenetic inheritance and have been reinforced across generations through social entrainment.

Having "the talk" should involve more than simply explaining how "it" works. It is equally important to work out the physical, emotional, and social consequences of "doing it." This is just as true for religious education as it is for sex education. We need a theological version of "the birds and the bees" that deals with the dynamics by which gods are reproduced in human minds, and the consequences of nurturing them in human groups. Part of the problem is that we are socialized not to ask where gods come from; we learn early that it is not polite to ask folks why they keep them around. When it comes to having the talk about where babies come from and what it takes to care for them, we know that waiting too long can have devastating effects. Of course, it can be equally devastating if the conversation makes people feel attacked, afraid, or ashamed. The activities that lead to sexual and religious reproduction can feel terrific to our bodies, but baring our souls about them can feel terribly vulnerable.

When discussing such intimate issues, it is important to be sensitive—but it is also important to be direct.

A growing number of scholars in the biocultural study of religion are arguing that the empirical findings in these fields do more than help explain the origin and evolution of belief in gods. They also provide adequate warrant for rejecting the existence of such culturally postulated disembodied intentional forces. As we will see, these sciences do not provide deductive logical arguments that *disprove* the existence of gods or inductive evidence that *invalidates* claims about their causal relevance, but they do offer powerful abductive and retroductive arguments that render their existence *implausible*. It makes more sense to think that shared imaginative intercourse with supernatural agents emerged over time as naturally evolved hypersensitive cognitive tendencies led to mistaken perceptions that slowly became entangled within erroneous collective judgments about the extent of the social field.

The reader might wonder why I so often engage *Christian* conceptions of GOD in my exploration of the challenges and opportunities for postpartum theology. First, a growing number of scientists in the biocultural study of religion go out of their way to single out this monotheistic religion for critique. Christianity was also the main target of Nietzsche's proclamations about "the death of God." So in this interdisciplinary context, it makes sense for me to use this tradition to illustrate the challenges and opportunities for theology after "the birth of God." A second reason for focusing on the way in which alleged supernatural agent revelations are interpreted and ritually engaged in Christianity is that this is my own religious "family of origin." In chapter 5, I will argue that one way to facilitate healthy conversations about religious reproduction is to maintain emotional contact with one's original "family system" while differentiating oneself from the triangulation of gods that binds anxiety within it. In our pluralistic, globalizing environment, however, it is becoming increasingly important to have "the talk" across religious boundaries. This is why I also often compare and contrast the religious conceptions of traditions that emerged in the East and South Asian axial age with the GOD of the West Asian monotheisms.

In many contexts, engendering atheism will be extremely difficult; in some contexts, it may turn out to be impossible. Letting the gods go can be a painful experience for those whose mental and social lives have been saturated and structured by shared imaginative engagement with them. Conceptions of gods, selves, and worlds come and go together; they hang together—that is, they hold together or they die together. This is why the very idea of the dissolution of the *gods* makes the *worlds* of human *selves* feel extremely vulnerable. The way in which one imagines the gods of one's group affects one's sense of self and one's sense of belonging in the world. Losing one's god(s) usually means the loss of status in one's group, and can even feel like losing one's mind. It is important for those who do not believe in gods to empathize with the sense of existential weightlessness that can arise when a person's imagination becomes disentangled from the supernatural agents that once secured his or her psychological and political worlds.

Especially for religious scholars who operate within monotheistic traditions, becoming conversant with the findings of the biocultural study of religion about the birth of God may well lead to a kind of theological postpartum depression. But there is no need to be depressed, or angry, or ashamed. Reproducing supernatural agents comes to us naturally because it served our Upper Paleolithic ancestors so well—helping them hold together in groups and survive long enough to reproduce natural agents. I am not proposing that theologians adopt atheism into their families like some alien child. Rather, I hope to show how theology itself has been bearing atheism all along—although it has not nourished it or encouraged it to reach its full potential. In light of the adaptive challenges facing humanity today, it is important for us to learn how to reflect more intentionally on the way we care for our theological intellectual offspring and the pragmatic implications of our religious reproductive strategies.

Chapter 2

Anthropomorphic Promiscuity and Sociographic Prudery

This chapter outlines a conceptual framework that can serve as a heuristic guide in an ongoing conversation about the ways in which our evolved cognitive and coalitional tendencies lead to the reproduction of gods in human minds and cultures. I have utilized this framework for a variety of purposes elsewhere,[1] but in this context I explicate its content and explore its implications in greater detail. It will be employed in the remaining chapters in a variety of ways. In chapter 3, the framework will help us drive a wedge between two distinctive trajectories within theology, the conflation of which has so annoyed scientists from other disciplines. Chapters 4 and 5 use it as a heuristic device to analyze the inferential and preferential systems that shape so much of the debate between atheists and theists, as well as debates among theologians bound to different religious "families." Finally, in chapters 6 and 7, this conceptual framework will be used to identify strategies for liberating an atheistic trajectory within theology that produces theolytic (god-dissolving) hypotheses, complementing the efforts of scientists within other fields whose research unveils the hidden mechanisms of theogonic reproduction.

In the first three sections of this chapter, I introduce some of the major themes and hypotheses related to the detection of supernatural agents and the protection of supernatural coalitions. The middle sections illustrate the integration of these theogonic forces in the work of three leading scholars who weave together both sorts of mechanism within their theoretical formulations. The last three sections explore some of the reasons for—and consequences of—attempting to bear GOD, that particularly problematic religious conception that was engendered and nurtured in the wake of the West Asian axial age. As the argument unfolds, it will be important to keep in mind that my overview of some of the empirical findings and theoretical developments within the bio-cultural study of religion has a primarily heuristic purpose: searching for new ways to respond—philosophically, psychologically, and politically—to the insights emerging out of this constellation of disciplines, especially as they bear on the discipline of theology. Now it's time for "the talk."

Where Do gods Come from—and Why Do We Keep Them Around?

The human predisposition for shared imaginative engagement with axi-ologically relevant supernatural agents is a result of the integration of cognitive and coalitional defaults that were reciprocally resolved and reinforced by selection pressures in early ancestral environments. This integration is indicated in the lower left quadrant of the coordinate sys-tem formed by the two axes of figure 2.1.

The level of generality at which human tendencies are depicted on this grid does not capture all of the nuances within (or between) the diverse scientific theories that have emerged within this multidisciplinary field.

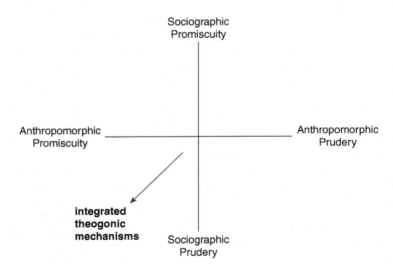

Figure 2.1   Theogonic Mechanisms

However, this framework does capture precisely what is needed to accomplish the general purpose for which it has been constructed: clarifying the relation between two basic kinds of bias that characterize our species, the integration of which leads to the reproduction of gods in groups. It has several other heuristic functions as well, and I will unpack the trajectories associated with the other three quadrants as we go along. The first step, however, is to clarify the concepts that form the grid itself.

Think of the horizontal line in figure 2.1 as a continuum on which one can mark a person's tendency to guess "human-like intentional force" when confronted with ambiguous phenomena in their natural environments. An anthropomorphically *promiscuous* person will always be on the lookout for intentional causes, jumping at explanations that appeal to "agency," even—or especially—when such inferences are not easily verifiable. The anthropomorphically *prudish*, on the other hand, are suspicious about such appeals. They prefer to reflect more carefully before giving in to their intuitive desire to grab at agential interpretations.

The vertical line represents a continuum on which one can register how tightly a person is bound to conventional modes of inscribing the social field, that is, to the proscriptions and prescriptions that regulate the evaluative practices and boundaries of the coalition(s) with which he or she primarily identifies. Sociographic *prudes* are strongly committed to the authorized social norms of their in-group, following and protecting them even at great cost to themselves. They are more likely to be suspicious of out-groups and to accept claims or demands that appeal to authorities within their own coalition. On the other hand, the sociographic *promiscuity* of those at the top of the continuum leads them to be more open to intercourse with out-groups about alternate normativities and to the pursuit of innovative modes of creative social inscription. Such persons are also less likely to accept restrictions or assertions that are based only (or even primarily) on appeals to tradition.

It is important to emphasize that these continua indicate proclivities within the mental and social space of human life, rather than judgments about the accuracy or adequacy of specific interpretive engagements. The horizontal axis has to do with a person's inferential *tendency* to detect intentional subjects, not with particular objects of detection. Many of the most important things that happen to us are indeed a result of embodied human (or human-like) agents, and so the anthropomorphic guess often turns out to be correct. Similarly, the lower end of the vertical axis refers not to particular normative behaviors but to one's preferential *tendency* to protect social inscriptions. Following conventional authorities is sometimes the safest and healthiest thing to do, and so sociographic prudery often promotes the wisest course of action.

The problem is that these mental and social habits are so deeply embedded in evolved default mechanisms that they operate automatically; it is difficult even to notice them—much less reflect on them critically. This does not mean they work "mechanically" in a deterministic or reductionist sense. When I refer to theogonic *mechanisms*, I mean more or less stable dynamic systems with recurrent patterns of causal relevance that produce a probability distribution over possible outcomes. Moreover, such mechanisms have a certain degree of plasticity, which means that it is indeed possible to move around the coordinate system depicted in figure 2.1. Shifting away from the lower left quadrant, however, requires significant reflective effort on the part of individuals and significant innovative investment within groups. Discerning when and how to contest these intuitive and conservative biases is becoming increasingly important as we learn to adapt together within an interconnected, globalizing environment.

The basic claim of theogonic reproduction theory is that supernatural agents continue to be born(e) in minds and cultures today because contemporary humans are automatically drawn into the biocultural gravitational force of the reciprocally reinforcing god-bearing mechanisms of anthropomorphic promiscuity and sociographic prudery. These easily integrated evolved defaults are part of our phylogenetic inheritance, and have been reinforced by millennia of social entrainment practices. In the environment of our early ancestors, the selective advantage went to hominids who were able to quickly *detect* relevant agents in the *natural* environment and whose groups were adequately *protected* from dissolution as a result of cheaters and defectors in the *social* environment. This is not a question of *either* biological *or* cultural inheritance; both contribute to the sensitivity level of any particular person's detective and protective tendencies and their distribution within any particular group.

As in all healthy and progressive fields of research, there are significant debates among scientists about the relative importance and functional relevance of the many factors that contribute to the arrival and nurture of god-conceptions within human coalitions. For example, scholars argue about whether "religious" traits emerged as a direct adaptation to challenges within the early ancestral environment or were merely the "by-product" of other adaptations. Those in the latter camp also differ in their answers to the question whether some of those by-product traits may have later become "exapatations" (adaptive for other reasons not connected to their original appearance). Other scientists argue over the extent to which natural selection operates only at the individual (or genetic) level or also at the group (or cultural) level. Ongoing research in archaeology, anthropology, psychology, and many other fields leads to continuous refinements of the various theories on offer within the biocultural study of religion and to fresh assessments of the dating of various shifts in cognitive capacity and coalitional complexity.

In the current context, however, I refrain from entering into the details of these debates because they can too easily distract from the main point that is central to my project, and from which such controversies do not detract: contemporary human beings are prone to share in imaginative engagement with supernatural agents as a result of a reciprocal intensification of evolved tendencies to (over)protect coalitions in a social milieu and (over)detect agents in a natural milieu. My philosophical extraction of a conceptual framework from this literature is empirically constrained and therefore vulnerable, as all good hypotheses should be. However, a retraction of the general claim of theogonic reproduction theory would be warranted only by a body of evidence that could outweigh the massive research across disciplines that overwhelmingly supports its plausibility.

The framework constructed by the two axes described above can help us more clearly delineate between four ways of integrating cognitive and coalitional tendencies, each of which promotes a different way of constructing (and different attitudes toward critiquing) hypotheses about the conditions for axiological engagement. How can we account for the binding normativity that shapes our pragmatic evaluations? What is it that conditions (originates, organizes, and/or orients) the human experience of valuing and being valued? The most common answer to this sort of question throughout the history of the human species has been "*our gods.*" This sort of answer comes to us intuitively because of naturally evolved and culturally reinforced *hyper*sensitive mechanisms that work together to promote widespread conceptions of disembodied intentional forces that are concerned about the behavior of members of an in-group.

The rest of this chapter introduces some of the theories that help to explain how and why these tendencies interact to reproduce "religious" traits that are apparently universal across cultures. Those of us trained primarily in the humanities and social sciences often develop an allergy to the term "universal," so much so that I was unable to resist adding the modifier "apparently" in the previous sentence. Most of the scientists operative in the biocultural sciences whose work we will explore below have no such allergic reaction. They confidently make claims like: "Interaction with imagined nonphysical agents (gods, spirits, ghosts, etc.) is a puzzling cultural *universal.*"[2] "In *every* society there are ... counterintuitive beliefs in supernatural agents."[3] In terms of cognitive architecture, "there is *only one* human religion with minor but strategically important variation in its conventional expressions."[4] "*All* religions entail some belief in supernatural entities, whether they be ancestors, spirits, gods or even less personal 'forces.'"[5] "... *Every* culture has emerged with collections of either ancestors or angels, demons or devils, ghosts or ghouls, or gods or golems possessing counterintuitive properties."[6]

The italics in these quotations are mine, but the boldness is the authors' own. Whence this confidence? As we will see, a vast array of empirical findings from multiple research fields points in the same direction, converging in support of a new message: the gods are born (cognitively)—and we have borne them (culturally).

Detecting Supernatural Agents

Where do gods come from? The basic answer arising from the biocultural study of religion is that mental conceptions of supernatural agents were (and are) engendered in human minds as a result of hypersensitive cognitive mechanisms that evolved to scan for relevant intentional forces in the natural world. Although it is widely used in the literature, the phrase "supernatural agents" is not without controversy and, for a variety of reasons, some scholars have proposed other adjectives like superhuman, spiritual, or special, as well as other nouns like forces, powers, or entities.[7] Each of these terms has its own potential problems; the important thing is to be clear about how we are making use of our designations. In what follows, I will continue using the terms god and supernatural agent in the sense outlined above: to refer to any putative disembodied (or contingently embodied) force that is attributed intentionality (or related person-like qualities) and imaginatively engaged in ways that bear on the evaluative judgments of a human coalition. How did such concepts first arise in the human mind?

Anthropologist Stewart Guthrie was one of the first scholars to use insights from cognitive science in the development of a new theory religion. Already in a 1980 article in *Current Anthropology*, he had outlined a new way to think about the relation between anthropomorphism and religion, but he set out his full theory in his 1993 book *Faces in the Clouds*.[8] More recent research in the biocultural sciences has confirmed his basic proposal, leading to a wide variety of complementary hypotheses, but Guthrie's book still provides one of the best places to begin when introducing the philosophical relevance of scientific insights into the prevalence and significance of anthropomorphism in human perception. Guthrie argues that the survival of early humans would have depended on their ability to quickly perceive any other agents—especially other people—who might be around. A hypersensitivity to human-like forms would have come in handy in the early ancestral environment by aiding in the quick detection of human enemies or other predators.

Many of the detections that result from this overactive perceptual strategy are false positives (e.g., faces in the clouds), but this strategy still would have been naturally selected because it provided a significant survival advantage. Our hunter-gatherer ancestors would often have been confronted with large, dark, and oddly shaped objects as they worked their way through the forest. Which of them would be more likely to survive an encounter with a real bear and live long enough to pass on their genes: those who immediately defaulted to guesses like "bear," although it was usually just a boulder, or those who always defaulted to guesses like "boulder," although it was occasionally a bear?

Guthrie defines anthropomorphism as the failure of a naturally evolved perceptual mechanism, that is, the *mis*-interpretation of an ambiguous phenomenon as a human-like form or force. He notes that religious anthropomorphism is often understood as consisting of the attribution of humanity to gods. Guthrie, however, turns this around: in fact, "gods consist of attributing humanity to the world."[9] Religion, he argues, involves *systematized* anthropomorphism. Perceptual uncertainty and the need to find relevant agents in the environment are the progenitors of all religions. Despite the obvious diversity of religious beliefs and practices, they were all engendered when some of the mistaken detections that necessarily occur as a result of the regular failure of an important perceptual strategy were taken seriously and made central to the ritual life of a coalition.

In this sense, argues Guthrie, all religions have gods; they all involve "ostensible communication with human-like, yet nonhuman, beings through some form of symbolic action."[10] Buddhism is often held up as a counterexample to such a claim, but this is based on a misguided Western stereotype about meditating monks. Guthrie's own ethnographic work was primarily among Japanese Buddhists, and he points out that, although there are some philosophical schools within Buddhism that do not emphasize supernatural agents, the vast majority of practicing Buddhists (including monks) are deeply entangled in shared imaginative engagement with all kinds of disembodied human-like intentional forces such as hell-ghosts, devas, bodhisattvas, and, of course, Buddhas.[11]

The last two decades of research in cognitive science have supported Guthrie's hypothesis, and further clarified the complexity and power of the evolved inferential systems that lead to god-detections. Human inferences naturally tend to follow the path of *most relevance* and the path of *least resistance*. If two interpretations of an ambiguous phenomenon have about the same processing cost, the mind will naturally default to the one with the richest inferential power. If two interpretations have about the same inferential power, the mind will naturally defer to the one with the least processing cost. Our ancestors would often find themselves in situations where they did not have time to reflect; too much reflection would mean getting eaten—or failing to eat. As Sperber and Wilson explain, in such contexts, "resources have to be allocated to the processing of information which is likely to bring about the greatest contribution to the mind's general cognitive goals at the smallest processing cost."[12] Balancing the criteria of facility and fecundity happens quickly, intuitively and automatically, triggering certain types of inferential systems that gave survival advantage to our ancestors.

Two of the most well known and most empirically tested of these cognitive systems are the Hypersensitive Agency Detection Device (HADD) and the Theory of Mind Mechanism (ToMM). The first is a phrase introduced by cognitive psychologist Justin Barrett, whose early experimental research focused on the perceptual strategy identified by Guthrie. Barrett's experiments, which have been expanded and duplicated cross-culturally, demonstrate how quickly HADD leads to the detection of "agency" when an object is perceived as violating intuitive assumptions about physical objects and moving in ways that seem to be goal-directed.[13] If an agent cannot be clearly identified, HADD automatically infers that the object is an agent, or that a hidden agent is responsible for its movement. At this point, other anthropomorphically sensitive cognitive tools, such as facial detectors and teleonomic reasoning, come into play. Very young infants scan for faces, and children quickly default to explanations that appeal to purpose. Why are rocks pointy? "So that animals won't sit on them."[14] All of this makes sense in light of evolution; such tendencies would have contributed to survival by helping early hominids quickly find (or avoid) relevant intentional agents.

Even if the agent detected by HADD is illusory, other mechanisms—such as ToMM—still go to work, generating additional inferences about the imagined entity. ToMM is related to what is sometimes called the "intentional stance," "hyperactive understanding of intentionality," or "mind reading."[15] Once we human beings imagine that we detect an agent, we immediately theorize that it has mental and emotional states somewhat like our own. We automatically infer that the imagined "other mind" is purposive, and easily attribute to it qualities such as an interest in communicating with us, a susceptibility to anger at us, etc. Our intuitive assumptions about how minds work shape our interpretation of movements that we perceive to be intentionally caused. Todd Tremlin offers the following example. When we see a woman holding a coat and purse walk into a kitchen, look all around, then throw up her arms, and walk out of the room, we naturally explain it with mentalistic notions: "She *wanted* something that she *believed* was in the kitchen and was *frustrated* when she couldn't find it."[16] Recent research suggests that the various interacting cognitive tendencies that predispose human minds toward religious belief often follow a particular order; mentalizing comes first, followed by mind-body dualism and teleology.[17] Such mechanisms may help us navigate our social worlds, but they can also lead to hyperactive inferences that impute mental and emotional states even when none are present; indeed, even when no agent is actually present.

Human beings have evolved with "hair-triggered" cognitive mechanisms for detecting intentional forces. The balance of facility and fecundity in these inferential biases means it is less costly and more relevant to assume that ambiguous phenomena, like perceived shapes or movements in the forest, really are caused by agents. Unless we take the time to contest these intuitive biases with critical reflection, we just keep on guessing "intentional force." I could not clearly identify an embodied bear, so perhaps it was a disembodied (or contingently embodied) bear-spirit. What did it want? Perhaps it was an ancestor-ghost who was upset with me for what I did yesterday. Where has it gone and what does it plan to do? All religions have such "gods" because of the aggregate of cognitive inferential systems that automatically work together to produce them in human minds. They operate not only on oddly shaped boulders in a shadowy forest, but also on unexpected noises, dreams, disease, weather anomalies, and anything else that we find difficult to explain.

Supernatural agents are portrayed in a variety of ways across human cultures but they commonly fall into the same sort of broad categories, such as predator, prey, protector, and partner. In other words, the features attributed to gods are typically those shared by the kind of agents that would have been most important for our early ancestors to detect. For example, hunter-gatherers would have had to be constantly on the watch for *predators* and *prey*. Hypersensitivity to the detection of agents, whether animals or other people, who might want to kill you, or whom you might need to kill, would clearly have provided a selective advantage. For the species to survive, however, humans also need to find *protectors* and *partners*. For example, infants automatically seek proximity to protectors, activating behavioral systems that detect and bond with caregivers. As we will see in our discussion of "attachment theory" in chapter 3, this sort of behavior, which served the adaptive function of ensuring that children receive sufficient care to survive long enough to procreate, continues to affect attachment in adulthood (even with gods). It should be obvious enough how scanning for, detecting, and attracting mating partners would also have been necessary for the survival of the species.

It is not surprising, then, that when supernatural agents are detected they are also often attributed these sorts of features. This is somewhat obvious in the case of the animal-spirits or ancestor-ghosts that are engaged in shamanic rituals within small-scale societies. Archaeological and ethnographic research suggest that such "gods" are naturally woven into human attempts to find and manipulate actual animals (or people) who are considered dangerous or delicious, or somehow relevant to the bearing of human offspring. These features are commonly found in the gods of groups from around the world. Limiting ourselves to examples from Christianity, we can point to the sort of images used to portray the central supernatural agents of the Bible, Yahweh and Christ: Father, husband, warrior, lion, lamb, etc. (Exodus 15:3, Deuteronomy 32:6, Hosea 3:1, Ezekiel 23, Matthew 25:1–6, 1 Corinthians 15:25, Ephesians 5:25–32, Revelation 5:5–6, 13:8, 19:7).

When confronted with ambiguous phenomena, evolved inferential systems intuitively follow the path that balances least resistance and most importance, which typically leads toward belief in disembodied intentional forces. However, the anthropomorphic promiscuity of cognitive detection devices is not the whole story. It is not enough for a god-conception to be facile and fecund. Supernatural agents may be *born* in the human mind as a result of the hypersensitive detection of cognitive mechanisms, but this does not explain why they are cared for and *borne* within human coalitions. When it comes to raising gods, it takes a village.

Protecting Supernatural Coalitions

Why do we keep gods around? Research in the biocultural study of religion suggests that shared imaginative engagement with supernatural agent conceptions (of a certain sort) improved the chances of survival for our early ancestors by reinforcing behaviors that protected the cohesion of their groups. The detection and interpretation of disembodied intentional forces—*revelations* in a broad sense—are not enough. The gods stay around only if groups engage them using practices—*rituals* in a broad sense—that bind the coalition together. Without the evolution of what we might call coalitional *preference* systems, the gods detected by cognitive *inference* systems would simply have dissipated. The idea that religion plays a significant role in social cohesion is not new; it goes back (at least) to Emile Durkheim's notion of the "collective effervescence" of a society and is central to Roy Rappaport's hypotheses about ritual as the foundry in which the "truth" about "reality" that maintains a social order is forged.[18] What distinguishes the more recent research that I will briefly summarize here from earlier proposals is the way in which it integrates insights from the cultural *and* the cognitive sciences.

From an evolutionary biological point of view, shared ritual engagement with gods does not initially sound like the sort of behavior that would promote the survival of an individual's genes. Assuming that malaria, for example, is really caused by parasites transmitted by mosquitoes, and not by angry ancestor-ghosts, it seems odd that natural selection would not have weeded out energy-intensive and apparently time-wasting activities like rituals that attempt to manipulate putative disembodied intentional forces in order to ward off disease or other misfortune. As it turns out, however, a group's shared engagement with "gods" that are interpreted as axiologically relevant to the strategic interests of persons within that group strengthens its social cohesion, which, in turn, grants a dispersed survival advantage to the individuals who comprise the in-group. The formation of imagined *supernatural coalitions* reinforces the tendency of their (human) members to conform to, prefer, and defend their familiar evaluative norms. In this context, I limit myself to some examples of ways in which "religious" behavior increases *cooperation* and *commitment* within such groups, which helps protect them from dissolving.

An individual might often be tempted to benefit from the productivity of his group without contributing, to cheat other members of the group, or even to take some of the resources of his group and defect to another. Although such actions may very well improve the individual's chances of surviving and passing on his genes, the group would fall apart if this sort of behavior became widespread. Groups hold together, in part, because (enough) individuals resist such temptations. Perhaps the strongest motivation for resisting is the fear of being caught and punished. One of the advantages of groups with gods is that they have more agents to watch out for—and punish—potential freeloaders, cheaters, and defectors.

Psychological experiments across cultures have demonstrated that priming individuals with thoughts about disembodied intentional forces—especially punishing gods—reduces their tendency to cheat and increases their tendency to follow the rules. Ethnographic research of small-scale societies that continue to live in niches similar to early ancestral environments has shown that supernatural agents who are able to appear out of nowhere and punish individuals (or their offspring) for violating conventional norms are among the most common sorts of gods ritually engaged in such groups. Scientists hypothesize that similar ritual practices within early hominid groups increased their members' sensitivity to *social surveillance*, as well as the number of potential surveyors they imagined might be watching, which in turn led to more cooperative behavior.[19] This helps to explain why punitive gods are still kept around within religious coalitions throughout the world.

Research within the biocultural study of religion on coalitional mechanisms also supports the claim that the emergence of shared ritual engagement with supernatural agents strengthened cooperation in early groups of humans by enhancing *social intelligence*. Based on a review of archaeological, ethnographic, and psychological research, Matt Rossano suggests that the capacity for participation in more intense social interaction was ratcheted up during the Upper Paleolithic as a result of the demand for more "ritual competence" in human groups. Maintaining increasingly complex social worlds would demand more complex rituals for trust building and intragroup cohesion. This demand in adult life gave a fitness advantage to more "ritually capable" individuals. Rossano argues that this would have manifested itself in mothers who were able to engage their infants in more extended socially and cognitively enriching interaction. Over time, this would have introduced more socially intelligent children into the population, a new variance that "was then available for further filtering by ritual selection pressure until increased working memory capacity was stabilized genetically in the population."[20]

Research related to children's interaction with imaginary friends suggests that the latter provide the former with the opportunity to test potential social scenarios "off-line." Several scholars have argued that imaginative engagement with supernatural agents could have increased our Paleolithic (and later our Neolithic) ancestors' capacity for more socially intelligent interaction (and greater cooperation) with embodied agents in the real world.[21]

As competition for resources among hominid groups increased in the early ancestral environment, survival would have required more than cooperation among its members. For a coalition to remain competitive, the individuals must also stay *committed* to one another. Psychological research shows that emotional bonds and shared intentionality are forged through the synchronic movement and arousal provided by religious rituals.[22] Moreover, many rituals, especially in small-scale societies, are often intended to mediate healing to members of the community, a function that would obviously have provided motivation to remain committed to the group. Such rituals do in fact have powerful stress-relieving and placebo effects that contribute to human longevity. The prominence of ritual healing in the ethnographic data leads Joseph Bulbulia to refer to religion as "Nature's Medicine." He hypothesizes that natural selection "amplified dispositions to believe in gods because such beliefs helped our ancestors live longer and healthier, leaving more god-believing progeny."[23] The binding power of healing (and other) rituals is also reinforced by the way in which they activate cognitive mechanisms that facilitate the ongoing detection of new revelations (or manifestations) of the group's gods.

It makes sense that people would stay committed to groups in which rituals contribute to physical health and emotional bonding. But what about all the unhealthy and even self-destructive things that religious people do to each other (and themselves)? To illustrate the sort of torturous and terrifying rituals that one finds throughout the world, Richard Sosis points out a practice among the Ilahita Arapesh in which adult males dressed like boars pin down boys (as young as three-years-old) and rub their genitals forcefully with stinging nettles. Similar sorts of abuse occur later in childhood, and newly married husbands lacerate their own penises in a public display after the couple's first night together. The descriptions of the molestations that must be suffered by the males in this coalition would make Hesiod blush and Chronos cringe.

It seems that natural selection would weed out such behaviors since they do not provide any obvious reproductive advantage, and waste energy that could be used in more productive ways. Sosis argues that this sort of ritual can be explained as a form of *costly signaling*.[24] Continuing to participate in such costly activities signals one's commitment to the group. The harder the signal is to fake, the more trustworthy it seems to others in the coalition. For the most part, and over the long run, the most convincing displays are by those who truly believe in the gods of their supernatural coalition and who are truly committed to its human members. The rituals weed out the noncommitted.

The evolution of religion enhanced cooperation and commitment within human societies—but these traits were naturally selected because they granted a *competitive* advantage. The other side of in-group cohesion is out-group hostility. The god-bearing groups that survived during the Upper Paleolithic were those that outcompeted other groups when resources were low. Religion can promote pro-social behavior, but such altruism is typically limited to members of one's own kith and kin or to regular trading partners. Shared imaginative engagement with supernatural agents provides motivation for putting "Us" ahead of "Me." As Joshua Greene points out in *Moral Tribes*, however, cooperation within and commitment to a religious tribe exacerbates conflicts between "Us" and "Them."[25]

The inclination to show aggression toward members of out-groups is intensified under stress. So is the inclination to believe in and reach out for the supernatural agents of one's own in-group. Mortality salience, for example, has been shown to increase both the tendency to protect one's own coalition by behaving violently toward cultural others and the tendency to detect the relevant gods who might be of help.[26] People who are primed to think about death (their own or others they love) are far more likely to experience a conservative shift, escalate their level of commitment, and insist on injuring those who have injured them.[27] Reflecting on religious revelations and participating in religious rituals commonly prime people to think intensely and even urgently about death (e.g., reading biblical texts about heaven and hell, symbolically "dying" with Christ in Baptism, remembering his death at the Eucharist, anticipating his imminent return to judge the living and the dead, etc.). The axial age religious traditions often emphasize love and compassion for all human beings (even all sentient beings) in their official doctrines, but engagement with even these sorts of ideals in a religious context spontaneously generates psychological processes that motivate participants to seek proximity to familiar attachment figures and that promote bigotry and aggression toward cultural others.[28]

This is exactly what we would expect if "religion" provided a survival advantage in the early ancestral environment by fostering attitudes that encouraged out-group antagonism and other behaviors that enhanced combat effectiveness (e.g., self-righteousness, dehumanizing the enemy, and exchanging natural cost-benefit concerns for supernatural ones).[29] The question facing us today is whether such attitudes and behaviors are adaptive in our contemporary environment. If not, what strategies can we develop to contest the evolved defaults that reinforce them?

Anthropomorphic promiscuity and sociographic prudery reinforce one another. The detection of gods promotes the protection of groups and vice versa. The theories with the most explanatory power are those that emphasize this empirically demonstrable reciprocity and include both sorts of theogonic mechanisms within their hypotheses about the evolution of religion. In the next three subsections, I briefly summarize some of the contributions of three influential scholars whose works illustrate this type of integrated theoretical modeling.

Interesting and Interested Parties

Pascal Boyer's *Religion Explained: The Human Instincts That Fashion Gods, Spirits and Ancestors* is one of the most discussed examples of a theoretical synthesis of cognitive and coalitional mechanisms in the biocultural study of religion. Although he relies heavily on anthropological research, Boyer's argument also integrates insights from cognitive science, evolutionary psychology, and archaeology as well as other disciplines. For Boyer, the recurrence of patterns in religious belief and behavior across cultures can best be explained as by-products of an aggregate of complex and independently evolved mental and social strategies, each of which in its own way contributed to the survival of early humans.[30]

In his earlier work, Boyer had distinguished four "repertoires" within religion: ontological assumptions, causal claims, episode types, and social categories.[31] In much of his later work, he has focused on the relation between cognitively constrained intuitive ontology and culturally restrained god concepts that help hold groups together.[32] The reciprocity between these (and other) evolved processes helps to explain why religions the world over are filled with supernatural agents that are both *interesting to* and *interested in* the members of the coalitions that imaginative engage them.

Human consciousness generates all sorts of bizarre images, but relatively few of them stick around in the human mind and are shared across generations. The god-conceptions one finds in the imaginative space of religions around the world have survived because they are easy to remember and inferentially rich enough to warrant transmission to others. Boyer argues that religious ideas are memorable because they are minimally counterintuitive. An idea is considered *intuitive* if it fits all the natural inferences normally connected to an ontological kind, such as ANIMAL, PERSON, PLANT, NATURAL OBJECT, or ARTIFACT. This intuitive ontology has evolved by reinforcing a set of principled expectations and inferential dispositions concerning various aspects of experience. So, for example, if a child is told that "zygoons are the only predators of hyenas," the attribution of predation will immediately lead her to place the new entry "zygoon" into the category ANIMAL. Once an idea is placed in an ontological category, the latter works as a template that automatically activates other inferences associated with objects in that category. Other important information will be imported into the zygoon entry, such as "zygoons cannot not be made, they are born of other zygoons" and "if you cut a zygoon in two it will probably die."[33] The child will infer that he or she too should be wary of zygoons. The ability to sort new entries into templates and quickly infer this sort of relevant information provides an obvious survival advantage.

A *minimally* counterintuitive (MCI) idea is one that *violates* some (usually only one or two) expectations or inferential dispositions normally activated by a template, but simultaneously *preserves* most of the others. Cross-cultural psychological experiments have demonstrated that such ideas are easier to remember over time than merely intuitive ideas or maximally counterintuitive ideas that violate too many natural inferences.[34] Religious ideas can (and do) minimally violate each of the ontological categories mentioned above; for example, a tree (PLANT) that remembers human actions, or a statue (ARTIFACT) that can hear prayers. Boyer argues that the most significant MCI ideas in religion are those that minimally violate the category PERSON, especially domain-level intuitions about bodily constraints and limited knowledge and power.[35] For example, the idea of an "ancestor-ghost" activates the PERSON template, preserving many inferences about persons (e.g., having emotions, memories, and desires), but violating the expectation that persons have bodies.

MCI concepts may be easily born in the human mind, but that is not enough to make them "religious." Mickey Mouse, an idea that minimally violates the category ANIMAL (a rodent who talks), is also interesting and easy to remember. For a counterintuitive agent to function religiously, however, it must be widely interpreted within a coalition as an entity that is *interested* in the thoughts and behavior of its members and has the power to intervene in their daily lives. For Boyer, the reason gods matter so much within groups is because they are conceived as "interested parties" whose potential to bring misfortune (or blessing) activates coalitional mechanisms that enhance cooperation. One of Boyer's favorite illustrations comes from the Fang tribes of Cameroon and Gabon, who believe in ancestor-ghosts who roam the bush and the villages, and can trip people in the forest or destroy crops. They also believe in witches who are born with an extra organ (called an *evur*) that can leave their bodies at night, fly on banana leaves, and make people sick or kill fetuses in the womb.[36]

Once an ancestor-ghost is *detected*, intuitive ontological inferences and other cognitive mechanisms (such as ToMM) are immediately activated, leading to the assumption that it is probably interested in what I am doing, may get angry, and could hurt me or my offspring. The cohesion of a Fang tribe is *protected* by shared ritual interaction with such counterintuitive agents because its members are less likely to cheat, freeload, or defect from the group. Cooperation is enhanced by increased social surveillance and social intelligence: be careful—the ancestor-ghosts could be watching and the witches are waiting to hurt those who cheat, freeload, or consider defecting from the group. Attempts to detect and interpret this sort of axiologically relevant supernatural agent reinforce prudent behavior within a coalition. At the same time, participation in synchronic, emotionally arousing, and socially binding rituals further activates the detection of the gods allegedly interested in the group.

Affective and Collective Security

Another influential example of theoretical integration in the biocultural study of religion is Scott Atran's *In Gods We Trust: The Evolutionary*

Landscape of Religion. Atran notes that in every known society, there are (1) widespread counterfactual—and counterintuitive—beliefs in supernatural agents like ghosts and goblins, (2) hard-to-fake public expressions of costly material commitments to those agents, which involve sacrifices of goods, time, or even life, (3) engagements with those agents in ways that master people's existential anxieties about death, disease, loneliness, etc., and (4) ritualized, rhythmic sensory coordination of (1), (2), and (3) in ways that enrich communion within the group. The convergence of these four societal features was canalized in the evolutionary landscape to produce "religion," that is, "passionate communal displays of costly commitments to counterintuitive worlds governed by supernatural agents."[37] Taking advantage of insights from a wide variety of disciplines, Atran develops a complex theory that integrates all four of these aspects of religion.

It initially seems odd, from an evolutionary perspective, that religion exists at all. The material sacrifice, emotional expenditure, and cognitive effort required by religious belief and practice do not obviously provide any survival advantage. On the contrary, it seems that "if people literally applied their counterfactual religious principles and prescriptions to factual navigation of everyday environments they would likely be either dead or in the afterlife in very short order—probably in too short an order for individuals to reproduce and the species to survive."[38] If religion is so costly, and a poor strategy for dealing with the factual world of physical and biological laws, then why is it so prevalent in human societies? Like Boyer, Atran recognizes that religion enhances *cooperation* within groups, but he focuses more on the way in which it also increases *commitment* to groups. Atran argues that the main reason that religion is so resilient, despite the advances of scientific naturalism and secular reasoning, is that it provides people with affective and collective security.

The reason people feel the need for such security is related to what Atran calls the "tragedy of cognition." Humans have an evolved tendency to interpret movements as telic event structures, that is, as processes that lead up to and have a terminal point. This perceptual strategy comes in handy when attempting to decipher movements like those shaped by the interactive goals of a predator-prey relationship. However, this teleological reasoning is applied automatically to all sorts of events, leading us to scan for and infer the presence of a CONTROLLING FORCE even—or especially—when its location or intentions cannot be specified. Such reasoning is also easily applied to the event of our life as a whole and the lives of those we love, which leads to an awareness of death as the final goal of the process of living, which in turn arouses existential anxiety and emotional stress. Atran argues that belief in gods and their supernatural realms provides an imaginative space in which stressful and even paralyzing anxiety can be evaded. Death is then converted into an event whose "goal state" can be conceived as an extended afterlife. This helps to explain why "humans are cognitively susceptible to invoke supernatural agents whenever emotionally eruptive events arise that have superficial characteristics of telic event structures with no apparent CONTROLLING FORCE."[39]

In several empirical studies, Atran and his colleagues have demonstrated the effect that inducing mortality salience has on people's tendency to detect supernatural agents and protect supernatural coalitions. Participants in psychological experiments who are primed with thoughts or images of death are more likely (compared to control groups) to express belief in God and the possibility of supernatural intervention.[40] Atran hypothesizes that nonnatural—or counterintuitive—beliefs in gods provide a "causal resolution to the existential fear of death by evoking possible worlds of avoidance."[41] Such beliefs provide *affective* security. When combined with ongoing involvement in religious rituals that require costly displays of commitment, they also provide *collective* security. Research on religious violence in contemporary societies has demonstrated that a greater willingness to die for one's god, and the belief that other religions are responsible for the world's problems, can be predicted by greater participation in the rituals of one's own in-group.[42] The between-group enmity aroused by religious belief and behavior would have helped small-scale societies survive in the early ancestral environment, but it is deeply problematic in our contemporary context.

In *Talking to the Enemy: Faith, Brotherhood and the (Un)Making of Terrorists*, Atran reports on his ethnographic work among terrorist groups in Palestine, Afghanistan, and Southeast Asia. He argues that (most) fundamentalists and jihadists are not naïve or sociopathic; they are devoted actors who, like the rest of us, are motivated by the evolved need to feel physically and emotionally safe in small-scale groups. Atran observes that their willingness to kill and die is usually not merely for an abstract Cause but for the cause of a specific group, their "imagined family of genetic strangers," whether brotherhood, fatherland, or tribal coalition. He maintains that it is concerns that arise at the *small-scale* level, such as raising families or playing soccer together, that trump almost everything else as people move through life.[43] For Atran, "collective commitment to the absurd is the greatest demonstration of group love that humans have devised," but costly displays of commitment to such "preposterous beliefs" unfortunately lead to enduring conflict between human groups.[44] Unfortunately, the most common reactions to terrorists in recent years have simply reinforced the spiraling effect of the theogonic mechanisms within the complex literate states that dominate our contemporary evolutionary landscape.

Consciousness and Social Contracts

My choice of David Lewis-Williams as a third example of theoretical integration in the biocultural study of religion provides me with an opportunity to introduce some empirical data sets that are not empha-sized by the first two exemplars. Like the others, he mines the vast anthropological literature. Lewis-Williams's own early work involved ethnographic research and archaeological analysis of the rock paintings of the San (Bushman) peoples of South Africa.[45] In his later work, how-ever, he explores a wider range of the archaeological record and focuses in more detail on the relevance of neuropsychology for understanding religion. Lewis-Williams provides a comprehensive presentation of his argument in *Conceiving God: The Cognitive Origin and Evolution of Religion.* Although he does not play with the idea of the "birth of God" in the same way, this title obviously fits well with the metaphor I am using to guide my current project. Because one of his main concerns in *Conceiving God* is challenging the discipline of theology, I will delay my exploration of that book to chapter 3 and limit myself here primarily to references to his earlier work.

In *The Mind in the Cave* Lewis-Williams focused on the cave art of Upper Paleolithic western Europe, especially what is now southern France. Based on archeological evidence, he hypothesizes that about 45,000 years ago, some bands of *Homo sapiens* moved into a region already inhabited by *Homo neanderthalensis*. The latter borrowed several practices, such as techniques for tool making, from their new neighbors. However, the Neanderthals did not adopt other practices, such as the elaborate burial of grave goods and image making. Lewis-Williams sug-gests that they *could* not adopt them because they did not have the same cognitive capacities. In contrast to the Neanderthals, the cave art and other evidence of complex ritual behavior left behind by the newcomers that invaded their territory indicate that they were not only anatomically, but also mentally and behaviorally, modern humans. Their cognitive capacity for abstract thinking and symbolic communication gave them a competitive advantage; by 35,000 years ago, they (i.e., we) were the only surviving hominid species.

Lewis-Williams emphasizes the ambivalence of this capacity: "reli-gious" art and ritual do indeed contribute to social cohesion but they do so by marking off groups from one another. "It was not cooperation but social *competition* and tension that triggered an ever-widening spiral of social, political and technological change that continued long after the last Neanderthal had died, indeed throughout human history."[46]

To defend this claim, Lewis-Williams weaves together research on altered states of consciousness, shamanic rituals in small-scale societies, and the three-tiered cosmology reflected in monumental architecture throughout later pre-modern cultures. He points out that both the cave art of the Upper Paleolithic and that of modern shamanic small-scale societies (such as South African San tribes) show evidence of the sort of hallucinations that normally result from the intensification of *introverted* altered states of consciousness. Whether induced by psychotropic substances, sleep deprivation, or in a neuropsychological laboratory, such experiences consistently lead to entopic phenomena (images that originate within eye-brain relation, such as light spots, zigzag lines, geometric patterns, and auras).

If the experience continues, the subject becomes more autistic (inner focused, cut off from the external world) and the imagery shifts to random hallucinations of objects, animals, and people. Finally, after an experience that is often described as a swirling vortex or rotating tunnel, the subject has iconic hallucinations that mix together the entopic and other images. This is exactly what one finds in shamanic art from the Upper Paleolithic to the present: animals or people (or beings that are part animal, part human) overlain with spots, lines, and auras. Lewis-Williams argues that what we typically call "religion" evolved as a result of early humans' mistakenly taking the effects of hypnagogic and hallucinatory experiences during altered states of consciousness as experiences of a real supernatural realm. The neurologically generated feelings of being pulled down into a hole (or tunnel) and sensations of floating (or flying) up in the sky were taken seriously as actual events in a tiered reality filled with strange spirits. This helps to explain the near-universality of three-tiered cosmologies in pre-modern societies. All religious experience presupposes contact with a supernatural realm, while in fact it is simply the result of "exploring the introverted end of the consciousness spectrum."[47]

In his collaboration with David Pearce in *Inside the Neolithic Mind*, Lewis-Williams extends this analysis to the art produced in the Neolithic age (which began around 12,000 years ago), during which many human groups domesticated animals, developed agriculture, and formed sedentary collectives. Here too one finds the same sorts of imagery, but now it is painted on (or carved into) constructed buildings rather than the walls of caves. During the Neolithic age, humans increasingly took intentional control of their experiences of introverted consciousness and wove them into social life. Lewis-Williams and Pearce hypothesize that they began to manipulate the world (including their housing and food sources) not primarily in response to environmental challenges, but because they wanted better control of their ritual mediation with supernatural agents.

The emergence of "social contracts," Lewis-Williams argues, presupposed a "consciousness contract." Early humans had to learn how to deal with the buzzing confusion of consciousness, which alternated between waking states of alert attention to the external world and other states closer to the introverted end of the consciousness spectrum (hypnagogic states, dreams, and intensified autistic states leading to hallucinations). All humans have neurologically generated experiences, but they have to be shared and regulated in a particular way before they can become the foundation for religion. Lewis-Williams suggests that "shamans" were likely those members of early human groups who were adept at (or susceptible to) having such experiences. The shamans and the other members of the group came to believe that during these experiences they actually engaged with (or even became) powerful spirit-beings, traveling within and across the tiers of the supernatural realm. As the regulation of the alleged interaction between supernatural agents and the other members of a coalition was increasingly taken over by shamans, social differentiation became more marked.

Religion was the "first tool of social discrimination" that was not based on physical strength, gender, or age.[48] Supernatural agent ideas were initially born when hallucinations generated by the electro-chemical functioning of the brain during altered states of consciousness were interpreted as real. The ideas that became and remained culture borne were those that played a role in authorizing and reinforcing the social discrimination practices of a group. Shared imaginative engagement with axiologically relevant supernatural agents (shamanic animal-spirits, ancestor-ghosts, etc.) intensified anthropomorphic promiscuity and sociographic prudery, which granted a competitive advantage to coalitions within the environments of our early ancestors. For Lewis-Williams, "the body provides raw material for what, in a variety of social contexts, is accepted as some sort of trafficking with supernatural forces or beings." In this sense, he observes, "the 'origin' of religion is always with us."[49]

How GOD Was Born

Human populations continued to grow and social discrimination became increasingly complex and hierarchically structured during the millennia that followed the Neolithic. Smaller societies congealed into (or were taken over by) larger coalitions, whose cohesion depended on the development of more powerful mechanisms that could keep its members from cheating, freeloading, or defecting. Bigger groups needed bigger gods to watch over them and punish those who failed to cooperate and commit. The affective and collective security provided by engagement with the relatively limited ancestor-ghosts or other interesting gods who were only interested in one tribe or extended clan was no longer enough. During the first millennium BCE, a new sort of supernatural agent coalition emerged among the Chinese warring states in the Yellow-Yangze valleys, the Magadha of the Ganga valley in India, and urban Jewish communities in the eastern Mediterranean. In addition to finite gods that could punish or bring misfortune, the traditions that emerged in these areas developed concepts of an ultimate disembodied Force that was axiologically relevant for everyone; for example, Dao in East Asia and Dharma in South Asia.

In the wake of the West Asian axial age, however, the major religious conception that emerged to serve this function was far more human-like and coalition-favoring. To avoid confusion with other uses of the word "God," I will use the term GOD (small capitals) to designate the idea, nurtured in all of the "Abrahamic" monotheistic religions, of a disembodied PERSON with unlimited knowledge and power. In other words, GOD is an attempt to represent the intentionality of an ultimate supernatural agent as infinite—or infinity itself as an intentional CONTROLLING FORCE. Wesley Wildman makes a helpful distinction between *super*-naturalism, the inclusion of discarnate intentional beings as items in one's ontological inventory, and *supra*-naturalism, which adds to this inventory a particular sort of item: an "ultimate reality" conceptualized as a "determinate, focally intentional entity," a being with qualities apart from its relation to other finite beings or the world as a whole.[50] I will adopt and adapt this distinction, referring to GOD as a *Supra-natural Agent* (always capitalized), that is, an infinite and intentional Force that creates all determinate finite forces and controls the destiny of every natural (and *super*-natural) coalition.

How was GOD born? The short answer: anthropomorphic promiscuity was pressed to infinity. As we have seen, when the intuitive functioning of human cognition breaks down, it tends to default to inferences that postulate human-like intentionality. Stewart Guthrie points out that it is relatively easy to weed out anthropomorphism and develop alternative interpretations in relation to particular things that are close to us, such as grass and wind. When cognition gets to work on objects that are farther away or more ambiguous, the task of weeding becomes Herculean. "Lacking a Hercules, we inhabit a world whose periphery is rankly overgrown." What happens when we approach the periphery and attempt to detect the cause of "everything?" Guthrie notes that our critical tools, such as science and philosophy, cannot penetrate this periphery. The human mind did not evolve to deal with the "whole of reality" but to solve practical problems related to survival. "When we press on nonetheless, we are thrown upon intuition: that is, upon hypotheses lacking alternatives. Such hypotheses typically posit human attributes."[51]

Imagining that the cause of "all finite things" is a Supranatural Agent initially feels both facile and fecund but, as we will see, reflection on this conception reveals it to be both theoretically incoherent and pragmatically irrelevant. The hyperattribution of human features to an infinite and ultimate reality in West Asian monotheisms is no doubt related to the way in which the identity of those traditions was shaped by their self-identification within a story about a single patriarch (Abraham) who was called by the one true god (Yahweh, Theos, Allah) to set in motion a plan to fix the problems caused by the first man he had created (Adam). For obvious reasons, none of the religions of South or East Asia trace the origin of humanity to the (Mesopotamian) Garden of Eden. Perhaps it makes more sense to refer to Judaism, Christianity, and Islam as *Adamic* rather than *Abrahamic* traditions.

The debates over how (or whether) to conceptualize the fusion of infinity and intentionality in their Supranatural Agent were also influenced by the Platonic conflation of the One and the Good. This conflation was taken over by the monotheistic traditions and superimposed onto GOD as the One source of Value—the absolute origin, condition, and goal for all human axiological engagement whatsoever. We have already seen the first major problem with this religious conception. Human beings do not have the cognitive capacity to think it. GOD is literally *inconceivable*.

This will come as no surprise to theologians associated with the monotheistic religions. Indeed, the major theologians of the Adamic traditions have always insisted that the nature of the divine is "beyond reason." One reason for the inconceivability of GOD is intrinsic to the concept itself. The notion of a Supranatural Agent (an infinite intentional Force) is incoherent. Being an "agent" involves being limited in relation to "patients," that is, to objects of knowledge or power that are *not* the agent. Intentionality entails being in tension, purposively oriented toward objects that condition one's intentions. It makes no sense to apply this to an infinite (unlimited) reality. To conceive of "infinity" as essentially related to that which limits it, that is, as defined *relative* to that which it is *not* (the finite) is not to conceive of *absolute* infinity, but of a *limited* object. In this sense, infinity cannot be "objectified" at all, much less objectified as an agent. To comprehend is to limit, to draw a line around, to capture within a category, to qualify as one being among others. This is why theologians insist that a God comprehended is no God. This insistence is evident even in Anselm's famous "ontological" argument for the necessary existence of a being than which nothing greater can be conceived. "O Lord, thou art not only that," Anselm prays, but "thou art a being greater than *can be* conceived" (Proslogium, XV).

The devotional context of Anselm's argument points us to a third reason that theologians insist GOD is inconceivable. In addition to the psychological and logical problems associated with thinking infinite intentionality or intentional infinity, such a conception is *doxologically* forbidden. GOD not only cannot—He *must not* be conceived. Attempting to imagine the infinite divine reality all too easily leads to idolatry. The worship of finite images (even those that putatively represent GOD) is an affront to the divine glory, which infinitely transcends any and all finite creaturely conceptions. On the other hand, monotheistic coalitions would not hold together unless there was shared imaginative engagement with their Supranatural Agent. Once the idea of a limitless cause of all limitation became an explicit object of reflection, theologians struggled to deal with the tension between their philosophical awareness that GOD is unthinkable (and the doxological demand that He remain so) and their naturally evolved tendency to attribute intentionality to a disembodied force that cares about their group. The inability of finite creatures to conceive the infinite (or even all finite things) suggested an infinite vacuum in human knowledge. Abhorred, the theogonic mechanisms quickly and easily filled it by detecting manifestations of a GOD who watches over any and all coalitions whatsoever.

These problems with conceiving GOD help to explain what Jason Slone calls "theological incorrectness."[52] Why do regular religious folk believe things they should not, that is, things that are inconsistent with the orthodox teaching of their coalitions? For example, classical Christian doctrine includes claims that describe GOD as unchanging, impassible, and in control of all things. Psychological experiments have shown that the same believers who are able to articulate such orthodox doctrines in situations where they are given time and space to reflect automatically default to theologically *incorrect* conceptions when given time constraints and asked to answer questions about narratives involving petitionary prayer.[53] In such experiments, which have been extended and repeated cross-culturally, individuals typically import finite god-conceptions into their interpretations of imaginative engagement with GOD and rate Him as having more knowledge about moral behaviors than about other events or entities.[54] It seems that "dumb gods" (supernatural agents with limited knowledge and power) are more effortlessly born within the mind because they are more relevant and easier to think than a Supranatural Agent whose knowledge encompasses everything and never changes. Moreover, the thought of an all-knowing and all-powerful GOD is a heavy political burden to bear.

How GOD Was Borne

If it is so difficult, even impossible—not to mention blasphemous—to conceive GOD, then why is this idea still kept around in contemporary religious coalitions? Indeed, why was GOD *borne* in the first place? The short answer: sociographic prudery was pressed to eternity. A longer answer requires more attention to the sort of coalition in which He has been engendered and nurtured. As we saw above, bigger groups needed bigger gods to watch over their expanding ranks and punish behavior that did not enhance cooperation, commitment, and proportional reciprocity.[55] As they took over this constitutive and regulative role, however, these bigger gods also demanded bigger groups, motivating and authorizing the expansion of empires. In the case of the West Asian monotheisms, the idea of an infinite GOD was correlated to the idea of an eternal GROUP. Supranatural Agents are borne by Supranatural Coalitions, that is, by complex social networks whose cohesion is dependent on the shared belief that its members have been called out by such an Agent and set apart as a HOLY PEOPLE. Members of monotheistic GROUPS often struggle to dedicate themselves to obedience and worship of a GOD whom they believe will dedicate for them a place with Him in a final social inscription. The idea of an eternal segregation enforced by a disembodied Entity obsessively interested in human behavior makes Him all the more interesting.

In the major religions of South and East Asian origin, one also finds belief in a coalitional afterlife, participation in which is dependent upon one's behavior within and commitment to one's group in this life (reincarnation, ancestral realms, etc.). Such traditions are also characterized by social inscriptions involving obvious segregations, such as the Hindu organization of "castes" and the Chinese organization of "occupations." These hierarchical distinctions within society might even be carried into the next life. In the Adamic traditions, however, a renewed Paradise is exclusively reserved for faithful members of a single GROUP, variously conceived in terms of the Jewish Nation, the Christian Church, or the Muslim Ummah. There are voices within these traditions that resist this sort of exclusivism, and call out for more inclusivist or pluralist conceptions of *eschatological* communion. Such calls often come from activists or mystics who are concerned about the oppressive political and psychological effects *here and now* of bearing GOD within a GROUP in ways that reinforce segregation within it or antagonism toward those outside it. As we will see in chapter 5, such efforts can only go so far. As long as attempts to alter religious conceptions and practices are bound up within religious "families of origin," they will continue to activate the theogonic mechanisms and intensify folk's detection of supernatural agents who can grant everlasting affective and collective security to their kith and kin.

The key point at this stage is the difference between the way in which a Supranatural Agent is borne within a Supranatural Coalition and the way in which gods are borne in the axial age religions that emerged in China and India. Like their West Asian counterparts, supernatural coalitions in (for example) Daoism and Hinduism are populated with a multitude of finite supernatural agents, imaginative engagement with whom helps hold natural coalitions together. In such contexts, however, neither Dao nor Dharma (nor any other conception of an "ultimate reality" that is considered axiologically relevant for all groups) is usually imagined as an infinite intentional Force. The GOD of a monotheistic GROUP is both more person-like and more coalition-favoring. The excessive anthropomorphic promiscuity of the Adamic religions reinforces their excessive sociographic prudery—and vice versa. Theologians within such traditions will object that all such limited (and limiting) human language about GOD must be negated because creatures cannot grasp the infinite mystery of a transcendent Creator. Laypeople may accept this objection when doxologically reflecting on the impassibility of the divine nature, but will intuitively fall back into the automatic cognitive inferential defaults when dealing with the passibility and passions of everyday life. It is much easier to find motivation in shared imaginative engagement with a passionate god who promises participation in a social contract that will secure a blissfully and permanently altered state of consciousness for us and those we love.

Another distinction between the religions of West Asian origin and their counterparts in East and South Asia is the way in which "ultimate reality" is imaginatively engaged to facilitate human transformation. A Confucian sage, for example, may attempt to balance cultivation with contentment, that is, ritual effort with effortless deference to the flow of the Dao. A Buddhist monk may attempt to balance enlightenment with loving-kindness, that is, meditative pursuit of an escape from suffering with compassion toward all suffering beings caught up in the determinations of Dharma. One of the dominant tensions that characterizes the Jewish, Christian, and Muslim struggle for transformation within a GROUP is the attempt to find a balance between justice and mercy, between following the rules and forgiving the rule-breakers as they relate to a GOD who is both just and merciful. Of course, other religions have both compulsory commands and calls for clemency, but that which conditions all finite entities and events is not (usually) conceived as a personal *law*-giver and *care*-giver in the same way one finds in the Adamic traditions. This difference has ramifications for the interpretation of revelation and the practice of ritual in monotheistic Supranatural Coalitions.

During the long process in which small-scale societies were combined and forged into imperial coalitions, it became increasingly important—and increasingly difficult—to be sure that everyone in these (ever bigger) groups knew how their (ever bigger) gods thought, acted, and felt about their behavior. The evolved cognitive and coalitional default mechanisms could not handle the pressure; they were not adapted for shared imaginative engagement within complex, large-scale social environments. The invention of writing and record-keeping was an important part of the solution to this problem. Literacy provided a way to maintain and transmit cultural narratives and values in a way that transcended the limited evolved capacities of human memory and social networking. [56] All religions that emerged within complex literate states have holy texts, but each of the West Asian monotheistic traditions bears a HOLY TEXT (Torah, Bible, Qur'an) that is allegedly authored by GOD and intended as a guide for His HOLY PEOPLE. Supranatural Coalitions are indeed people of THE BOOK, which provides a literary scaffolding for their wider shared imaginative engagement with a Supranatural Agent.

But it is not quite that easy to bear GOD. How does one know how to interpret the HOLY TEXT and how to organize ritual practices that bind the GROUP together? Monotheistic traditions clearly illustrate what Harvey Whitehouse calls the "doctrinal" mode of religiosity. The *imagistic* mode of religious transmission relies on episodic memory and is characterized by high arousal, low-frequency rituals. This sort of ritual engagement works well in local small-scale societies, but does not spread easily to other groups. The *doctrinal* mode, on the other hand, relies more on semantic memory and is characterized by low arousal, high-frequency rituals. This sort of ritual engagement works better in large-scale societies and spreads more easily to new groups. However, the doctrinal mode requires more centralization and a hierarchy of religious leaders who can codify and police the ritual practices within the Coalition. The constant repetition of and relative lack of arousal within its rituals, however, easily lead to what Whitehouse calls a "tedium" effect.

If this sort of religious transmission is to continue—if GOD is to remain culturally borne within a monotheistic GROUP—the tediousness of its routinized rituals must be counterbalanced. Whitehouse argues that the tedium effect is overcome, in part, by a bifurcation of memory systems: explicit semantic schemas play the dominant role when remembering religious teaching, but implicit scripts that operate automatically play the dominant role during the actual repetition of rituals. Explicit religious knowledge involves the repetition of official dogma, which does not necessarily entail a reflective process. People may repeat the orthodox interpretations given by the rabbi, priest, or imam, but the intuitive cognitive mechanisms of implicit memory take over when the shared ritual practices begin. As Whitehouse points out in his analysis of research on Christian groups, members of religious coalitions characterized by the doctrinal mode of transmission have little occasion for doubt. Because they are rarely encouraged to consider the contradictions between implicit and explicit forms of religious knowledge, they "are capable of being profoundly unreflexive participants in their religions."[57]

In other words, it does not matter so much whether the idea of GOD makes sense as long as a monotheistic GROUP is regularly engaged in rituals that activate the evolved cognitive and coalitional mechanisms that hold its members together in small groups. Costly signaling theory helps clarify why and how this works. Psychological experiments, social surveys, and ethnographic observations suggest that one of the most important variables that effects whether an individual will continue to bear the beliefs postulated by a group is the extent to which he or she is confronted with what Joseph Henrich calls *credibility enhancing displays* (CREDs).[58] The human mind is predisposed to grant credibility to people who display powerful emotions and costly behaviors connected to what they claim to believe. If a person grows up in a context where he or she is not exposed to CREDs related to (otherwise incredible) religious claims, he or she is less likely to believe. This helps to explain the prevalence of atheism in contexts such as Scandinavia, where GOD sometimes hangs ambiguously in the cultural air but is not widely borne.[59]

Unveiling Theogonic Mechanisms

In the majority of the world's population, however, gods are continually born in human minds and carefully borne in human cultures. As ongoing research within the biocultural study of religion continues to disclose the naturally evolved cognitive and coalitional tendencies that drive religious reproduction, this new message will have a more powerful effect in the marketplace of ideas, and even on the churches, than Nietzsche's message about the death of God. Why? Because unveiling the mechanisms that reproduce the "birth of God" in human minds and cultures automatically *weakens* them.

This enervating effect can be clarified by comparing and contrasting what I have been calling theogonic mechanisms with Rene Girard's treatment of the *scapegoat* mechanism. Even if we cannot accept all the details of his description of this mechanism, or the universal prescription he proposes, we can acknowledge that Girard has illuminated the dynamics of an important process within some societies. People's desires tend to mimic the desires of those around them; they want what others want (or have). This desire plays a role in holding an in-group together. As mimetic desire escalates, however, it can easily lead to manipulative and even violent behavior that, if left alone, can threaten the cohesion or even the existence of the group. The scapegoat mechanism provides a way for coalitions to dissipate this threat. One individual (or subgroup) is identified by the majority of the coalition as the cause of the problem, the culpable source of the disorder. All of the coalition's violence is focused on the scapegoat, who is removed or destroyed. This process can re-establish solidarity within the coalition, whose members temporarily feel united against "evil."[60]

There are several important differences between Girard's analysis of the scapegoat mechanism and my analysis of theogonic mechanisms. Girard's theory has been criticized for its lack of empirical warrant, its overly broad application to ancient mythical texts, and its narrow focus on ritual practices that are privileged within patriarchal societies.[61] Moreover, his proposed solution for dissolving the scapegoat mechanism appeals to the revelation of a particular monotheistic coalition (Christianity). The basic claims of theogonic reproduction theory, on the other hand, are massively supported by empirical research across a wide variety of scientific disciplines and do not appeal to shared imaginative engagement with the gods of any group. Another important difference is material: the *scapegoat* mechanism leads to the empirical identification and victimization of more or less embodied vulnerable agents, who must be cursed, sent away, or destroyed in order to rid the community of violence, sin, or evil. The *theogonic* mechanisms, on the other hand, lead to the putative identification and valorization of more or less invulnerable disembodied agents, who must be manipulated or appeased in some way in order to avoid misfortune or acquire blessing.

However, there are also some interesting similarities. In one sense, what Girard calls the scapegoat mechanism is one example of the kind of theogonic mechanism we have been discussing, insofar as the former involves the detection of an ambiguous intentional force that must be dealt with in order to diffuse tension and maintain the psychological and social cohesion of members of an in-group. Another similarity is the way in which both theogonic and scapegoating mechanisms "work," in the sense that (some) persons within the in-group often feel better and their communities often survive longer because of them. In each case, however, their "working" actually makes things worse. Removing or destroying *scapegoats* reinforces the powerful belief that our problems can be solved by more violence against natural agents. Detecting and protecting *gods* reinforce the powerful belief that our problems can be solved by maintaining coalitions with supernatural agents.

The most important similarity, however, has to do with the *effect* of the process of unveiling. Girard points out that the scapegoat mechanism only works well when it is hidden, that is, when those who are caught up in its operation are not fully aware of what they are doing. In fact, using violence against scapegoats does not rid the community of violence—it only reinforces it. Once people come to see that the cohesion of their in-group is being secured by a violence toward scapegoats, that they are not ridding the community of "evil" but only reinforcing it, it becomes harder to participate in the scapegoating. When we begin to recognize what we are doing to scapegoats, and what our scapegoating is doing to us, the process no longer automatically has the effect of (temporarily) calming us psychologically and politically. This is true of other coalitional mechanisms as well. Racism, sexism, and classism have all played a role in holding together selves in groups for millennia. However painful this may have been for some, few people questioned the violent mechanisms by which affluent European males, for example, maintained their rule over women and slaves. As Aristotle put it, this sort of ruling just seems "natural" (*Politics*, 1.12).

As such mechanisms are increasingly unveiled, their effectiveness wanes and they can more easily be contested and altered. The more one sees the negative effects and biases driving the oppression of minorities, women, and the poor, the harder it is to continue participating in the systems that reproduce this oppression. We have evolved not to reflect critically on such conventions, but it is harder to follow our default biases the more we are faced with their consequences. In a similar way, as we begin to see how gods are born(e) in human cognition and culture, such conceptions can more easily become the object of our critical reflection rather than surreptitiously shaping our subjectivity and sociality. For the reasons outlined in previous sections, evolution has predisposed us to think, feel, and act in ways that keep these mechanisms hidden. Pulling back the veil and talking about the dynamics of god-bearing not only make them less mysterious, but also enable us to engage them more intentionally.

In other words, having "the talk" about theogonic mechanisms promotes, or at least allows, analytic *reflection* on processes that usually operate *intuitively* and automatically at an affective or emotional level. Research in the biocultural study of religion has overwhelmingly demonstrated a correlation between atheism and variables such as reflective cognitive style, intelligence, and the enjoyment of rational analysis. Atheistic individuals also tend to be better at identifying and analyzing their emotions and to be less prone to illusory agency detection in biological motion-perception tasks.[62] Psychological experiments also suggest that the repetitive procedures characteristic of religious rituals activate default causal assumptions about intentionality, which contribute to believers' interpretation of the efficacy of supernatural agents. In other words, ritual engagement generates intuitive cognitive processes that lead to increased self-reported belief in God.[63]

Anthropomorphic promiscuity and sociographic prudery function intuitively and automatically reinforce one another. Contesting these cognitive and coalitional tendencies requires more intentional reflective effort but, as we will see, once they begin to gain momentum the forces of anthropomorphic prudery and sociographic promiscuity are also mutually stimulating. This will be important to remember as we engage in the maieutic task of facilitating atheist conceptions. The theogonic mechanisms are being unveiled by scientists operating within the fields that make up the biocultural study of religion. For the most part, theology has helped hold up the veil up around the reproductive activities of particular monotheistic traditions. But is that all it can do?

Chapter 3

The Scientific Discipline of Theology

For any human coalition to hold together, some sort of discipline is required. This applies to religious groups bound together by shared imaginative engagement with supernatural agents as well as to extended families linked together by genetic and matrimonial bonds. It is quite common for disciplinary practices within the latter to play a central role in the formation of disciples in the former. A very different sort of discipline—mental and social—is necessary for maintaining academic networks that are held together by shared research interests and goals. In this chapter, I use the conceptual framework introduced in chapter 2 to clarify the difference between theology (as it is usually practiced) and other academic fields. Like scientists in most other disciplines, scholars who operate within the fields that make up the biocultural study of religion place a high value on arguments that are based on empirical analysis and critical conceptual reflection that can be assessed by those outside their own research group.

To a growing number of these scientists, it seems that theologians coddle rather than critique their religious conceptions, nurturing them in the safety of their own supernatural coalitions. In descriptions of contemporary *popular* forms of religious belief and practice, especially in small-scale societies, the tone one commonly picks up in the scientific literature on religion is a mixture of mild fascination and patient incredulity. However, when it comes to the *professional* activities of religious specialists, philosophers, and theologians committed to Supranatural Agent Coalitions in complex literate states, one increasingly finds expressions of disdain and even outright alarm among scholars in the biocultural study of religion. Many doubt that theology deserves to be called an academic discipline. Some argue that theology deserves contempt or even censure because of the deleterious effects of its psychological and political machinations.

This chapter provides an overview of some of the most caustic criticisms of the discipline. A glance at the subheadings of the central sections, which are phrases constructed from the terminology used by some scientists to define or describe "theology," indicates the level of their aggravation. When theology is conceptualized in this way, we can understand why so many scholars want to keep it out of sight from the academy and away from the public sphere. Rather than protecting theology from such critique, I want to set it under the harshest light we can find in order to clearly reveal the mechanisms at work within it, so that we can deal with them more intentionally. Utilizing a conceptual crowbar constructed out of insights from the biocultural sciences, we may then be able to pry apart two very different sorts of strategies within the field of theology, one of which has dominated and domesticated the other ever since the axial age.

First, however, we need to clarify some of the mechanisms at work within other academic fields, mechanisms that have contributed to the escalation of calls for disciplinary action toward—and sometimes even for the death of—the erstwhile queen of the sciences.

From Interdisciplinary Revolt to Regicide

During the high Middle Ages in Europe, philosophy was widely considered the "handmaiden of theology" (*ancilla theologiae*). It was allowed to serve as long as it did not challenge the reigning dogmas of Mother Church or the ambitions of the Papal See for expanding the family of GOD. As other scientific disciplines emerged during the Renaissance, the Reformation, and early modern periods, they had to distinguish themselves in an academic court ruled by theology. Almost all European scientists in the sixteenth century, and most well into the seventeenth and eighteenth centuries, took it for granted that their research into "the book of Nature" was wholly consistent with faith in, and was even authorized by, a Supranatural Agent whose intentions for an eschatological Supranatural Coalition of those who professed faith in Christ had been clearly revealed in "the book of Scripture." Christian theology focused on the sacred field of its HOLY TEXT and permitted other sciences to plow their (mundane) fields as long as their empirical and intellectual toil did not unearth anything that threatened to weaken the cohesion of its monotheistic GROUP.

Slowly, but surely, the various sciences have extricated themselves from the controlling oversight of the Christian religion. Scholars of nature and society came to realize that they did not need the hypothesis GOD in their theoretical explanations of the physical world (e.g., Laplace) or their practical proposals for organizing the social world (e.g., Grotius). From the Galileo affair to the Scopes monkey trial, there have been fabulous flash points and surprising setbacks in this long process of liberation, but today (for the most part, in most contexts) scientists do their work without worrying about theology. It may not be clear exactly when or how it happened, but the queen has been dethroned. In fact, her status in the academic court is seriously in question. Most scientists ignore her. Many are willing to nod toward her, as long as she stays out of the way. Some tease and make fun of her. A growing chorus, however, is calling for her head.

Some of the most clarion voices in this choir are the "new atheists." Richard Dawkins, for example, refers to theology as "self-indulgent thought-denying skyhookery," filled with grotesque pieces of reasoning that appear out of the sky and only serve to support what is already believed.[1] Sam Harris finds the writings of some theologians so bizarre that he sardonically wonders if they might be "carefully constructed nonsense...pseudo-science, pseudo-scholarship and pseudo-reasoning" intentionally employed to embarrass the religious establishment.[2] Daniel Dennett suggests theological discussion and "research" is an intellectual exercise that "scratches the skeptical itch of those few people who are uncomfortable with the creeds they were taught as children, and is ignored by everybody else." If that were all it did, we could go on ignoring it. However, Dennett argues that we should hold accountable moderate theologians who provide a "cloak of respectability" to their fanatical coreligionists.[3]

For the purposes of this project, I will focus on critiques that have arisen among scientists operative within the wider research field I have been calling the biocultural study of religion. As we will see below, their assessments of the academic discipline of theology are no less (and sometimes more) harsh than those of the new atheists. Limiting myself in this way makes it easier to keep our attention on the underlying cognitive and coalitional tendencies at work in theology—and its critics. I suggest that the acrimony toward theology can be explained, in part, by the fact that scientists are trained to contest both types of theogonic mechanism. Like most scholars in the academy, researchers in the biocultural study of religion work hard to resist the defaults that automatically detect intentionality when confronted with ambiguous natural phenomena and that automatically protect the cohesion of an in-group by accepting claims based on conventional authority.

Most scientists—at least when they are doing science—are *anthropomorphic prudes*. As Scott Atran points out, scientific explanations differ from religious (or even common sense) interpretations of ambiguous events "by *excluding* rather than *conjuring up* agent-based accounts."[4] In their analysis of religious rituals, Lawson and McCauley observe that "the religious world *increases* the number and influence of intentional agents while science ultimately aims to *minimize* both by seeking alternative accounts of affairs in terms of underlying, predictable, non-intentional mechanisms."[5] This is perhaps most obvious in disciplines like physics and chemistry, but it is equally true of social sciences in which human intentionality is quite often causally relevant and a necessary component of an adequate explanation. Scholars working in such fields still try to minimize rather than conjure up agent-based accounts, going out of their way to detect nonintentional factors at work within the social systems they analyze. All academic disciplines (except traditional theology) are hesitant to postulate gods as actual causal forces within an interpretation. This is the hallmark of *methodological naturalism*: rejection of appeals to supernatural agency in theoretical explanations of the world.

Moreover, scientists are also (or at least they long to be) *sociographically promiscuous*. They are open to intercourse with other research coalitions even—or especially—when members of those coalitions are critical of the experimental designs or conceptual arguments of their own. Scientists welcome such interactions because the cross-pollenation of ideas can lead to more plausible hypotheses and more feasible research methodologies. In fact, the academy fosters a suspicion of in-group bias. Scientists learn to be wary of research that is heavily funded by coalitions that have a strong interest in the outcome. The salutary effect of a drug may be as astonishing as the study funded by the pharmaceutical company that produces it suggests. Most scientists will defer judgment until and unless the research is duplicated by less potentially prejudiced parties. Scientists are human too, so of course they are often blind to their own biases. Ideally, however, members of an academic community learn to value the unveiling of such biases through critical engagement with those from opposing schools of thought. Insofar as it is possible, they strive to overcome the temptation to submit to the pressures of convention—particularly religious convention—when arranging the arena of social inquiry. This is the hallmark of what I will refer to in chapter 6 as *methodological secularism*: rejection of appeals to supernatural authority in normative prescriptions for the social world.

Scientists, like most other people, fully expect theologians to be partisan defenders of their own GROUP in discussions of the values that should shape social engagement in the public sphere. They also expect theologians to talk about their own GOD (and other coalitional "gods," such as angels, demons, or jinn) in discussions of the forces that actually shape the causal nexus of human life. It is not hard to see why a growing number of scholars, especially in the biocultural study of religion, believe that theology has no serious role to play in scientific or public discourse. Insofar as it is borne along by the integrated mechanisms of anthropomorphic promiscuity and sociographic prudery, theology seems diametrically opposed to the course taken by science—and inevitably fractious in pluralistic contexts. As we will see, some scientists are nervous about publically supporting *metaphysical* versions of naturalism and secularism.

However, even when they do not *intend* (or intend *not*) to deny the existence of GOD (or gods), the findings and formulations of scientists within the biocultural study of religion unveil the forces of theogonic reproduction. As the mechanisms by which supernatural agents are born(e) within supernatural coalitions are increasingly exposed, they lose their reproductive power. They only work well when they are hidden, when members of religious groups do not reflect on the intellectual coherence or the practical consequences of their god-bearing. The forces that are integrated in the upper right quadrant of figure 3.1, on the other hand, may be referred to as *theolytic* mechanisms. As we will see, these two tendencies are also mutually reinforcing as they work together to loosen or dissolve (*lysis*) the hold that conceptions of gods (*theōn*) have on human minds and groups.

I will return in chapter 6 to the other two quadrants of this diagram in the context of a discussion of arguments for and against "letting gods go."

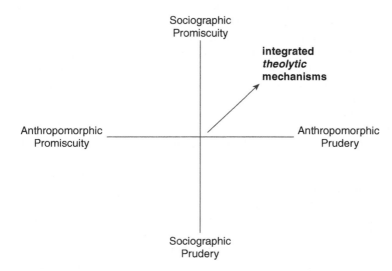

Figure 3.1   Theolytic Mechanisms

At this stage, the important point is the tension between theolytic and theogonic mechanisms, especially when they are integrated in the upper right and lower left quadrants of our conceptual grid. This helps us understand why many scientists and philosophers find the discipline of theology so annoying. Rather than simply murdering the former queen, however, I suggest that the critical conceptual tools provided by the biocultural study of religion can help us differentiate between two distinct skill sets she possesses. No doubt she has worked hard over the centuries to protect a particular monotheistic GROUP, and exhausted herself in engendering (in ever more minds and cultures) conceptions of a GOD who is supposed to have created Adam and called Abraham and whose revelation is mediated by Moses, Christ, and/or Mohammed. However, if she too can escape the biocultural gravitational pull of "religion," she might have a unique contribution to make in the ongoing disclosure of theogonic mechanisms and the creative production of theolytic hypotheses.

Sacerdotal and Iconoclastic Trajectories in Theology

I suggested in chapter 1 that theology can be reconceptualized as the critique and construction of hypotheses about the existential conditions for axiological engagement, a task that I will take up in earnest at the end of this chapter and throughout chapter 4. In chapter 2, I observed that for most of the history of our species attempts to account for and orient the evaluative interactions that shape human life arose in small-scale coalitions and involved appeals to supernatural agents. After the rise of complex literate states, and in the wake of the West Asian axial age, a new kind of hypothesis emerged that appealed to a Supranatural Agent. The major traditions that originated in East and South Asia have their own versions of "theology," but in this context I am interested primarily in the dominant sort of hypothesizing that came to characterize the Adamic religions: all axiological engagement whatsoever is conditioned by an infinite intentional Force, a GOD revealed to and ritually engaged by a particular GROUP.

This kind of hypothesis, which is borne along by the natural integration of theogonic mechanisms, follows what I call the *sacerdotal* trajectory of theology. The word "sacerdotal" refers to the mediation (or making) of the sacred (that which is holy, or set apart), and usually carries connotations related to the ministrations of a priestly class in a monotheistic tradition. In this context, I am using the term to designate the trajectory followed by the majority of Jewish, Muslim, and especially Christian theologians in the formulation of claims about the origination, organization, and orientation of human valuation. The hypotheses that flow out of this trajectory presuppose the authority of a HOLY TEXT and propagate the making-sacred of a HOLY PEOPLE. The overwhelming dominance of the sacerdotal trajectory has led many scholars within the fields of the biocultural study of religion to assume that this is all that theology does and all that it can do.

As we have already noted in earlier chapters, however, there have always been other forces at work in theology. Intellectuals within the West Asian traditions have also generated other sorts of arguments that challenge the coherence and credibility of the concept of an infinitely just GOD whose mercy is limited to only one GROUP. For reasons we will explore in chapter 4, these often arose in response to the so-called problem of evil. But alternate hypotheses emerged in theology for other reasons as well, whenever there was critical reflection on the idea of an infinite Supranatural Agent (or an eternal Supranatural Coalition). Insofar as *an* agent or *a* being (of any kind) is defined relative to that which it is *not* (other beings, whether agents or patients), it cannot be considered absolutely *infinite*. To think of a Supranatural Agent as transcending (being above or beyond) nature is to distinguish that Agent from that which it is not (nature). Being intentional (or having intentions) requires being distinct from that which is potentially (or actually) intended.

But such distinctions introduce conditions of limitation (or negation) and therefore render that which one is trying to think *finite*. The concept of an infinite intentional Force makes no sense. If one cannot imagine GOD as a PERSON because it introduces limitation into the divine, *a forteriori* one cannot think of "Him" as favoring one GROUP over others. This is one reason why the "image" of Supranatural Agency must be broken; it pretends to signify infinity *iconically*—a logically impossible task. This kind of hypothesizing follows what I call the *iconoclastic* trajectory of theology. The term "iconoclastic" also has strong connotations, and is often linked to particular historical periods in Christianity (e.g., early medieval Byzantium). My use of the term here, however, is philosophical. It refers to the tendency to resist what Gilles Deleuze calls the Platonic domain of representation, the Eidetic sphere in which images are judged as true copies (icons) or false copies (simulacra) based on their alleged conformity to (or participation in the being of) ideal models. Elsewhere, I have explored the destructive *and* constructive process of "overturning Platonism," utilizing the metaphor of "hammering theology."[6]

In this context, I will continue to use the distinction between sacerdotal and iconoclastic, but, in accordance with the primary metaphor guiding this book on "postpartum theology," I will often also focus on the way in which these trajectories generate GOD-bearing or GOD-dissolving hypotheses about the conditions for axiological engagement. When operating under the influence of the theogonic mechanisms, theologians follow the *sacerdotal* trajectory, codifying and policing the way in which GOD is imaginatively engaged within a particular monotheistic GROUP. When they follow the *iconoclastic* trajectory, on the other hand, their hypothesizing resists person-like and coalition-favoring images (figure 3.2).

It is important to emphasize that the theolytic forces that motivate the iconoclastic trajectory do not necessarily lead to the dissolution of groups or all of the evaluative practices that hold them together. Both trajectories generate arguments about the conditions of (and for) the human experience of valuing and being valued. The iconoclastic trajectory is distinguished from its sacerdotal counterpart by its repulsion of hypotheses that rely on and reinforce appeals to the revelation and ritual practices of a Supranatural Agent Coalition.

The problems with traditional sacerdotal hypotheses have been openly and widely discussed throughout the centuries by leading intellectuals in all three monotheistic traditions. Long before the emergence of the biocultural sciences, theologians have been pointing out the philosophical flaws in (and, more rarely, the psychological and political distress caused by) the concept of a GOD who sets apart a GROUP. It is tempting to give a list of names of Christian theologians who have

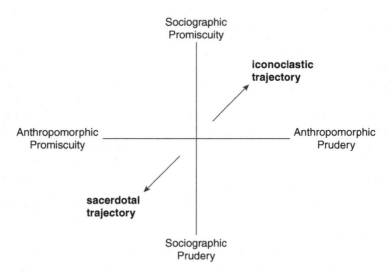

Figure 3.2   Sacerdotal and Iconoclastic Trajectories

pointed out the inconceivability of (and difficulty in bearing) such religious conceptions, but such a list would contain virtually every major theologian since, and including, St. Paul. OK, maybe just a short list of some of the most well-known: Irenaeus, Gregory of Nyssa, Augustine, Anselm, Thomas Aquinas, Duns Scotus, William of Occam, Martin Luther, John Calvin, Jonathan Edwards, Friedrich Schleiermacher, and Paul Tillich. The problem, however, is that even those in this list who most powerfully resisted the idea of God as a PERSON who exists in a determinate and intentional relation to the finite world, that is, GOD, still approved or even encouraged the use of anthropomorphic language in the context of pastoral care and sacramental practice within the religious coalition itself, further reinforcing the sociographic prudery of the GROUP.

In other words, the vast majority of Christian theologians have felt the pull of the theolytic mechanisms, but have been dragged back by the biocultural gravitational force of the theogonic mechanisms. When the preferred religious images of a Supranatural Agent begin to crack in a way that threatens the cohesion of a Supranatural Coalition, the sacerdotal forces go into overdrive to suppress the iconoclastic trajectory. Up until the last few centuries, it has not been that hard to suppress. For a long time, appeals to "mystery"—reminders of the unlimited glory of the divine nature and of the limits of sinful human nature—were enough to secure a veil of ambiguity behind which theogonic reproduction could run wild. It makes good sense to say that the human mind cannot grasp infinity the way it grasps finite things, but this philosophical observation has all too often been appropriated for religious purposes, *domesticating* critical reflection on infinity and intentionality within a particular sacerdotal community. Most theologians have tried to develop both sorts of hypothesis at the same time.

This seems to be what most annoys scholars from other disciplines. On the one hand, theologians have often provided reflective arguments that press in the direction of anthropomorphic prudery and sociographic promiscuity, but, on the other hand, they have also protected their own religious coalition's supernatural agent detections. This undermines their credibility when they try to participate in serious academic conversations. If theologians can escape the forces of the sacerdotal trajectory, however, they may be able to contribute to "the talk" about religious reproduction in a way that *complements* the efforts of scientists in the biocultural study of religion to unveil the theogonic mechanisms. Bearing gods comes naturally, but bearing GOD does not. I will argue that demonstrating the implausibility (and infeasibility) of conceiving a *Supranatural* Agent can have an enervating effect on the power of the theogonic mechanisms to generate shared imaginative engagement with *supernatural* agents as well.

How can we free the iconoclastic trajectory from its domestication within particular religious in-groups by the forces of the sacerdotal trajectory? How can we pry apart GOD-dissolving hypotheses from the GOD-bearing hypotheses that have overshadowed and subjugated them for so long? We can find resources for the construction of conceptual tools for such an extraction within the writings of some of the most vocal critics of theology in the biocultural study of religion, including the three scholars whose theoretical integrations were introduced in chapter 2.

Commodified Parasitic Knowledge of Airy Nothing

When treating religious beliefs and behaviors within small-scale societies like the Fang tribes, Pascal Boyer expresses himself in a tone that is relatively unruffled, although one senses that he is often writing tongue in cheek. This is in stark contrast to the tongue-lashing critique he gives to intellectual and political leaders of large-scale religious traditions in complex literate states. In *The Fracture of an Illusion: Science and the Dissolution of Religion*, Boyer observes that polytheistic shamans are far more tolerant than monotheistic priests. The former are generally content to provide their services locally, whereas the latter are part of expansive institutionalized guilds trying to grab more of the market share for their own religion. Boyer insists, however, that there is "no such thing as religion." Of course there are cognitive representations of nonphysical agents, ceremonies, and other ritual practices that bind people together emotionally, strategies for enforcing social norms, etc. But the "packaging" of these things into "religion" is the invention of religious officers in "cartels" that have bundled their ministrations into a "brand," a stabilized set of beliefs (doctrines) and services (sacraments) that they can control. In this sense, a "religion" is just a slogan, a "marketing ploy" of ecclesiastical and theological guilds.[7]

The terminology that makes up the heading for this subsection is derived from Boyer's earlier book *Religion Explained*. He notes that it has been said of poetry that it "gives to 'airy nothing' a local habitation and a name."[8] Boyer suggests that this remark is even more applicable to the supernatural imagination. In that context, he uses the term "religion" as a label for describing "the ideas, actions, rules and objects that have to do with the existence and properties of superhuman agents like God" (11). Boyer argues that religion is a by-product of other cognitive and coalitional processes that evolved for other reasons. This is why he calls religious knowledge "parasitic." It can only exist by feeding off other evolutionarily stabilized mechanisms such as moral intuitions that already hold selves and groups together. Science, insists Boyer, has shown that there is some-thing "dramatically flawed *in principle* about religion as a way of knowing things, and that there is a better way of gathering reliable information about the world" (369).

What distinguishes theology from religious imagination in general is that it *commodifies* this parasitic knowledge of airy nothing. Over time, literate religious guilds tried to replace local supernatural agents with ideas of abstract gods, but the latter are cognitively costly and not clearly rel-evant to daily life. It was difficult to convince people that they needed the special services provided by such guilds, when it was so much easier to go to their local shaman. This placed literate groups of religious specialists in a precarious position. The only way to sustain their group, which required rigorous training for its members, was somehow to guarantee that people would continue to need their services. Religious scholars had to develop new strategies for maintaining the demand for their commodities in order to compete with local specialists who offered religious services that were (cognitively) more accessible. Boyer notes that the marketing strategy that seems to have worked best for priestly guilds involved gaining leverage within a large-scale political organization and offering "supernatural justi-fications for the established order" (317).

What appears to upset Boyer most is not the attempts by religious specialists to develop more or less coherent doctrines, but the way in which they "spawn abstruse and paradoxical theology as well, that is, lit-erate versions of the supernatural concepts that do not connect with any of the supernatural templates... and do not activate inference systems either." In their reflective attempts to make sense of the intuitive concep-tions borne in the religious community, theologians construct *maximally* counterintuitive ideas, that is, ideas that combine multiple violations of the assumptions and expectations that structure intuitive ontology. For example, GOD is like a PERSON but is impassible, simple, omniscient, omnipotent, infallible, transcendent, etc. When pressed on the inco-herence of such ideas, theologians often use "mystical contemplation to escape puzzles they create" (319). Convincing people, or keeping them convinced, that they need to believe things that are difficult to understand, and engage in behaviors that are not obviously useful, is an arduous task. It is hard to connect everyday religious behavior to "the rarefied intellectual atmosphere of literate theology" (99).

This contributes to what Boyer calls "the tragedy of the theologian." Pointing to some of the literature we reviewed in chapter 2 on the way in which people may repeat "theologically correct" answers, but default to more minimally counterintuitive ideas under time constraints, Boyer expresses a little sympathy for theologians. Powerful evolutionary mechanisms make their job very difficult. But his sympathy does not extend very far. Boyer is particularly irritated by the contemporary "science and religion" dialog, in which the asymmetry between the explanatory power of science and (sacerdotal) theology is too often ignored. He charges the doctrinal directors of Christianity with making "the crucial mistake of meddling in empirical statements of fact, providing us with a long list of particular precise, official and officially compelling statements about the cosmos and biology, supposedly guaranteed by Revelation, that we now know to be false." Boyer argues that in every case where the church has offered "its own description of what happens in the world *and* there was some scientific alternative on the very same topic, the latter has proved better. Every battle has been lost and conclusively so" (368).

In his earlier book on *The Naturalness of Religion*, Boyer had challenged what he called a *theologistic bias* in cultural anthropology. This "theologism" is the combination of two mistakes. The first error is taking for granted the systemic connections between religious ideas, which are, for the most part, invented by theologians, and presupposing that these links are a necessary part of religious representation. The second mistake is thinking that these representations can be best described by "postulating some abstract intellectual entities," such as symbol systems or webs of meaning, that allegedly underpin the connections. This theologistic bias has led many anthropologists to project these (imagined) systems of meaning onto people's explanations of particular religious objects such as material tokens. In light of cognitive psychology, Boyer argues, it makes more sense to say that these objects are simply used to orient people's attention, as "cues" for selecting and strengthening interpretations relevant within a particular context. Written theological productions, he insists, do not "contain" a "meaning"; rather, they are "overextended cues" that can generate a higher specificity of inference than other cues.[9]

We will address these issues again in chapter 4, as part of a larger discussion about the role of inductive, deductive, abductive, and retroductive inference in science, religion, and theology. At this stage, the main point is to acknowledge the aptness of Boyer's critique, which clearly applies to the sacerdotal trajectory of theology. The theogonic forces integrated within the latter have (so far) succeeded in domesticating the iconoclastic trajectory whenever it begins to threaten the cohesion of a religious coalition within one of the monotheistic traditions.

Half-Baked Representations of Logically Impossible Worlds

As we saw in chapter 2, one of Scott Atran's main interests is the function that religious costly signaling plays in fostering commitment in groups, and especially in big groups with big gods. In *Talking to the Enemy*, he explored the connection between the evolution of monotheistic coalitions, large-scale cooperation, and enduring group conflict. Atran argued in that context that costly religion and the problem of fostering cooperation in expanding coalitions resolved one another in a process of "cultural coevolution." This coevolution depended upon "costly communal commitment to absurd, counterintuitive ideas that have no consistent logical or empirical connection to everyday reality."[10] Early human populations survived by cooperating, but, as they expanded in size, they came into conflict with other groups over resources. Atran suggests that the increase in *the scope and cost of religious belief* was "both the cause and consequence of this increasing group cooperation, expansion and competition."[11] In other words, expansive doctrinal religions like the Adamic monotheisms not only facilitate large-scale cooperation, but also intensify competition among groups, increasing people's willingness to kill or die for "the Cause," which is all too obvious in the so-called war on terror.

What does this have to do with theology? In *In Gods We Trust*, Atran argued that religious doctrines are only public representations of "quasi-propositional beliefs" whose meaning can never be fixed because they are based on counterintuitive, supernatural concepts. Theological statements about ultimate postulates or foundational myths have the superficial characteristics of ordinary logical or factual propositions (e.g., a subject-predicate structure), but they are nonpropositional—at least if they include any reference to supernatural agents. "The violations of intuitive categories that any supernatural phenomena manifests preclude any possibility of inferential consistency and completeness."[12] This preclusion provides and protects an imaginative space in which believers can ignore ordinary relevance criteria when dealing with religious communications such as holy texts or theological doctrines. "To be sure, people interpret God's message in particular ways for specific contexts, but they have no reason to ever *stop* interpreting." Doctrinal theological assertions can *never* be logically integrated or empirically relevant in the way normal assertions are; their cognitive role is to "mobilize a more or less fluid and open-textured network of ordinary commonsense beliefs in order to build *logically and factually impossible worlds* that are readily conceivable, memorable, and transmissible."[13]

Atran had spelled out this argument in more detail in his earlier *Cognitive Foundations of Natural History.* One of his main tasks in that context was clarifying the distinction and interrelation between what he calls common sense, symbolism, and science. His overall argument was that common sense (and cognitively universal) conceptions of the living world are both historically prior to and psychologically necessary for any elaboration of that world, whether symbolic or scientific. Adapting terminology developed by Dan Sperber and others, Atran argues that a *symbolic* utterance is *nonpropositional* in the sense that no logical, fixed meaning could be assigned to it that would permit a coherent evaluation of its empirical entailments, and no determinate factual content could be experienced that would definitively confirm or disconfirm it. "In multiplying senses and metaphors, symbolism leaves the interpretation of an utterance significantly 'open-ended.'"[14] The goal of such forms of knowledge is not to determine facts but to incite and keep on inciting evocations: "The quasi-propositions of symbolism are always open to contradictory interpretations of meaning and experience." The propositions of *science*, on the other hand, are, at least in principle, "semantically precise and empirically testable."[15]

Both scientific and mythico-religious symbolic utterances are elaborations of *common sense*, which operate intuitively with ontological assumptions about natural kinds that are universal across cultures. The difference lies in the way in which these two modes of elaboration deal with new ideas. In the everyday process of learning, when an idea is introduced, the mind engages in second-order speculations, attempting to make sense of the idea and assimilate it into a broader understanding of the empirical world. Forming ideas about these half-understood ideas "allows the construction of conceptual stages towards a full understanding." This is how children come to terms with the world as they assimilate new words. The cognitive capacity for *meta-representation* is what enables humans to "entertain, recognize and evaluate the difference between true and false beliefs." In addition to rapid and complex learning, however, this capacity to imagine counterfactual states of affairs and communicate about them also makes it possible for humans to lie, cheat, and obsess about death. Human beings use "their 'susceptibilities' to 'meta-representation,' that is, the capacity to form representations of representations, so as to retain half-understood ideas. By embedding *half-baked notions* in ideas we can have about them, they can be extended into full knowledge or otherwise further conceptually articulated."[16]

However, the passage from meta-representation to assimilation of new knowledge is not always easy; learning new ideas in a scientific discipline, for example, is hard work. In some cases, however, assimilation is not even *possible*. In mythico-religious symbolism, argues Atran, knowledge remains "*forever half-baked* (meta-representational) notions about ideas." Second-order cognitions about ideas derived from doctrinal formulations, religious rites, or liturgies are never fully baked. Religious beliefs are always held meta-representationally, endlessly discussed, taught, and reinterpreted in religious coalitions. The fact that they "do not lend themselves to any kind of clear and final comprehension allows their learning, their teaching and their *exegeses to go on forever*."[17] As in a child's normal process of acquiring ordinary knowledge, science uses the capacity to form second-order representations to "play with the idea of an idea" in a way that constructs conceptual stages toward a full understanding. The goal of science is to "extend factual knowledge, resolve phenomenal paradoxes or increasingly restrict the scope of interesting conceptual puzzles." Mythico-religious elaborations, on the other hand, are continuously developing open-ended reconstruals of a symbolic world that is "always open to contradictory interpretations of meaning and experience." Religious cognitions are sustained on this path by "faith in the authority of those charged with the task of continually reinterpreting the truth and fitting it to new circumstances."[18]

For Atran, the trunk of the "tree of knowledge" is formed by common sense dispositions shared by all human beings. The tree permits of elaboration in a way that forms two distinctive branches, one in which cognitive susceptibilities lead in the direction of "the relatively unfettered growth of symbolism," and one that follows "the direction of well-pruned scientific graftings." This helps to explain the different ways in which biblical creationists and evolutionary scientists, for example, elaborate the ordinary common-sense meaning attached to species as natural kinds. He argues that the symbolic and scientific modes of elaborating second-order speculation about the empirical world "tend to be *diametrically opposed*."[19] It is quite clear on which branch Atran locates theology. Even if one were to assess doctrinal sentences by the criteria of "fuzzy logic" they would still be too open-textured to "reliably generate intuitions of truth, falsity, verisimilitude, likelihood probability, warrantedness, or justifiability."[20] No doubt the sacerdotal trajectory of theology thrives only as long as it follows the symbolic "branch," on which it is relatively easy to nurture half-baked ideas involving supernatural agents as long as they feed the imagination of a religious coalition. The iconoclastic trajectory, however, draws theologians out onto the more carefully trimmed limbs of the scientific "branch," where they come to realize that they cannot have their half-baked doctrinal ideas and eat them too.

Factitious Enigmas of Complaisant
Religious Pundits

Boyer and Atran both make strong distinctions between science and theology and are clearly concerned about the psychological and political problems associated with the role of the latter in monotheistic coalitions. Lewis-Williams is more than concerned: he is alarmed by theology and straightforwardly attacks it. Well aware that it was once regarded as the queen of the sciences, he insists that theology now "stands no chance of being reinstated in that exalted position."[21] Lewis-Williams views theology as a dangerous, perhaps even criminal, endeavor that must be exposed and eradicated. In *The Mind in the Cave*, he compared the visions of Hildegard of Bingen, a medieval Roman Catholic mystic, with the shamanic art produced during the Upper Paleolithic and other contexts. Hildegard interpreted entopic phenomena and iconic hallucinations, most likely caused by migraines, as God's revelation to her about the actual material structure of the universe. During these intensified introverted states of consciousness, she saw hallucinations of angels and creatures suggested to her by scripture and medieval wall paintings, whereas an Inuit shaman, for example, "sees" talking polar bears and seals.[22] The problem with theologians in monotheistic contexts is not just that they take such experiences seriously, but that they establish themselves as arbiters of the belief of religious practitioners. In *Inside the Neolithic Mind*, Lewis-Williams complained about the way in which theologians "manipulate the systems of belief that they construct to include or exclude groups of people, as the church fathers did at Nicea."[23]

In his latest book on *Conceiving God*, however, Lewis-Williams takes off the kid gloves. In that context, he describes theology as "a continuously tended and trimmed hedge that screens off fundamental and really quite straightforward matters."[24] Science advances by using empirical analysis and logic to get rid of outmoded explanations and adopt new ones. In theology, on the other hand, logic is "perverted to become a weapon of exclusion, rather than clarification" (64). Scientists should not accept theological claims because the latter always presuppose the revelation of a realm of supernatural agents, belief in which is simply a misinterpretation of certain kinds of neurological activity. "Once we allow for the possibility of divine revelation of special knowledge...we are adrift on a logically stormy sea. All that theologians can then do is try to explain and clarify supposed divine revelations." Theology cannot be taken seriously;

it is simply "what religion says about itself" and "therefore the product of spin-doctors" (116). Lewis-Williams is particularly agitated by the way in which theologians start by trying to prove illogical or paradoxical beliefs with "convoluted justifications," but then always end up appealing to mystery.

Such "mysteries" are merely "factitious enigmas" that are "created by religious belief and that become raw material for the theological industry" (271). Theology is an "industry" in more than a metaphorical sense. Incorporated within a monotheistic institution like the Roman Catholic Church, argues Lewis-Williams, theology is also industrial in a capitalist sense. An elite group (a priestly hierarchy) controls the resources (revealed knowledge, access to sacraments) and the means of production (e.g., cathedrals, schools). "The public at large buys the product (salvation, peace of mind) and thus enriches the elite (witness the wealth of the Vatican and other major religious denominations)."[25] Theological justifications of supposed divine revelations are always ad hoc, reacting complaisantly to changes in scientific and cultural understandings of the world in order to reinforce the "power base for clergy and theologians" (274). Theologians are religious pundits who invent and play with puzzling doctrines, altering them as necessary to maintain their elite status. Because religion, at least in its large-scale, monotheistic manifestations, intensifies competition for power and influence based on special revelation controlled by particular groups, it is a problem, not a solution, for discussions about how to live together in pluralistic contexts. "Supernaturalism is the death knell of multiculturalism" (286).

Lewis-Williams is not only kicking ass, he is also taking names, and Augustine and Aquinas are at the top of his list. Citing Augustine's suggestion that scientific inquisitiveness is a "diseased craving," as well as his attitudes toward slaves and pagan religions, Lewis-Williams concludes he was a "bully, a bigot and an obscurantist...his sins after his conversion were more heinous—certainly more far-reaching—than the peccadilloes and debaucheries of his youth" (57). Patristic and medieval theologians wove together biblical references about Satan and demons and developed a complex demonology and angelology in relation to which people were supposed to understand their own lives. Lewis-Williams notes Augustine's belief in lesser demons who could have sex with human beings, and Thomas Aquinas's descriptions of Succubi who could bring a dead woman's body to life, have sex with a man, and then turn into an Incubus in order to impregnate another woman with the sperm of the man. "When we read this sort of horrific, indeed wicked, nonsense, we wonder why the Church continues to admire people like Augustine and

Aquinas. They were not merely 'of their time.' Their obsessed, twisted minds verged on madness" (181).

If theology is the problem, science is the solution. He credits Thales and other sixth-century (BCE) Ionian philosophers with introducing a new mode of critical thinking into human life. Their efforts contributed to the emergence of what we today call science, which involves empirical observations and conceptual explanations that are always open to criticism. This was only possible, argues Lewis-Williams, because Ionia was not "priest-ridden." Thales and company were not beholden to a priestly class with vested interests in the status quo, whose members insist "that some knowledge is not to be questioned—the knowledge that they themselves possess and guard" (28). Lewis-Williams complains that theology today is "massively fertilized" by the "religion *versus* science debate" (117), a debate that he finds neither necessary nor beneficial. Science has repeatedly modified religion and never vice versa. Trying to appease religionists through "dialogue" with science merely keeps up a façade, behind which imaginative engagement with spirit-beings continues undisturbed. Lewis-Williams argues that there can be no reconciliation between science and religion, because they are diametrically opposed when it comes to questions about the existence of supernatural realms and the validity of the alleged revelation of supernatural agents.

In the last chapter of *Conceiving God,* Lewis-Williams anticipates the objection that he should distinguish between fundamentalist ravers and the sophisticated arguments of theologians. However, he sees such distinctions as side-stepping a basic issue that he insists should no longer be evaded in a world where religion can do so much damage. Even debates about "belief in God" and "spirituality" are red herrings. "Simple" people the world over can indeed understand this issue: Do supernatural entities exist who can intervene in daily life? When "subtle" theologians dismiss naïve ideas about an anthropomorphic being in the sky and replace them with complex ideas about the Trinity as a model for human relationships or about a divine consciousness that apprehends all possible worlds, they are obscuring the core question upon which religion depends: Are there supernatural agent coalitions—or not? "The *most important* question is: Can we today, after all that has happened since Thales...believe that there is a supernatural realm peopled by beings and forces who are interested in the lives of those who live on planet earth and who, at least from time to time, intervene in both natural and human affairs?"[26] His answer is a resounding no, ruling "theology" out of the bounds of serious academic inquiry.

Ockham's Shaving Foam on Divine Attachment Figures

One of the basic insights of "attachment theory," first developed by John Bowlby and others in the 1960s and 1970s, is that early childhood relationships with "attachment figures" (or primary caregivers, usually the parents) shape a person's capacity for and style of relating to others throughout life.[27] The evolution of an "attachment behavioral system," whose activation leads a stressed infant to seek proximity to such figures, and these figures to provide protection and comfort, contributed to the survival of the species. The formation of a *secure* attachment contributes not only to surviving, but also to thriving: the attachment figure is experienced as a "safe haven" to which the child can turn when anxious, and as a "secure base" from which the child can set off to explore the world. A child who is unable to seek (or does not receive) proximity early in life can become *insecurely* attached, anxiously hyperactivating or avoidantly deactivating the behavioral system. Early in life, children develop "internal working models" of others (and the self) based on their relationship to their primary caregivers. These models are then automatically applied to others (and the self) in adolescence and adulthood, powerfully shaping interpretations and reactions in relationships with romantic partners, friends, employers, and even strangers in larger social networks, especially under stressful conditions.[28]

Over the last two decades, Lee A. Kirkpatrick and Pehr Granqvist have been at the forefront of the attempt to apply attachment theory to religion. In *Attachment, Evolution and the Psychology of Religion*, Kirkpatrick summarizes (and theoretically integrates) dozens of studies that have explored the connection between relationships to early attachment figures and "attachment to God."[29] Granqvist has expanded this research field by also exploring the impact of early attachments on forms of spirituality that do not involve such obviously anthropomorphic gods, as in some New Age movements and some "mystical" experiences.[30] Along with many others, these scholars have demonstrated how the internal working models that develop in childhood activate people's attachment behavioral machinery in adolescence and adulthood, powerfully affecting their perceptions of themselves and others both in human relationships and in their imaginative engagement with supernatural agents (including, and even especially, GOD).

Experimental and clinical research suggests that there are two different "developmental pathways" that lead to adult relationships with a divine

attachment figure, both of which involve the application of internal working models acquired through early childhood experiences of caregivers
to GOD (or gods).[31] The *correspondence* pathway is more common among
individuals who developed a secure attachment with their early caregivers. They are more likely to perceive GOD as sensitive, nurturing, and
trustworthy. In such cases, the internal working model for "others" is activated and applied to a supernatural "Other," who might be experienced
as providing an eternally secure base. For others, however, the pathway to
religion involves *compensation* for earlier experiences of insecure attachment. In such cases, persons with anxious or avoidant attachment styles
might seek out proximity with a divine attachment figure who can provide what they did not receive as children. Their internal working models
have hindered them from finding a safe haven in the natural (and social)
world, and they deal with this anxiety by turning to a surrogate—an idealized supernatural caregiver. Sudden religious conversions in adulthood,
for example, are most common among those with anxious or "preoccu-
pied" attachment styles.

Compared to securely attached individuals, those with insecure
attachment styles tend to be less focused on GOD when they enter new
romantic relationships and more focused on GOD when they break up. "If
there is a recipe for attachment to God in adulthood," suggests Kirkpatrick,
"it might be the combination of an anxious/preoccupied attachment
style and an avoidant romantic partner."[32] The compensation pathway is
clearly illustrated in the findings of a research study by Thomas Ross on
men in an evangelical Christian setting. The results suggested that men
who scored low on the scales of self-concept and self-efficacy, and scored
high on the scales for dependence on immediate narcissistic gratification,
magnificent self-representation, symbiotic self-protection, and pining for
a powerful, radiant, mighty, and stimulating ideal self-object were using
GOD as a compensatory attachment figure to make up for their own sense
of individual weakness or their longing for security.[33]

Neither Kirkpatrick nor Granqvist is as hostile toward theology (or
religion) as Boyer, Atran, or Lewis-Williams, but they do go out of their
way to distinguish it strongly from science. Kirkpatrick describes theology
as the effort of religious experts to wrestle with "fundamental paradoxes
and apparent logical inconsistencies in their belief system." He insists that
personal beliefs about such things are "extra-scientific," and should not
be included in scientific discussions.[34] Granqvist feels a bit more strongly
about separating the disciplines. When it comes to scientific discussions
of religion, he implores: "will theology please be left out?" Science and
religion are "incommensurable" and any attempts to integrate them
"should probably be abandoned in the first step, as it seems to be doing

both disciplines more harm than good." Theology, which he describes as "anything dealing with the ontology of God," is outside the boundaries of scientific inquiry.

Science, argues Granqvist, is based on materialist metaphysics and physical causation. When engaging any phenomenon, it uses Occam's razor to shave away unnecessary factors (or "substances") that are not necessary for developing explanations, descriptions, or taxonomies. Religion, on the other hand, is "based on immaterialist metaphysics and teleological causation, engaging in values and existential props, while *applying Occam's shaving foam*."[35] Granqvist has a point. The sacerdotal trajectory of theology generously lathers layers of unnecessary immaterial substances onto its descriptions of a hidden Supernatural Agent. However, it is important to point out that Occam himself was a theologian. In fact, he is an excellent example, perhaps the most important late medieval example, of the iconoclastic trajectory within theology. Occam found the concept of GOD existentially troubling and logically incoherent. In his analysis of the concept of predestination, for example, he wondered how GOD could know and will everything for all eternity and still hold human beings responsible for their actions? Unfortunately, even Occam finally failed to use his own razor when it came to his faith in the divine attachment Figure of the religious GROUP to which he was bound.

Management of Ritual Failure through Excess Conceptual Control

As we noted in chapter 2, shared *ritual* engagement with supernatural agents plays a major role in holding religious in-groups together. The costly signaling involved in participating in such rituals can buy affective and collective security, but it also purchases an increase in the felt need to protect one's own group and a stronger bias toward detecting one's own gods (especially when under stress). This helps to explain why the forces of the sacerdotal trajectory are able to pull otherwise reflective theologians back into the intuitive theogonic reproduction of the coalitions in which they are ritual participants. In one of the earliest books in the field, *Rethinking Religion: Connecting Cognition and Culture* (1990), Thomas Lawson and Robert McCauley developed a cognitive theory of religious rituals, which they defined as "those religious actions whose structural descriptions include a logical object and appeal to a culturally postulated superhuman agent's action somewhere within their overall structural description."[36] One of the most significant contributions of their theory is the analysis of the formal function of cognitive representations of *action* in participants' representations of the role of culturally postulated superhuman (CPS) *agents* in rituals.

In this context, however, I want to focus on their broader treatment of the role of theological interpretations of rituals within religious coalitions. Lawson and McCauley observe that theologians typically "adopt a protectionist stance toward their object of study."[37] In other words, theologically oriented analyses of ritual are rarely interested in *explanatory* questions, but rather are usually content to *interpret* the religious ritual as "a relationship" between the human participants and the CPS-agents that the rituals allegedly engage. Ordinary cognitive assumptions about agency may constrain the *form* of religious rituals, but they argue that the unusual metaphysical presumptions about the *objects* of religious worlds (such as CPS-agents) mean that theological interpretations are "practically *flexible without limit*, possessing resources that are sufficient to persist in the face of virtually any challenge."

In fact, Lawson and McCauley argue that the failure of the "Death of God" movement was, in part, a result of its inability to maintain this flexibility and creativity. Its leaders denigrated the most central transcendent symbols of the Christian religious world, because their putative referents had "died," and attempted to force the remaining symbols to refer to immanent "objects and events in the everyday world," linking them to a particular time and place (late 1960s' America). However, religious groups survive only if their imaginative religious worlds include "groundless symbols" that can be endlessly manipulated and applied to new contexts. "Death of God" theology dissipated because it tied itself to a particular religion's symbolic world, but excised the sort of symbol that keeps people engaged. This movement did not have the creative flexibility required to facilitate ongoing ritual interaction with complicitous CPS-agents who are *unconstrained* by the spatial and temporal limitations of the empirical world.[38]

In *Bringing Ritual to Mind: Psychological Foundations of Cultural Forms*, McCauley and Lawson critically engaged Whitehouse's theory of "ritual modes," to which we briefly alluded in the last chapter. The theory of "ritual form" they developed in this second co-authored book attends not only to the relationship between frequency of repetition and sensory pageantry, but also to the action role attributed to CPS-agents in religious rituals. They argue that it is the participants' *representations* of how CPS-agents are implicated in their rituals (e.g., the extent to which they are represented as immediately present and active) that determine how (and whether) the rituals are repeated, as well as the sort of mnemonic dynamics and emotional arousal involved.[39] McCauley and Lawson also explore what Whitehouse called the "tedium effect" in doctrinal religions: people lose interest if rituals are frequently repeated but do not arouse the cognitive and coalitional mechanisms that motivate religious selves and hold religious groups together. They often use Christianity to illustrate the sort of "balanced" ritual system that helps a large-scale coalition survive by providing a mix of rituals that are adequately arousing.

McCauley and Lawson point out that all religious groups, regardless of size, must deal with a similar hermeneutical problem: how to make sense of apparent ritual failure. If a CPS-agent is allegedly acting (or promises to act) in a ritual, then participants' cognitive representation of "agency" leads them to expect to detect *some* effect of its action in the real world. If the ritual continually fails as, for example, in the millennial rituals of splinter groups that are intended to welcome back ancestor-ghosts (or invite the return of Christ), then the religious coalition becomes unstable. When splinter groups fail, they are usually re-integrated into the coalition from which they dissented or dissolved by mass suicide—or by wholesale slaughter as in the conflicts between and among Roman Catholics and Protestants after the Reformation. How then did the earliest Christian groups succeed even when Christ did not return as they expected? McCauley and Lawson argue that, in order for such splinter groups to survive the failure of their innovative CPS-agent rituals, they must develop *"religious conceptual schemes that can avert these rituals' failures."*

This "conceptual control" works only if the schemes "provide conceptual resources for characterizing the consequences of these rituals as fundamental transformations that result from the actions of CPS-agents *without necessitating any empirically detectable changes in the world that the religious system cannot control."*[40] McCauley and Lawson illustrate this in a variety of religious groups, including Christianity. In the latter, conceptual control is called "theology." The tedium effect can be reintroduced into this sort of doctrinal coalition if theologians or religious leaders exert too much control. What they call *excess conceptual control* reduces sensory pageantry and emotional arousal in *all* of the group's rituals. They hypothesize that the increasing concern among Christian theologians in the West "with theological niceties and intellectual nuance" is a result of the challenges they have faced over the last centuries from "a larger secular society armed with modern science." McCauley and Lawson suggest that the anguish of "theological elites" associated with the languishing mainstream denominations can be explained in part by the tension between "their religious allegiances and their commitments to rational reflection."[41]

In a more recent single-authored volume, *Why Religion Is Natural and Science Is Not*, McCauley deals with several of the issues we have been exploring in the last two chapters. He also offers a more direct assessment of the difference between science and theology. McCauley does not think religion and science will ever be reconciled. Why? "(1) The findings of science concern the (intersubjectively available) empirical world. (2) Almost all gods are (alleged to be) empirically inaccessible almost all of the time. Therefore: (3) Scientific findings, indeed empirical findings of any sort, will not ordinarily have any direct bearing on claims about those god's existence." As McCauley points out, however, the problem is that "religious people, *including theologians*, regularly backslide about the truth of that argument's second premise." Violations of premise (2) often come with "theological defenses to *insulate* their claims from empirical refutation."

This sort of theological dodging drains doctrinal claims "of all empirical refutability and, thus, of all empirical interest, but that has no impact on their continuing cognitive (and religious) appeal." The "theological constables" of doctrinal religions, who are often champions of "bloodless, abstract religious thought," have shown throughout history an ingenuity that can accommodate almost any challenge, devising "intellectual means for tolerating even the most revolutionary scientific claims." However, they succeed only by vacillating about "the empirical detectability of the gods' works and of the gods themselves."[42] This is effective within a religious coalition only so long as theologians remain within the flow of the sacerdotal trajectory, whose reproductive power easily and "naturally" keeps human minds occupied in imaginative engagement with alleged disembodied agents who are interested in their in-group.

Reactionary Immunization of Foundational Sacred Texts

In chapter 2, we saw how rituals and revelation—broadly conceived—work together within the shared imaginative worlds of religious groups. In the case of the monotheistic traditions that emerged in the wake of the West Asian axial age, the *revelation* of GOD is more or less tightly bound to the HOLY TEXT of a HOLY GROUP. Among the scholars operating in the fields of the biocultural study of religion, none has engaged the actual content and procedures of Christian theology more than Ilkka Pyysiäinen. His formal education was in theology before he turned his attention to comparative religion and the cognitive sciences. In *Supernatural Agents: Why We Believe in Souls, Gods and Buddhas*, Pyysiäinen engages the work of Christian theologians like Thomas Aquinas and Paul Tillich in some detail, arguing that even their most abstract claims about God are still empirically unconstrained elaborations of folk-psychology (animacy and mentality attributed to disembodied forces). Like most of the other scholars introduced above, he also emphasizes the importance of both cognitive and cultural perspectives in research on religion: "(T)he world's religious traditions are comparable across cultures" because *cognitive* mechanisms like HADD and ToMM "sustain a cross-culturally recurrent pattern of perception and reasoning." Insofar as supernatural agent representations are "related to the need to understand the ways others understand the minds of others, [they] are intimately linked with the organization of human *societies*."[43]

My primary interest in this section is on Pyysiäinen's analysis of the function of theology within a religious coalition, especially as it bears on the interpretation of sacred texts. In *Supernatural Agents,* he argued that "theology is only reactionary" (185). As more knowledge about physical reality adds new constraints to the religious imagination, theologians constantly reinterpret the idea of GOD. These reinterpretations are always connected to a foundational text—in the case of Christianity, the Bible. Pyysiäinen notes the importance of the Protestant principle of *sola scriptura,* according to which the Bible should be viewed as the only authoritative arbiter of truth and capable of "interpreting itself." The authority of the Bible is not dependent on the church (or anything else) and it cannot be understood or judged by extra-biblical standards. This circularity leads Pyysiäinen to suggest that, were it not for sacred texts, theology would apparently "be about nothing" (121).

In his earlier book on *Magic, Miracles and Religion,* Pyysiäinen explored the relation between theology and Scripture in more detail. In a chapter called "Holy Book: The Invention of Writing and Religious Cognition," he described the change in the transmission of religious ideas that came along with the emergence of sacred texts. Religious specialists "began to strive for a *coherent and complete* doctrinal system that was supposed to be universally valid and independent of time and place and ended up with circular reasoning and paradoxes." As oral traditions were written down and canons were formed, "mythology" was "turned into theology." But the dialectic between a foundational sacred text and attempts at logically explicating its meaning inevitably led to hermeneutical contradictions that could only be "quarantined" in the hope that they might eventually be solved through further reflection on revelation. Religions that rely on theological interpretations of canonical literature are not "more evolved" than nonliterate small-scale religions; they are on the same continuum of folk belief, but "use a new device—writing—to transmit cultural representations." The reliance on a foundational sacred text, however, "leads to endless symbolic exegesis" because of the tension between *"the logical impossibility and the theological necessity* of having foundational knowledge that *also* has a foundation."[44]

Pyysiäinen argues that biblical exegesis and theological reflection can function endlessly within a religious coalition because of the nature of religious meta-representation. Critical reflection on a belief requires that one detach it from its meta-representational context and "copy" it into a temporary mental "buffer." In everyday situations, one *suspends* the semantic relation between an extensional truth claim "X" (e.g., "There is a beer in the fridge") and the intensional context in which a person says "X" (e.g., "Tom says there is a beer in the fridge"). This suspension leads to a *restriction* of empirically relevant inferences; one may not infer that there actually is a beer in the fridge from Tom's saying so (Tom may be lying or simply mistaken, or he may have had one too many). In other words, in normal reflective processes, one distinguishes between the representation "beer in the fridge" and its original meta-representational context "Tom says so." In *religious* meta-representation, however, "semantic relations are *not suspended* and inferences are *not restricted*."[45] This means that in religious situations believers automatically accept the veracity of extensional claims, whose truth they intuitively take as following directly from their intensional context: the HOLY TEXT says so.

Although theologians (and regular believers) may disagree on what the Bible *means*, they typically agree that if "the Bible says X" then "X is true." Whether the issue is the acceptance or prohibition of, for example, women in ministry, slavery, or homosexuality, theologians on both sides have quoted the Bible in support of their positions. However, as long as both sides accept the insularity and inviolability of the authority of the Bible (the foundational meta-representational context), such hermeneutical debates can go on forever. Pyysiäinen argues that this is a characteristic of *ideology*, which is "typically based on the prohibition on detaching certain beliefs from their context and subjecting them to critical refection." This prohibition, which is assumed rather than argued, "leads to a situation where ideology is totally *immune* to criticism, because all criticism not based on a shared meta-representational context is merely taken as an example of how people always get the ideology wrong as long as they are outside of its scope."[46]

When confronted by non-Christians (or "heretics" who claim to be Christians) with inconsistencies in the Bible or in their own interpretations, "true" believers might comfort themselves by reminding each other that out-group members cannot understand the Word of God which, after all, is not addressed to them. Members of a different HOLY GROUP will say the same thing about their HOLY TEXT. In *How Religion Works: Towards a New Cognitive Science of Religion*, Pyysiäinen suggests that

Christians (or Buddhists, or any other sort of religious believer) *cannot* represent their religious beliefs outside of a religious situational context, in which they are immunized by an authoritatively "intensional" text, without destroying what makes them *religious*. Critically reflecting on them meta-representationally suspends the assurance that they are true (even if one does not understand them fully) and restricts their inferential relevance in daily life (even if one sees no obvious effects). This helps to explain why theologians are more often tempted by unbelief than laypeople. It also helps to explain why the paradoxes that arise when attempting to make sense of religious beliefs usually "force the theologian too finally to adopt a situation theory of religious knowledge."[47]

What differentiates Christian theology from the sciences, insists Pyysiäinen, is that the former operates on "a different domain of phenomena and employs causal mechanisms that cannot be verified or falsified." He acknowledges that science, like theology, can be used for ideological purposes. It can also function as an authority in some contexts. But there is a difference: "Whereas theology cherishes static truths that are not called into question, the authority of science cherishes the principle of calling everything into question." Pyysiäinen recognizes that theologians are often, perhaps even usually, driven by a desire to reflect critically on the religious beliefs of their coalition. This weakens the power of religious representations. In this sense, he suggests, "theology tends to be as much a *cause* as a *consequence* of 'secularism.'"[48] This leaves open the possibility that the intensification of theological resistance to the theogonic mechanisms of the sacerdotal trajectory might have other, even more serious, consequences.

What Is Theology "about"?

The dethroning of the queen of the sciences has led to a more open, democratic, and productive academic court. But must her deposal be followed by excommunication or extermination? Perhaps, it is best to ignore her and let her work alone as long as she does not get in the way. This would be a tempting alternative if theology were really only about an "airy nothing," or about nothing but "sacred texts." As we have seen, many atheist (or nonreligious) scientists and philosophers are suspicious that this "discipline" is only and always about the supposed status and function of GOD (and gods, such as angels or the Spirit of Christ) in the shared imaginative life of a religious GROUP. If we look only at the reproductive processes within its sacerdotal trajectory, this suspicion is not difficult to understand. However, the god-bearing forces are not the only mechanisms at work in the field of theology. Liberating the long-suppressed forces of its iconoclastic trajectory may enable theologians to contribute in their own way to the generation of productive atheist conceptions in cognition and culture.

As I will argue in more detail in chapter 4, ever since the axial age, this disciplined mode of inquiry has produced *retroductive* hypotheses about the *existential* conditions for axiological engagement. True, most of those hypotheses have incorporated references to the Supranatural Agent of a monotheistic Coalition. Others, however, have not. Some theological hypotheses have operated within constructive arguments about the conditioning of human evaluative interaction that have not appealed to the supernatural agents of any religious coalition. As we will see below, such hypotheses can already be found, for example, in the "theological" writings of Plato, Aristotle, and other ancient philosophers. In the *theologia tripartita* developed by some of the Stoics, we find a distinction between the mythical theology of the poets, the political theology of the state cultus, and the *cosmological* theology of the philosophers.[49] The theological hypotheses constructed by the latter were not at all "religious," in the sense we have been using the term. Even if one were to define theology simply as reflection (*logos*) on the gods (*theōn*), the outcome of theological inquiry might very well be that there are not any—or, if there are, they are completely unintelligible and irrelevant. This was the conclusion of Epicurean theology.

In any case, theology is too important to leave to theists. Some modern *atheist* philosophers have continued to use the term "theology" to describe aspects of their constructive proposals, even though they explicitly reject the concept of GOD and resist the oppressive power of religious GROUPS in their conjectures about the conditions for the real, empirical experience of evaluating and being evaluated.[50] There may well come a time when this sort of hypothesizing is no longer called this—or even called for—but for the time being, in this context and for the purposes of this interdisciplinary conversation, I will keep calling it "theology." Many atheists show little empathy toward theologians in the past who have followed the sacerdotal trajectory. How can we respect them when they gave in so easily to the forces of anthropomorphic promiscuity and sociographic prudery? But, after all, they were human—all too human— members of the species *Homo sapiens* whose phylogenetic inheritance overwhelmingly disposed them in this direction. The fact that theologians of various traditions wrote things now considered ridiculous is not a point against the discipline as a whole any more than the fact that scientists once believed in phlogiston or phrenology. The problem, rather, is continuing to defend such ideas *today*.

In its broadest sense, then, theology theorizes "about" the intense experience of being-conditioned, the being-limited of human knowing, acting, and feeling. It is (more or less disciplined) reflection on the empirical experience of axiological limitation. What could be more empirically relevant than the conditions of every conceivable empirical encounter? Theology deals with the evaluations that arise as we encounter the limits of existence. It operates "at the limits" of intentionality, critiquing and constructing hypotheses about the conditions of (and for) valuable engagements within the existential bounds of human life. It is true that the "object" of theology is not like the objects of other disciplines. The relation between intentionality and infinity cannot be objectified like the relations between finite objects or events.

Rather than using this ambiguous limitation of thought as an excuse for appealing to the mysterious supernatural agency imaginatively engaged within a particular religious coalition, postpartum theology can explore other ways of making sense of this being-limited of thought—or this being-thought of limitation—which can indeed be "objectified" (as the reader is currently doing). The limitation of thinking, acting, and feeling is an objective force in our lives with rather obvious inferential relevance. What are we to think, to do, and to feel about our bounded existence? The sacerdotal trajectory leads to the reactionary protection of supernatural agent detections, but the iconoclastic trajectory promotes the search for correctable criteria for evaluating hypotheses that intelligibly and productively engage the existential intensity encountered at the limits of our natural agency.

It seems that the most "objective" thing that can be thought in regard to the limitation of finite thought is that an objective infinite "thing" that limits finite thought is inconceivable. Our mental capacities have evolved so that they work relatively well in the categorization of finite objects, but there would have been no survival advantage to being able to think about the value of the "whole" of finite reality. Even if we could develop the capacity for such thinking, we would still not be able to conceptualize "the infinite" as an "intentional" force in relation to finitude because, as we have seen, such a concept is intrinsically incoherent. Thought will always "break on the infinite,"[51] because infinity cannot be represented as *an* object (much less *a* person who prefers *a* polity) over against the whole of finitude—else it would be limited and therefore not in-finite. However, this breaking is itself an "object" of thought that has objective force in our lives, precisely by forcing upon us the thought of our own limitation.

Sacerdotal theologians will insist that, behind or beyond this breaking, there exists an infinite intentional Force that cares about human political groupings.

Iconoclastic theologians, on the other hand, will work to de-personify, de-politicize, and, in a sense, even de-objectify (or de-commodify) "infinity" in order to liberate human intentionality. Is there any sense in which such theological critique and construction can operate "objectively?" The scare quotes here are well deserved. It (almost) goes without saying in an academic milieu saturated by postpositivistic and postcolonial concerns that pure objectivity is neither possible nor desirable. However, we can give up the pretentious idea of pure objectivity without pretending that we are not interested in the pragmatic ideal of developing arguments that are intersubjectively and transcommunally plausible. Humans are fallible subjects with biased norms, but the history of philosophy and science illustrates how valuable critical reflection and correctable experimentation can be, especially during periods of rapid ecological or social change. Acknowledging that all of our objectifications are relative to our embodied social contexts does not mean that we are unable to relate more or less "objectively" to others. Indeed, our surviving—and thriving—depends on it.

We can also ask what theology is "about" in a pragmatic sense—what can it *do*? After the "birth of God," what practical function can theology serve? I propose a conception (and practice) of theology as the critique and construction of hypotheses about the existential conditions of (and for) axiological engagement. *Constructive* iconoclastic theological hypotheses will follow the same trajectory that animates other scholars in the academy. Elsewhere, I have explored the hypotheses of Gilles Deleuze as one example of a productive iconoclastic theology.[52] In this book, however, I have focused—and will continue to focus—on the theological *criticism* of hypotheses that appeal to the Supranatural Agent of a monotheistic Coalition. I will argue that postpartum theological critiques of the plausibility of sacerdotal conceptions of an infinite GOD who eternally cares for a religious GROUP can complement the efforts of scientists within the biocultural study of religion who criticize the plausibility of belief in the finite gods imaginatively engaged in the quotidian existence of supernatural coalitions.

Chapter 4

Arguing about Axiological Engagement

Like other complex organisms, we human beings navigate our environments by fighting, fleeing, feeding, and copulating (the four "f"s). That is not all we do, but if we do not do those things well we will not survive to pass on our genes and cultures. Often we do these things without thinking. In fact, things often go better for us if we do not think too much (or too long) about them in moments of stress or excitement; just do what comes naturally. On the other hand, it is also important to learn how to adequately evaluate the appropriateness of each "f" as we engage other complex organisms. And so sometimes we reflect on the relative value of things, and on the potentially good or bad effects of our past and prospective engagements. Occasionally—or, if we are philosophically oriented scientists or theologians, regularly—we also think, and even argue about, the conditions for our (more or less thoughtful) evaluations.

For the reasons we have been exploring, shared imaginative engagement with axiologically relevant supernatural agents has played a central role throughout human history in reflection on and argumentation about the origination, organization, and orientation of "morality." Since the axial age, most debates about value judgments—intellectual and aesthetic, as well as ethical—have been carried out on terrain governed by religious interests. Since the early modern period, however, this territory has been increasingly occupied by anthropomorphically prudish and sociographically promiscuous *scientific* arguments about the conditions for the evolution of human axiological engagement. In the context of the evolutionary and social sciences, the concept of "religion" functions within scientific hypotheses that help to make sense of human behavior. Theological conceptions of axiological conditions, on the other hand, have tradition-ally functioned within *religious* hypotheses that help reproduce gods in groups. In other words, they have followed the sacerdotal trajectory.

In this chapter, I argue that one way to facilitate the liberation of the iconoclastic trajectory within theology is to pay more atten-tion to the role of the modes of inference in arguments between (and among) theologians and scientists about the conditions for axiological engagement. As we will see, Christian theologians (and philosophers) have traditionally focused primarily on deduction and induction, which draws attention away from the supernatural agent *abductions* that estab-lish the imaginative worlds of religious representation within which their argumentation operates. This distraction has made it easier for them to ignore or evade challenges from evolutionary science and other atheistic objections. I suggest that we evaluate claims about the exis-tence and alleged axiological relevance of gods (or GOD) not in terms of their provability (deduction) or probability (induction) but in terms of their *plausibility* as abductive and retroductive hypotheses.

I will compare and contrast scientific and (sacerdotal) theological modes of argumentation by exploring the different ways in which they approach the problem(s) of "good" and "evil." Why do bad things happen to good people? Answers to this kind of question in religious contexts typically involve some reference to supernatural agents, whose entangle-ment within a coalition helps to explain why misfortune befalls its mem-bers. In monotheistic religions, this question is complicated by the idea of a Supranatural Agent who is believed to be omnipotent, omniscient, and omnibenevolent. This leads to the well-known *problem of evil*. If all things are conditioned by an infinitely good, intentional Force (GOD), then why are there evils in the world?

For evolutionary scientists, however, it is quite easy to explain those happenings that people consider bad (for them). The answer is natural selection. Organisms that live long enough to reproduce pass on those variable traits that gave them a competitive advantage for survival in a particular environment. Competition often, indeed usually, means that one organism behaves badly toward another. Why, then, do naturally egoistic people do good things? Altruistic behavior toward other people, especially toward those who are not probable caregivers (or lawgivers), appears to lessen one's chances for survival. Evolutionary theories have to address what we might call the *problem of good*.

These are not merely intellectual problems. Arguing about the condi-tions for axiological engagement has pragmatic effects in the "real world," because it can alter the way we evaluate our engagements with others (including the four "f's"). Having "the talk" about religious reproduction will go better if we can learn to argue well. When we think about such things, we are *intuitively* drawn to infer the presence of supernatural agents who are evaluating our evaluations. Making (or having) a good argument may very well involve intuition, but it also requires critical *reflection* on the structure and strength of our inferences.

Modes of Inference

In the formal sense of the term, an *argument* is simply an attempt to provide *warrant* for making an inference—to move thought from some *grounds* to the acceptance of some *claim*. Once we start reflecting on the sort of claim that is being made and the reasons for accepting the grounds in the first place, however, things begin to get complicated. The limited goal of the following succinct summary of inferential modes is to provide the context for setting out my own claim about the value of moving beyond deduction and induction, and toward abduction and retroduction, in the critique and construction of theological hypotheses. For this reason, I am going to oversimplify matters greatly, focusing primarily on the distinct ways in which these four different modes of inference operate in determining *conditions* within an argument (figure 4.1). To some extent, albeit to varying degrees and with different purposes, scholars in all academic disciplines utilize these four modes of inference even, or especially, when they are not thinking about it.

Briefly, then, a *deductive* inference engages propositions (or sentences, categorical assertions, etc.), assessing their syllogistic form in order to determine the conditions for the logical necessity of a claim. Deduction moves toward one proposition (a conclusion) that allegedly follows from

mode of inference	engages	to determine conditions for
deductive	propositions	logical necessity
inductive	observations	empirical generalizability
abductive	ambiguities	interpretational plausibility
retroductive	suppositions	existential actuality

Figure 4.1 Modes of Inference

another set of propositions (premises). The success of a deductive argument depends on the formal relations between the propositions; its validity can be tested using the rules of formal logic. If the premises of a well-formed, valid deductive argument are true, then the truth of the conclusion necessarily follows logically. For example, take modus ponens: $(p \rightarrow q, p, \therefore q)$. If the propositions in both the major and minor premise are true, that is, if it is in fact the case that p implies q, and that p, then one can deduce that the proposition q is also true. Under these conditions, the truth of the conclusion can be proven based on the form of the argument itself. Of course, the intrinsic limitation of all deductive inferences is glaring: How can we know if the premises are true?

An *inductive* argument moves from multiple observations of particular cases to general claims about other nonobserved cases. This mode of inference does not lead to necessary conclusions, but to (more or less probable) generalizations about empirical phenomena. After observing one million white swans, I might infer that all swans are white. I would have some warrant for accepting the claim: the next swan you see will also be white. But the truth of that claim does not necessarily follow from the grounds (my earlier observations). If I had been traveling to Australia with Willem Vlamingh in 1697 when this claim was made, it would have turned out to be false. Black swans abound down under. The value of claims based on inductive inferences depends on the quality and quantity of the observations that support them, and their validity can be assessed through probabilistic analysis, statistics, and other means. However, this mode of inference only deals with the conditions for empirical generalizability, not logical necessity.

Charles S. Peirce used the term *abduction* to refer to the process by which we develop hypothetical conjectures that are intended to make sense of ambiguous phenomena. "The surprising fact, C, is observed; But if A were true, C would be a matter of course; Hence, there is reason to suspect that A is true."[1] The sort of conclusion that emerges in such conjectures may be based on earlier observations and utilized in later logical formalizations, but an abductive inference cannot be "proven" like deductions or "validated" like inductions. The criteria for accepting a claim that results from this kind of inference have to do with *plausibility*. How compelling is the hypothesis; how well does it make sense of the ambiguous C? Naturally, evaluations of the plausibility of an abductive inference will be shaped by the biocultural heritage of the interpreter and the context within which (and purpose for which) she makes an interpretation. Abduction begins, suggested Peirce, with a "guess": C might make sense if A were true. Such guesses occur all the time in everyday life, often requiring little or no reflection. The glass is broken . . . that would make sense if my dog knocked it over.

The tall grass is moving... that would make sense if a tiger were hiding in there. The hypothesis "tiger" emerges as a possible way to interpret a surprising movement in the jungle. Abductions involving complex theoretical conceptualizations take longer, of course, and may require extensive background knowledge and training. A cognitive scientist, for example, might use the hypothesis "hypersensitive predator detection module" to interpret surprising human reactions to movements in the jungle. Scientific abductions may begin as "educated guesses," but they are typically formulated as hypotheses whose plausibility can then be critically evaluated through creative conceptual or empirical analysis, or some combination of both, depending on disciplinary context. The plausibility of abductions is usually reinforced by the extent to which a newly developed (or applied) hypothesis also "leads away from" (*ab-ducere*) old and toward new insightful deductions and inductions.

Peirce often used the term *retroduction* in a way that was basically synonymous with abduction, but he was not always consistent.[2] For my purposes, I reserve the former term for inferences that are intended to "lead back" (*retro-ducere*) from more or less plausible and stable abductive inferences to that which conditions the existence of the interpreted phenomenon itself. In other words, retroductive inferences lead to claims about what makes a phenomenon possible, or better, the conditions for its *actualization*. Like abduction, retroduction involves the formation of hypotheses. However, retroductive conjectures are about the conditions without which a phenomenon could not *be* (or *become*) as it is. By saying that this mode of inference engages "suppositions," I do not mean that it begins with undefended assumptions. A *pre*-supposition may very well function as a premise in a deductive argument. A *supposition*, in the sense I am using the term, is a claim about the conditions for the actualization of a phenomenon about which a relatively stable and plausible abductive hypothesis has been formed.

Retroductions do not pre-suppose the truth of any abductive interpretation of a surprising phenomenon; rather, they treat such hypotheses meta-representationally, critically reflecting on the conditions for the existence of that which is supposed in (or by) the interpretation. In this sense, abduction and retroduction overlap and work together. Moreover, deductive and inductive inferences are wrapped up within, and generated by, retroductive inferences concerning abductions. Abduction attempts to make sense of a perceptually ambiguous phenomenon by (re)conceptualizing it in light of an interpretive hypothesis. Retroduction attempts to make sense of that which conditions the phenomenon supposedly interpreted by an abductive inference. This means that retroductive argumentation can also *alter* the conditions that affect the plausibility and stability of an abductive hypothesis.

The bulk of this chapter explores some of the typical ways in which the modes of inference function within the arguments of scholars in the evolutionary sciences and scholars in the monotheistic religions as they make conjectures about the conditions for human axiological engagement. Even—or especially—when they have not been explicitly thematized, supernatural agent *abductions* have played a powerful role in holding together religious coalitions and reinforcing the dominance of the sacerdotal trajectory of theology. Like most scientists in other academic disciplines, theologians who follow the iconoclastic trajectory resist the forces of theogonic reproduction as they critique and construct arguments in their field. But what, exactly, is this "field?"

Existential Conditions

Scientists not only develop abductive hypotheses in order to make sense of ambiguous phenomena, but they also often make retroductive inferences about the existential conditions for the emergence or persistence of those phenomena. For example, in order to make sense of their observations of the behavior of light, nineteenth-century scientists hypothesized the existence of "ether," an invisible medium through which it moved. Today, most scientists think that Einstein's conjectures about general and special relativity offer a more adequate account of photic phenomena. They retroductively infer that ether does not exist. In this sense, scientists try to determine the conditions under which a phenomenon could become *what* it is or function in the *way* it does. As we will see, scholars in the biocultural study of religion work hard to make sense of the conditions for the evolution of the phenomenon of "altruistic" human behavior.

Theologians, in the broad sense in which I have been using the term, are interested in hypotheses about particular finite phenomena too, but they also make retroductive inferences about that which conditions existence itself. In other words, they try to make sense of the fact *that* a phenomenon is—or the very fact that there *are* phenomena. Theologians explore the conditions for the becoming of the "field" of being (and beings). What are the conditions for the *existence* of axiological engagement? This level of abstraction may not be of interest to every scientist, just as the level of concretion at which some scientists operate may not be of interest to every theologian. This does not mean they have nothing to say to each other. When it comes to unveiling theogonic mechanisms, theological arguments can complement other theolytic hypotheses in the biocultural study of religion—*if* theologians can persist in the Herculean weeding (to borrow Stewart Guthrie's phrase) required at the limits of human knowledge and follow out the retroductive implications of the iconoclastic trajectory.

One might wonder why people have any interest at all in theological argumentation. We have already noted the psychological and political role that it has played in holding together doctrinal coalitions in the monotheistic traditions that arose in West Asia. Even when it is entangled within the repressive and oppressive structures of a sacerdotal religion, theological reflection about the conditions for existence is *intense*. Many people find theology compelling because its hypotheses about the "field" of being—or becoming—are also about *existential* conditions in a different sense. It is part and (in moments of existential intensity) parcel of the human condition to feel *the limits* of axiological engagement. Arguments about the conditions for our evaluative interactions are not merely theoretical exercises. They have powerful pragmatic effects that bear on the actual valuations that form everyday life, reinforcing or altering the complex axiological webs in which our shared evaluative engagements are entangled.

Our lives are characterized by the ongoing formation and transformation of hypotheses, or "conjectures," about how to make sense of what is going on and what it makes sense to do next. To survive and thrive, we must learn to evaluate not only the plausibility but also the *feasibility* of such conjectures. Under what conditions will my engagement with others "work" to enhance the value of life? We do not escape from the value-laden (and value-buoyant) matrix of human experience when we reflect critically on the *conditions* for axiological engagement, but such reflection can open up new opportunities for intentionally altering our valuations. This means that theology is "about" the pragmatic conditions *for* axiological engagement as well. That is to say, insofar as its theoretical hypothesizing is wrapped up within and around the *abductive* inferences that shape the actual practices of human coalitions, theological *retroduction* can make a difference in the composition of value. In this sense, theology can engender *new* conditions for axiological engagement. This is true of all sorts of theological hypothesizing, whichever trajectory it may follow.

Among the most philosophically and pragmatically influential "theological" hypotheses to emerge in the axial age were those of Plato and Aristotle. Perhaps Plato's most important conjectures about the conditions for axiological engagement were those that led to the claim that the surprising fact that human epistemic evaluations are fallible would be a matter of course if all temporal knowledge was conditioned by its relation to (and "participation" in) an eternal realm of intelligible Ideas. This abductive hypothesis helped Plato account for the problems he encountered when trying to judge between competing mental images. An ideal realm of unchanging Forms, ultimately determined by the Idea of the Good, would provide the conditions for adjudicating between true images (icons) and false images (phantasms) of ideal models, if the latter were retroductively supposed to exist in that realm. The mind and the ideal objects of its knowledge are "good," Plato hypothesized, but because immaterial souls have fallen into the sensible realm they must learn to harness their appetites and use their rational powers to ascend once again to the intelligible realm.

Aristotle used the term "theology" to describe the highest theoretical science, or first philosophy: the field of study that considers being *qua* being (*Meta.* 1026^{a}30). His most influential theological hypothesis postulated the existence of an Unmoved Mover, an ultimate "final" cause toward which all being is aesthetically drawn. As "thought thinking itself," the Unmoved Mover is the perfect, simple, and unchanging condition for all imperfect, complex, and changing axiological engagement. Both the "Idea of the Good" and the "Unmoved Mover" are somewhat human-like, at least in the broad sense that they are "ideational" and imaginatively conceived as grounding human knowledge and values. However, they are not "gods" in the narrower sense used in the biocultural study of religion; they are not supernatural agents watching over a coalition and waiting to punish those whose cooperation and commitment are suspect. In ancient Greek philosophy, that sort of thing was usually left to Zeus, or sometimes even left out of ethical considerations altogether.

Both Plato's and Aristotle's conceptions of the existential conditions for axiological engagement were maximally counterintuitive and did not function well when it came to holding together *religious* groups. Nevertheless, these conjectures were existentially intense for the philosophers who engaged them in search of the "good life" (eudaimonia, virtue, etc.). And they powerfully shaped the landscape of moral discourse and practice in the West. Their influence became pervasive once they were taken up within the Adamic religious traditions. Such grand hypotheses were not necessary when all humans lived in small-scale societies; arguing about values could occur while hunting and gathering with one's kith and kin. As we have seen, the large-scale religious traditions of East and South Asian origin developed a variety of theological hypotheses (like Dao and Dharma) to account for the evaluative interaction of all finite entities (even the gods). Within the monotheistic religions that trace their roots to the West Asian axial age, however, theologians came to suppose that the all-determining Condition for axiological engagement was an *infinite intentional* Force, whose intellect and will encompassed all things.

Ex hypothesi, that which originates, orders, and orients all finite valuation is a Supranatural Agent whose intention in creating the world was the formation of a Supranatural Coalition. The plan for calling this GROUP into eternal relationship with GOD began with Adam, continued with Abraham, and will end in a final judgment that discloses whether membership actually depends on following the law delivered by Moses, believing in Jesus Christ, or obeying the will of Allah as interpreted by Muhammad. This is all confusing enough, but things really got complicated as theologians in these traditions embraced key aspects of Plato's and Aristotle's hypotheses about "ultimate reality." For example, applying Platonic categories to their Supranatural Agent led many sacerdotal theologians to conceive of GOD as an eternally static, rational causative substance. But of what relevance is this to the everyday evaluative interactions within a GROUP composed of temporally dynamic, embodied, and differentiated human beings? It is not hard to understand why theological incorrectness prevails among the religious masses.

Friedrich Nietzsche's claim that "God is dead" was only one component of his broader *atheist* argumentation about the conditions for axiological engagement. Few philosophers have done more to overturn the Platonic-Aristotelian-Christian suppositions that have dominated and constrained thoughtful evaluations in the West. Nietzsche conjectured that it is the "will to power" that engenders values: he called for a transvaluation of values in place of the "slave morality" of Christianity. Few "theological" hypotheses have been more existentially intense than Nietzsche's. As we have seen, however, the intuitive functioning of the forces of theogonic reproduction has made it relatively easy for sacerdotal theologians to evade his critique. The claim that GOD is born(e) will not be so easy to dismiss, especially if we keep focused on the plausibility and feasibility of such supernatural agent abductions.

In *On the Genealogy of Morals,* Nietzsche presses us to reflect more intensely on the conditions that lead to our evaluations of "good and evil." Making judgments about what is good and *bad* is inevitable—a natural part of life. The translation of this distinction into judgments about good and *evil,* however, was a result of what Nietzsche calls a "slave revolt" in morality. This "priestly" mode of valuation that defines the threatening other as "evil" arose out of the *ressentiment* of the weak toward the noble and powerful. It is no surprise that lambs do not like great birds of prey. But this is not a ground for reproaching the latter for bearing off members of their flock:

> And if the lambs say among themselves: "these birds of prey are evil; and whoever is least like a bird of prey, but rather its opposite, a lamb—would

he not be good?" there is no reason to find fault with this institution of an ideal, except that the birds of prey might view it a little ironically and say: "*we* don't dislike them at all, these good little lambs; we even love them: nothing is more tasty than a tender lamb."[3]

Whether one judges the outcome of a particular predation as good or bad (or evil) depends on one's position in relation to the redness of teeth and claws.

This sort of imagery was offensive to Victorian (and Christian) sensibilities, especially for those who wanted to maintain a strong dichotomy between animals and humans in the order of divine creation. Writing in the aftermath of Darwinian theory, Nietzsche added insult to injury by provocatively referring to "good and evil" as a distinction within "herd" morality. This terminology is particularly suggestive in light of hypotheses within the biocultural study of religion that claim the imaginative expansion of the social field to include supernatural agents played a significant role in the complexification of coalitional organization within early groups of *Homo sapiens*.

The Problem of Good in the Evolutionary Sciences

If natural selection favors traits that enhance the capacity of an individual organism, such as a human being, to pass on his or her genes, why do individuals sometimes behave in ways that appear "bad" for them but "good" for others in their herd? Scholars who work in the evolutionary sciences have to construct abductive hypotheses to account for the surprising fact that humans occasionally sacrifice time and energy (or even their lives) in order to help others. Such behavior does not have any obvious survival benefit; indeed, it seems to diminish (or destroy) a person's chances for survival. Behaviors are often evaluated based on the extent to which they facilitate the acquisition of *goods*. All organisms are faced with the task of engaging their natural environment in ways that procure the material objects necessary for adequate nutrition and safety. It is "bad" for the organism if it does not obtain the relevant goods. The competition that is inherent to natural selection helps to explain why bad things happen to good people (actually, to all organisms).

Humans live in complex social environments in which the struggle for goods leads to evaluative judgments about others based on the extent to which they help or hinder their acquisition. All too easily we evaluate competitive others as essentially evil—as they so easily evaluate us. The value we place on others depends, in part, on their role in our survival strategy; an active shepherd is good for the lamb, but bad for the bird of prey. The groups that survive are those whose members develop adaptive mechanisms that enable enough of them to acquire enough goods and to live long enough to reproduce enough offspring. From the point of view of the biocultural sciences, it seems that the emergence of mechanisms related to "religion" contributed to the emergence of forms of human herding (and being herded) that gave a competitive advantage to our early ancestors.

There are three main sorts of evolutionary hypothesis that attempt to make sense of the "altruistic" behavior of human beings, that is, of ways of engaging others that do not evidently contribute to the individual's own survival. The first is the theory of *kin selection*. It makes sense that evolution would naturally select the trait of caring for one's children. In order for genes to be passed on, it is not enough to have offspring; they must survive long enough to have their own children. In the early ancestral environment, the children who lived to pass on their genes were those whose parents who were willing to risk their own safety in order to care for them. But what about acts that involve the provision of care to, sharing of resources with, or self-endangerment for the sake of non-kin? The tendency to behave in this way has no apparent survival advantage. This sort of trait is explained by a second hypothesis: *reciprocal altruism*. In the context of early hunter-gatherer coalitions, acquiring the necessary goods for the survival of one's offspring (and oneself) was often difficult. It would have paid off to maintain relationships with non-kin who might be able to help when things got tough. I'll scratch your back if you scratch mine (and my children's). Behaviors that promoted reciprocity of care beyond kin-relationships would have been naturally selected in such ecological environments.

However, as groups got larger and more complex it became increasingly difficult to know whether others *would* reciprocate—what if they are free-riders, cheaters, or secretly planning to defect? Caring for or sharing with such persons is not likely to contribute to the survival of an individual's genes. Yet, some individuals do behave in astonishingly selfless ways, risking their own lives for total strangers. Reflection on this surprising fact led to a third sort of hypothesis: *indirect reciprocity*. People who consistently act altruistically develop a reputation within the group. Even if they are taken advantage of by nonreciprocators who are the beneficiaries of their altruism, *other* members of their coalition might step in to care for them (or their children). One way to signal to others that one is a trustworthy reciprocator—and worthy of reciprocation—is to engage in costly (and sufficiently public) displays of altruism. Developing a reputation over time for indiscriminate caregiving can encourage others to signal back and provide care; even if the reciprocity is indirect, this strategy can still grant a survival advantage to one's offspring.

Altruistic behavior is not limited to the human species. Care for offspring (kin selection) is evident in all mammals, care for non-kin (reciprocal altruism) in some eusocial insects and other animals, and at least intimations of reputation-building care for others (indirect reciprocity) in a few primate species. All of this has contributed to the revival of "group selection" hypotheses, which had been all but abandoned in the mid-twentieth century. The basic idea here is that natural selection works not only at the level of the individual, but also at the level of the group. In some environments, coalitions whose members (whether birds, bees, or humans) can cooperate and remain committed to the group are able to out-compete other groups, which grants a dispersed survival advantage to the genetic pool. Individual behaviors that benefit the group as a whole would then be selected over the long term, even if they do not help the individual survive in the short term. Other animals have hypersensitive mechanisms that lead them to detect agents and protect their groups, but it seems that shared imaginative engagement with axiologically relevant supernatural agents has only evolved as a dominant trait within human groups.[4]

The fact that basic "altruistic" behavior existed in the animal kingdom for millions of years before the emergence of *Homo sapiens* suggests that religion per se cannot be the only condition for the evolution of morality. The independence and primacy of naturally evolved cooperative and committed behaviors in relation to shared imaginative engagement with supernatural agents are further supported by the fact that the former are characteristic of living primate species, just as they were of other hominid groups long before the appearance of anatomically modern humans. Moreover, human babies seem to be born with an innate sense of "morality," in the sense that they manifest a rudimentary sense of justice, express empathy and compassion to those in distress, and judge other's actions as good or bad, well before they can walk or talk, much less reflect on culturally postulated disembodied intentional forces.[5] "Religion," in the sense I have been using the term, is not a necessary condition for altruism.

As we saw in chapters 2 and 3, however, empirical findings and theoretical developments within a wide variety of disciplines that contribute to the biocultural study of religion have converged in support of the hypothesis that ritual engagement around ambiguous supernatural revelations *enhanced* the cooperative and committed behavior necessary for securing the overall good (and survival) of members of early human coalitions. In other words, for most scientists in these fields, the evolution of "religion" is the best educated guess for making sense of the tenacity, prevalence, and distinctive features of this sort of behavior among contemporary humans. It seems that human cognition is always and already "normative," but religion has played, and continues to play, a principal role in the formation and enculturation of human moral agency.[6] For our purposes here, the important point to notice is that such *arguments* contribute to the plausibility of the claim that the dominance of religiously oriented *axiological* judgments across human cultures today is a result of the natural selection of survival enhancing modes of evaluative *engagement* within the early ancestral environment.

Evolutionary hypotheses can shed light not only on the problem of why people are "good" but also on the surprising fact that people disagree in their evaluations of what constitutes good or "moral" behavior. Many early theories in moral psychology focused on studying the moral *reasoning* of *individuals* as they make judgments about the rights of people to fair (and just) treatment and the importance of providing care (protection from harm) to vulnerable persons. Based on extensive cross-cultural research, Jonathan Haidt has argued that this approach is based on a far too narrow conception of morality. In addition to justice/fairness and care/harm, there are at least three other dimensions (or evolved intuitive foundations) for moral judgment that are more *affectively* charged and *group* oriented: in-group/loyalty (coalitional psychology), authority/respect (hierarchy within groups), and purity/sanctity (which includes disgust-related taboos). Haidt's research shows that self-described "liberals" tend to endorse only the first two foundations or dimensions of morality. In other words, they are mostly concerned about protecting individuals from each other so they can function as autonomous agents. Self-described "conservatives," on the other hand, make moral judgments based on all five dimensions. They are more likely to evaluate behavior in light of the criteria for in-group loyalty, obedience to authority, and living in a "sanctified" way (as defined by their coalition).[7]

In *Supernatural Selection*, Matt Rossano argues that the last three of Haidt's dimensions of morality were reinforced in human evolution through the "supernaturalizing" of social life. Expanding the group to include gods provided supernatural incentives for following coalitional norms. The purity/sanctity axis was strengthened by the imagined presence of supernatural agents who "kept a close eye on them, ready to pounce on the first signs of deviance," thereby increasing compliance to taboos about what could be eaten, said, or done by members of the group. The authority/respect axis was also reinforced by a spiritual sanctioning of human hierarchy: "as hunter-gatherer bands coalesced into tribes, shamans became priests who bestowed supernatural authority on chiefs and kings." Finally, the group/loyalty axis was fortified by divine commandments that helped to maintain in-group stability (no coveting a neighbor's wife or property), and to regulate out-group relations (no intermarriage with infidels).

In light of archaeological, neurobiological, psychological, and ethnographic research, Rossano argues that during the Upper Paleolithic some of our ancestors envisioned a world inhabited by spirits who were watching them. "The idea was an evolutionary winner. Groups who had it fanned out across the globe and quickly overwhelmed those who didn't."[8] This is just one more example of the sort of hypothesis we explored in chapter 2. These scientific abductive inferences lead to ever more refined empirical observations and ever more precise logical propositions, all of which strengthen the plausibility of the conjecture that altruistic behavior would be a matter of course if it were true that "religion" played a role in enhancing cooperative and committed behavior in the evolution of human groups.

But what about *retroduction*? Theorists in the biocultural sciences make all sorts of claims about the existence of genetic structures, biological configurations, social and ecological systems, and other factors that are supposed to condition the actualization of evolved human traits such as those aggregated within "religion." However, many hesitate when it comes to the existence of gods or GOD. Rossano, for example, explicitly evades the question; he proposes that we simply accept that the question of the existence of supernatural agents is "irresolvable" and move on.[9] In chapter 6 we will return to this strange exemption given to the gods by so many evolutionary scientists in their retroductive arguments. As we have seen, there are a growing number of scholars in these disciplines (such as Guthrie, Boyer, Atran, Lewis-Williams, and Pyysiäinen) who are willing to make claims (publically) about the implausibility of the actual existence of disembodied intentional forces as conditions for human axiological engagement. I will argue that the plausibility and feasibility of such theolytic retroductive hypotheses provide us with adequate warrant for letting the gods go.

Religious Hypotheses

I have proposed (re)conceptualizing "religion" as shared imaginative engagement with axiologically relevant supernatural agents. As we have seen, scholars in the evolutionary sciences use religion *as* a hypothesis in their attempts to make sense of surprising facts such as altruistic behavior. However, they also argue about the nature and structure of hypothesizing *in* religion. What distinguishes *religious* abductive inferences is the way in which such conjectures appeal to the causal relevance of interesting gods who are interested in a group. This sort of abduction is prevalent today across human cultures because of the inherited cognitive and coalitional tendencies that we have been exploring. Guessing that an ambiguous phenomenon is conditioned by disembodied (and probably punitive) intentional forces comes intuitively as a result of the predisposition to over-detect agents who are somewhat "like us" in the natural world and to over-protect "our" way of inscribing the social field. As Stewart Guthrie argues, it is not that religious people develop anthropomorphic hypotheses *about* gods; rather, the guess "god" *is* a faulty perceptual interpretation—a mistaken abduction.

It is important to emphasize the "naturalness" of this sort of intuitive hypothesizing. The reciprocal reinforcement of evolved inferential and preferential systems automatically generates such conjectures, which come quite naturally to people, especially in the context of their own religious coalition. Beliefs about supernatural agents are not usually held onto as "hypothetical" in the narrower sense of postulates that might or might not be true, because everyone in the group "knows" about the powers of the disembodied intentional forces they ritually engage. However, they are "hypotheses" in the broader sense we have been discussing. They are abductive inferences or "best guesses" that are shaped by culturally moderated cognitive dispositions whose plausibility depends on their ongoing mental and social usefulness within religious coalitions. In such contexts, these hypotheses "work." They hold religious selves and groups together by strengthening sociographically relevant anthropomorphic interpretations of a shared imaginative world.

Several of the scientists whose work we explored in chapter 3 go out of their way to emphasize that religious knowledge is *not* based primarily on either deduction or induction. Scott Atran, for example, argues that "religious beliefs and experiences cannot be consistently validated by social consensus either through *deductive* or *inductive* inference. Validation occurs only by satisfying the very emotions that motivate religious beliefs and experiences." Deductive inferences do not work normally in religion, because supernatural conceptions are quasi-propositional and violate intuitive ontological categories. Inductive inferences in religion do not involve cumulative weight of evidence, repeated testing of observations, or multiple comparisons, but may be justified in relation to "a singular happening, such as a *supposed* miracle or revelation."[10] Similarly, Ilkka Pyysiäinen insists that religious inferences are not "*inductive* generalizations from observations or *deductions* from some general principles, but rather *abductions* from emotion-provoking mythical prototypes."[11]

Pascal Boyer has spelled out the *abductive* nature and structure of religious knowledge in far more detail. Like Atran, Pyysiäinen, and others, Boyer rejects the idea that recurrent belief in supernatural agents is a result of *inductive* inference, that is, of repeated observations of instances of apparent disembodied agency, which lead over time lead to generalizations about gods. As we saw in chapter 3, he is also critical of once popular claims in cultural anthropology about the *deductive* nature of religious inference, which he argues is the result of a "theologistic" bias. In other words, belief in and engagement with gods is not primarily the result of inferences derived from multiple observations (the last hundred ancestor-ghosts I saw were white, so. . . .) nor of inferences that lead to necessary conclusions (only ancestor-ghosts can walk through walls, Jesus walked through a wall, so . . .). Instead, religious conceptions are engendered through abductive inferences, which involve, in his words, "putting forward conjectural assumptions that, if true, would account for the data observed . . . the main purpose of abduction is to make surprising data unsurprising by positing an assumption, of which the data would be a normal consequence."[12]

For Boyer, two features of (everyday) abductive inference are particularly important for understanding the surprising fact that people explain some aspects of their worlds by appealing to invisible agents. First, the *explanans* in an abductive conjecture is often an *unobserved* state of affairs (e.g., that broken glass would make sense "if my dog had knocked it over"). In the case of religious abductions, however, the *explanans* is unobserved in principle; supernatural agents can never be observed like natural agents. Second, abductive inferences are not normally motivated by a desire to construct theoretical systems but by the need to make sense of some pragmatically relevant phenomenon in a concrete situation. Psychological experiments and ethnographic research suggest that abductive religious inferences only need to be "relatively satisfactory" in a "limited context."[13] When engaging in a ritual practice, for example, participants are not making deductive or inductive inferences about the presence of gods or the capacities of shamans or priests. They are going with the "guess" that is most facile and most fecund in such settings.

Boyer illustrates religious abduction by describing the way in which ritual participants interpret the role of a ritual officer. The lay members of a religious coalition do not identify the special power of a PRIEST or SHAMAN through logical deduction (from a "theologistic" system) or through empirical induction (repeated observations of causal effects over time). Rather, they automatically identify such officers as belonging to a certain social category of persons with a special power because, in that context, that is the easiest way to make sense of what is going on and leads to the richest set of social inferences. Religious abductions "establish a connection between a *condition* (possession of some unobservable property) and what is taken as an *outcome* of that condition (in this case, the performance observed)."[14] If it were true that the ritual officer fits into this category of special mediators for supernatural agents, then the situation being observed would not be surprising. It would be a "matter of course." Boyer concludes that religious claims are entertained widely in a group to the "extent that (1) they are tacitly enriched by (and therefore constrained by) intuitive ontological assumptions, and (2) they can provide abductive explanations for particular situations." Such claims are not deductive applications of "cultural axioms," but abductive inferences or "problem-driven explanatory conjectures."[15]

Religious people normally have no need to consider whether or not the gods actually exist. They do not wonder about the plausibility of the idea that an ancestor-ghost or the Spirit of Christ is watching them, or is currently being engaged by the SHAMAN or PRIEST in a ritual. There is no need for considering and wondering because the hypotheses "work" in ritual contexts and over time give meaning to people's lives, granting them affective and collective security. If retroductive reflection does arise in such contexts, it immediately defaults to acceptance of the supposition that the gods are causally relevant existential conditions. Religious ideas are relatively immune to inductive challenges, because they can live forever in meta-representational limbo and can never be empirically falsified through observation. They are relatively immune to deductive challenges because a symbolic religious representational context is so open-textured and counterintuitive that an endless array of quasi-propositions can be generated to qualify and protect the presuppositions and conclusions of a religious in-group.

However, something happened to religion during the slow emergence of complex literate states. As bigger groups got bigger gods, and some people got bigger chunks of time to think about them, *theology* was born. On the one hand, the formulation of doctrines helped promote cooperation and commitment in large-scale coalitions. On the other hand, it opened the door for reflection on the coherence of religious ideas and the plausibility of appealing to disembodied intentional forces to make sense of the world. The attempt—and failure—to conceive GOD altered the intellectual landscape in a way that made space for the emergence of atheism. In this sense, theological hypothesizing was a condition for the actualization of atheist conceptions.

Theological Hypotheses

I have proposed that we (re)conceptualize "theology" as the disciplined construction and critique of abductive and retroductive hypotheses about the existential conditions for axiological engagement. Most people only occassionally take time to reflect on the boundaries of their intentionality and the intrinsic limitations of their evaluations. Theologians make a habit of it. Whatever else it may include, thinking theologically involves making conjectures about the relation between intentionality and infinity—more or less plausible "guesses" about the *existential* conditions for the actualization of finite evaluative judgments. This means attending not only to existing constraints on empirical objects but also to the existence of empirically constrained objectification. How can we assess the plausibility of our theoretical interpretations of this limitation, this radically empirical experience of the constraints of thought? How can we determine the feasibility of our pragmatic hypotheses for dealing with this intense experience of being conditioned "at the limits" of valuation?

In their attempts to answer such questions, sacerdotal theologians have typically allowed the *intuitions* expressed in their own religious traditions to trump their critical *reflections*. This happens not so much at the level of ongoing deduction (proof) or induction (probability) as at the level of abduction (plausibility). Theologians do indeed often argue about the plausibility of this or that interpretation of the religious conceptions borne within their coalitions, but they rarely reflect on the plausibility of the underlying supernatural agent abductions upon which all such argumentation depends. Spontaneously—yet surreptitiously—generated by the evolved theogonic mechanisms, these "natural" religious conceptions are coddled, rather than subjected to disciplined critique, and so they easily go on reproducing retroductive inferences about GOD within the GROUP.

Theologians have always been shaped by (and often even shaped) the philosophical debates within their own cultural contexts about what it means to make a good argument. During the thirteenth century, Thomas Aquinas took over an Aristotelian conception of theoretical "science" (*scientia*) and applied it to theology. "As other sciences do not argue in proof of their principles, but argue from their principles to demonstrate other truths in these sciences: so this discipline (*sacra doctrina*) does not argue in proof of its principles, which are the articles of faith, but from them it goes on to prove something else." The *deductive* mode of inference is clearly dominant in this understanding of theological argumentation. One begins with premises, which are "received on faith," and argues *from* them to deduce the truth of other propositions. Like the "other sciences" in the Middle Ages, theology did not need to prove its axioms. In fact, its principles and premises were the most secure, since they were based on the highest possible authority—divine revelation in the "canonical books" of Scripture (*Summa Theologica*, I.1.8).

In the late nineteenth century, Charles Hodge had quite a different view of science, which led to quite a different way of thinking about theological argumentation. In the introduction to his *Systematic Theology*, he insisted that the method of theology "agrees in everything essential with the inductive method as applied to the natural sciences." In the proto-positivistic milieu in which he operated, Hodge was able to claim that "it is the fundamental principle of all sciences, and of theology among the rest, that theory is to be determined by facts, and not facts by theory." Where does one go to observe the facts one needs to develop one's theological theory? "The Bible is to the theologian what nature is to the man of science. It is his store-house of facts." Indeed, the Scriptures contain "all the Facts" of theology. Moreover, the theologian's method of ascertaining what the Bible teaches "is the same as that which the natural philosopher adopts to ascertain what nature teaches," that is, *induction*.[16]

Both Aquinas and Hodge started with a particular HOLY TEXT, accepted rather uncrically by a HOLY GROUP as the revelation of GOD. Critical reflection, whether deductive or inductive, began only *after* they had accepted the supernatural abductive inferences that held their religious coalition together. The behavior of the people around me (e.g., medieval monks or Princeton seminarians) would be a "matter of course" if the Supranatural Agent in whom they all profess belief and with whom they ritually engage actually existed and had written a Book with all the Principles or Facts. These Christian theologians developed all sorts of hypotheses about how to interpret the Bible (and how to practice the sacraments) that were based on their logical deductions or inductive observations. However, they did not challenge the primal, intuitive religious abduction upon which all of that reflection was based: an anthropomorphically promiscuous guess about an infinite intentional Force who had inspired a text to guide the sociographically prudish behavior of their own coalition. Their god-bearing and group-founding supernatural abductions were immunized from critique, which allowed the undisciplined theogonic reproductive frenzy within their coalitions to continue, unnoticed and unchecked, behind the veil of disciplined sacerdotal reflection.

Of course, many Christian theologians have moved beyond medieval and positivist construals of the nature of "scientific" method, and developed other ways of arguing theologically that take the hypothetical nature of knowledge more seriously. Perhaps no modern, Christian theologian has gone as far as Wolfhart Pannenberg in this direction. In his *Theology and the Philosophy of Science,* he suggested that because theological statements "adopt a critical attitude to claims of a self-communication of divine reality in religious awareness, they must be third-order hypotheses: *hypotheses about hypotheses about hypotheses.*" More precisely, theological claims are "about the truth and/or untruth of constructions of religious awareness: that is, they are about the *relation* of the implications about meaning contained in experience of reality in its most varied forms... to the understanding of life as whole."[17] Unfortunately, even Pannenberg fails to notice the theogonic forces at work in the production of the abductive religious claims *that* there is a self-*communication* of divine reality (anthropomorphic promiscuity) and *that* theology can appropriately limit itself to hypothesizing about the implications of meaning within *one historical tradition* (sociographic prudery).

In his analysis of the similarities and differences between science and theology, Robert McCauley acknowledges that theologians avail themselves of some of the same tools as scientists. For example, they can be "experts at conceptual analysis and at carrying out the same forms of deductive inference" one finds in science. Theologians often "generate convoluted, abstract religious representations that are no easier to understand than esoteric scientific ideas are."[18] In this sense, theology is, like science, "unnatural" compared to religion, which comes intuitively. What distinguishes science from theology, however, is the way the former is fixated on the obligation to criticize theories both logically and empirically, demanding the "public availability" of its hypotheses and the "replicability" of its findings by other research coalitions.

McCauley observes that theology and science have both drifted away from the "maturationally natural moorings" of human cognition from which they emerged. Unlike science, however, "theology is largely devoted to making sense of and bringing some logical order *to* the claims of a popular religion." Science, on the other hand, "follows wherever its inquiries lead and that has reliably been *away* from the automatic deliverances of the maturationally natural mental systems" that evolved in the early ancestral environment. Based upon the current state of publically available evidence, and without "epistemologically troublesome coercion," scientists around the world often come to provisional consensus on a variety of issues. No religion, however, "has yet made a case for its truth that comparatively disinterested observers from around the world find persuasive."[19] In chapter 5 we will focus on this and other problems within the dialogue among theologians who come from different religious "families of origin."

At this stage, I want to emphasize the importance of the distinction between the two trajectories described in chapter 3 for making sense of the surprising fact that theological hypothesizing has for so long been characterized by an irresolvable tension between "religious" intuition and "scientific" reflection. Neither philosophically oriented scientists nor ritually engaged believers are really sure what to make of theologians. The stark contrast between the theogonic and theolytic mechanisms can help us understand why. While engaging within the imaginative world of a religious coalition, theologians "naturally" default to the cognitive and coalitional tendency to bear the gods of their group. While engaging within an academic community of inquirers, they "unnaturally" strive to resist these defaults.

When they try to engage in *reflection* on the *intuitions* of their own religious group, theologians are pulled both ways at the same time. The sacerdotal forces have almost always won in the tug-o-war with the iconoclastic forces. Most theological hypotheses have indeed been GOD–bearing. However, the implausibility (and infeasibility) of this religious idea has simultaneously led to the production of GOD-dissolving hypotheses. Among the most robust of these atheist conceptions have been those engendered by reflection on the logical and existential impasses in a problem that has been *created* by the birth of GOD within the major religious traditions of West Asian origin.

The Problem of Evil in the Monotheistic Religions

We have seen how evolutionary scientists have had to develop hypotheses within the biocultural study of religion in order to deal with the problem of good(s). Theologians committed to a monotheistic religious coalition, on the other hand, are more likely to find themselves faced with the problem of evil(s). If the infinite Creator of all finite reality is good, then it is no surprise to find goodness in the creation. But how does one account for the existence of *evil*? This is not a problem for belief in finite gods in small-scale societies; the stupidity and spitefulness of supernatural agents may very well help to make sense of the surprising fact that bad things happen to good people. However, one might expect an infinitely wise and perfectly good disembodied intentional Force to do a better job when creating (and providentially upholding) the existential conditions for human axiological engagement.

Most religious people are less concerned about abstract debates over *how* their supernatural agents act than the extent to which that alleged agency is related to any series of (un)fortunate events that impacts their own lives. Hypothetical arguments about the existence of evil and the goodness of GOD are rarely comforting or compelling under stress, during actual axiological engagements with concrete evils. Our evolved cognitive defaults do not normally lead us to leap to questions like: Does evil have its own existence or is it merely a privation of the good? Or: Is the existence of evils a necessary condition for human freedom? On the contrary, people's inferential (and preferential) systems quickly jump to find answers to more intuitive questions like: Why did *this* evil thing happen to (our) good people? Why didn't our supernatural agent protect us from *that*?

Theologians in monotheistic traditions are also faced with the problem of evils *in* religion, that is, with the need to explain why participants in their coalition fail to do "good" and sometimes do "evil." Why do (our) people do bad things? Christian theologians, for example, need some way of making sense of the medieval slaughtering of religious out-groups during the Crusades, the torture of alleged in-group defectors during the Inquisition, and other modern atrocities carried out "in the name of God."

As I noted in chapter 2, the popular habit of referring to Judaism, Christianity, and Islam as "Abrahamic" religions is somewhat misleading because it obscures a deeper presupposition they share. Theologians in all of these traditions have argued that making sense of the conditions for axiological engagement requires attention not only to the divine call of Abram (with Sarai) to leave the Town of Ur, but also to the divine expulsion of Adam (with Eve) from the Garden of Eden. The religious traditions that originated in East and South Asia do not trace the origin of human (im)morality back to a primal pair's disobedient decision regarding forbidden fruit in a Mesopotamian paradise. Especially when dealing with the problem of evil, it really makes more sense to refer to the West Asian monotheistic religions as *Adamic*.

There are indeed many theological treatments of the creation narratives that reject literal interpretations of its anthropomorphic imagery, such as its description of a god "walking in the garden" (Genesis 3:8). Many theologians within the Adamic traditions also resist sociographically prudish interpretations of these texts that are used to authorize the patriarchal domination of women. But such reflective readings of these religious myths still pre-suppose a prior supernatural agent abduction: the conjecture *that* a GOD has authorized this HOLY TEXT, the interpretation of which is relevant for the axiological organization of a particular HOLY GROUP.

It is important to notice that neither of the two creation stories in the early chapters of Genesis contain any explanation for (or even express any interest in) the existence of evil or dis-order within—or even before—creation.

The watery chaos and formless void in the first story and the crafty serpent in the second are simply taken for granted. In the Qur'an as well, Satan and the tempting tree are already present in the Garden (Surah 2.30–39). In fact, the story of Adam and Eve in the garden is just the sort of narrative we would expect to emerge as a result of the hypersensitive cognitive and coalitional mechanisms that intensified and congealed in the Upper Paleolithic. After giving in to the temptation to cheat, freeload, and defect, the original pair hears surprising sounds at dusk, "at the time of the evening breeze" when it is particularly difficult to interpret ambiguous phenomena. They are afraid that the human-like god who set up the favorable conditions for their coalition will discover their deceit and so they hide. But the god finds them, sees what they had done, and punishes them by banning them from the easily accessible resources of the Garden and imposing unpleasant conditions on childbirth and agriculture.

For most religious believers within these traditions, this sort of biblical text is not problematic until a theologian tells them it is. The so-called problem of evil within the Adamic religions arises only on the supposition that an *infinitely* Good *intentional* Force is the condition for all axiological engagement whatsoever. It is the conception of GOD as an omnipotent, omniscient, and omnibenevolent PERSON who has an eternal plan for a GROUP that *engenders* the problem of evil. If such a GOD exists, whence evil (*unde malum*)? My interest here is not in summarizing or contributing to the vast literature on this problem, but in drawing attention to the role of the modes of inference within the most common sorts of argument that characterize the debate. Philosophers of religion and theologians operating within monotheistic traditions, especially Christianity, typically focus on the logical or evidential problems of evil. As we will see below, these arguments primarily utilize the *deductive* and *inductive* modes of inference. Does the existence of evil entail that the nonexistence of GOD is logically *necessary*? Do our repeated observations of evils provide evidence that the nonexistence of GOD is quite *likely*?

In other words, a theodicy—a justification (*dikaiōsē*) of god (*theos*) —is usually an attempt to defend against deductive and inductive inferences that would challenge the possibility or probability of GOD's existence. This defensive strategy makes sense in light of the inferential structure of the arguments that so many philosophical opponents of monotheistic religion have used in their attacks against it. I want to suggest that paying more attention to the role of *abduction* (as well as retroduction) can alter the nature and structure of the whole debate. As we have seen, empirical research and theoretical developments in the biocultural study of religion suggest that the tendency to guess "supernatural agent" when confronted with surprising facts contributed to the cohesion of early human coalitions by enhancing cooperation and commitment, increasing their competitive advantage over other groups. This is why religion is so easily borne across human cultures today.

The notion of an infinite Supranatural Agent who eternally favors a particular Coalition, however, is more difficult to bear. Nevertheless, the cohesion of large-scale monotheistic religions depends on the reproduction of GOD within the shared imaginative world of the GROUP. Most believers in these traditions do not find such GOD-conceptions compelling. Nor do they need to. Their "theologically incorrect" intuitive detection of limited supernatural agency overrides concerns about the plausibility of the idea of a limitless GOD. Further reflection is hardly ever necessary, although it is often forced upon individuals when something bad happens to them (or to those they love), leading them to ask a rabbi, priest or imam: "Why?" The doctrinally correct answers they receive are the result of anthropomorphically promiscuous and sociographically prudish conjectures about the conditions for the existence of finite evaluative processes. At the limits of knowledge and valuation, ambiguity collides and colludes with infinity, and the theogonic forces run wild. This helps to explain why theologians bound to the Adamic religions continue to burden themselves with the task of analyzing "the problem of evil," which flows naturally after the birth of GOD.

Justifying a Supranatural Agent

Once supernatural agents are imaginatively detected and widely postulated within a culture, their actions may need to be justified. Such justifications are usually called for when ritual engagements with such agents do not have the expected or desired outcome or when some misfortune befalls the group. It is important to notice how easily *super*-natural agents are justified. When a shamanic healing ritual fails, this rarely challenges belief in animal-spirits or ancestor-ghosts. If a group believes in a relatively good and relatively powerful god whom they expect to protect them from harm, his failure to do so can be justified in any number of ways: he is upset with us for some reason, another bad supernatural agent is at work in a way we don't understand, etc. In fact, evils can be *explained* by appealing to some kinds of gods; jinn, for example, play tricks on people because they are bored or just nasty.

Justifying a Supranatural Agent, however, is a whole new ball game. If an all-good GOD is the all-determining condition for everything, then why is there *any* evil? At the very least, if one accepts the existence of such a Creative Agent it is a surprising fact that its created patients are plagued with such a large quantity of qualitatively horrid evils. The most common arguments in defense of GOD typically fall into two categories. The first type responds to the *logical* problem of evil. Such arguments seek to block a deductive inference that appears to follow from the following propositions: an omniscient being would know all about evils; an omnipotent being would have the capacity to eliminate evil; an omnibenevolent being would eliminate evil if it could; evils exist. Therefore, it seems logically necessary that such a being (GOD) does not exist.

Given the limits of human knowledge in the face of an indeterminate number of compossible worlds, it is very difficult indeed to prove the necessary *impossibility* of any premise much less one involving an abstract concept like GOD. This helps to explain why most opponents of the concept seem to focus more energy on rendering it highly *improbable*. This provokes a second type of defensive argument, which responds to the *evidential* problem of evil. In this case inductive inference plays the primary role. Does our observation of so many (quantitative) evils, or such horrible (qualitative) evils, render it unlikely that GOD exists?

Defenders of the concept of GOD, whether as a premise or as a possibility, most often develop strategies that tweak the concept of evil and/or the divine attributes. Irenaeus focused on tweaking the latter. He argued that divine *power* in relation to creation was limited in a certain sense by the divine *knowledge* that the goodness of a world with free creatures would require the existence of evils. In other words, evil was *necessary* in order to provide the conditions under which (some) creatures could mature into responsible fellowship with GOD and one another in an eschatological consummation of the divine plan for a GROUP (the Church). Augustine, on the other hand, focused on tweaking the concept of evil. He famously argued that evil is only the *privation* of good; it has no real existence of its own. Augustine assured believers that once they attained a heavenly perspective they would see clearly that what appeared to be evil and ugly on earth was merely the shadow side of a brilliant divine strategy for saving (some of) humanity. He also often reminded his readers that divine *knowledge* is mysterious and beyond their ken, and urged them to have faith that divine *power* will prevail in the end. In all such approaches to the problem of evil, GOD is still conceived as a PERSON with (maximally counterintuitive) mentality and animacy.

Some scholars within the Adamic traditions find the very idea of defending an abstract theological concept through logical and evidential arguments in the face of evil somewhat offensive. They develop a different strategy by focusing on what might be called the *pastoral* problem of evil. For those who have faith in GOD, they insist, the encounter with evil should lead not primarily to defending divinity but to helping humanity. The main "problem" is not theoretical but practical. Arguing whether the nature of evil is privative or preparative is insensitive and unhelpful; the existence of concrete evils should provoke us to participate in redemptive action toward those who are suffering. In most of these arguments, however, one still finds appeals either to the limits of human knowledge in relation to the divine plan or promises of eschatological consummation that will be of infinitely higher value than even the most horrendous evils.

All three of these strategies work (more or less well) *within* religious coalitions, but are rarely convincing to those outside them. Our review of theoretical developments within the biocultural study of religion helps to explain why. Each of these approaches can function to reinforce the abductive inferences already dominant in the mental and social space of those committed to the tradition. Even if (or precisely because) most people do not understand why the idea of an infinite intentional Force is important to theologians, they do not find arguments about the justification of a Supranatural Agent either worrisome or compelling. They simply default to the hypothesis "supernatural agent," which comes easily and hardly needs any justification. Evaluations of retroductive inferences of this type will be shaped, of course, by a whole host of factors, not least of which is the way we are bound together with others through the axiological inscriptions that constitute and regulate our social lives.

Simply bringing the findings of the biocultural sciences into the dialogue will not end the debates over whether one can prove that GOD does not exist (is not logically possible) or demonstrate the statistical unlikelihood that GOD will ever be observed (is not empirically probable). These ways of framing the issues have always resulted in an impasse, and there are no signs that such arguments will ever be resolved or rescinded. Moreover, scientific hypotheses about the role of religion in the evolution of morality will not have much immediate bearing on sacerdotal approaches to the *pastoral* problem of evil either. Like those who focus on logical or evidential issues, proponents of this third sacerdotal strategy can always appeal to mystery. The latter will almost always suffice as "justification" within the coalition because its participants are held together (psychologically and politically) by abductively inferring the presence and purposiveness of a GOD who is already and always watching over their GROUP.

Unveiling the theogonic mechanisms that generate the problem of evil in monotheistic coalitions is a useful starting point when having "the talk" about religious reproduction in our contemporary context. However, it will also be important to shift the focus of the conversation away from the necessity of deductive inferences and the probability of inductive inferences and onto the *plausibility* (and feasibility) of the abductive inferences that surreptitiously subtend sacerdotal justifications. Research in the biocultural study of religion continues to undermine the plausibility of conjectures about "supernatural agents." Unlike religious specialists in small-scale societies, theologians in the Adamic religions have always found *their own* hypotheses about an infinite intentional disembodied Force deeply problematic for logical, psychological and doxological reasons. If the hypothesis GOD fails so miserably as a way of making sense of the surprising fact that bad things keep happening to us, why do theologians keep defending it? In other words, what may one reasonably suppose to be the conditions for the *existence* of theodicy-hypothesizing itself? What makes possible the ambiguous phenomena *of* religious abductions that interpret evil in relation to the hypothesis "Supranatural Agent?"

Sanctifying a Supranatural Coalition

Here too we can see the way in which sociographic prudery and anthropomorphic promiscuity reinforce one another. Hypotheses involving supernatural agents are relatively easily justified not only because of hyper-sensitive cognitive mechanisms for the detection of agency but also because of coalitional mechanisms that make us hyper-protective of our own coalitions. Attempts to sanctify (*sanctificare*, set-apart, make-holy) religious in-groups are as "natural" as attempts to justify the gods. However, protecting the boundaries of a Supranatural Coalition of the sort that emerged in the wake of the West Asian axial age does not come so easily. It takes just as much (if not more) effort as it does to convince people they can detect a Supranatural Agent. Holding together a HOLY GROUP requires complex cultural scaffolding, such as written expressions of doctrinal belief and rules about ritual practice that are coded by religious scholars and policed by a priestly class. My task in this context is not to evaluate particular religious moral codes, but to point out the way in which this sort of religious moral overcoding amplifies evaluations of "good" and "bad."

What does this have to do with the problem of evil? The intensification of sociographic prudery within monotheistic traditions after the birth of GOD amplified the natural tendency to evaluate one's own group as good (or pure) and other groups as bad (or impure).[20] The "surprising fact" of an eternal segregation between believers and unbelievers would be a "matter of course" if the in-group is HOLY and all out-groups are EVIL. What practical value could such attributions possibly have for those within the Supranatural Coalition? First, ramping up anxiety about the ultimate importance of a group boundary led to the hyperactivation of the evolved coalitional mechanisms that *sanctify* members of religious in-groups, holding them together by holding them apart from out-groups. In this case, however, an ultimate parting of the groups was postulated: everlasting reward for holy people (believers) and everlasting punishment for evil people (infidels). Second, this boosting of sociographic prudery made it easier to *sanction* violence toward out-groups and defectors. These are two of the most significant pragmatic effects of the amplification of hypersensitive coalitional protection mechanisms in the construction and maintenance of Supranatural Coalitions.

John Teehan deals with both the sanctification of in-groups and the sanctioning of violence against out-groups in his book *In the Name of God: The Evolutionary Origins of Religious Ethics and Violence*. He notes that altruism *and* violence are naturally evolved behavioral strategies that were selected because they contributed to the emergence of systems of cooperative reciprocity and reinforced group cohesion. Teehan emphasizes the way in which religion escalates these strategies. What happens when minimally counterintuitive concepts are introduced into the moral matrix? The putative presence of gods heightens the sense of the significance of—and obligation to—the group. In the case of monotheistic traditions, religious coalitions are bound together by shared belief in a divine legislator and righteous enforcer of a moral code. This often fosters astonishing acts of altruism. However, it also leads to horrific acts of violence. Out-group members are not simply "other," but insofar as they are aligned against GOD, they are "in league with *evil* itself. Inter-group conflict is no longer simply a competition between two groups seeking to promote their own interests, it is now a cosmic struggle with no middle ground available, and nothing short of victory acceptable."[21]

In light of costly signaling theory and other theoretical insights from the biocultural study of religion, Teehan argues that it is the same moral logic that sanctions both the death penalty for in-group members and violence against out-groupers.[22] As we have seen, "moral" intuitions are not dependent on belief in supernatural agents. However, religion has the power to *amplify* the inferential and preferential dispositions that generate cooperative *and* competitive behavior. Teehan analyzes the moral codes of Judaism and Christianity and demonstrates that the ethical systems of both traditions are based on the same psychology of reciprocation evident in other religious groups. The commands, admonitions, and warnings that fill the Hebrew Bible and the New Testament are cultural expressions of underlying evolved cognitive processes that were selected in the Upper Paleolithic because of the survival advantage they granted to the groups that bore them. Even Jesus's call to "love your enemy," which appears to break the leash of evolutionary psychology, is explicitly motivated by the logic of reciprocal altruism: "and your reward will be great, and you will be sons of the Most High" (Luke 6:35–36). Teehan also points to the "perversity in the level of hatred and blood-lust" in the book of Revelation, which promises a punishment for out-group members that is so grievous they beg for death—and are denied it, suffering endlessly "in the presence of the holy angels and of the Lamb" (Revelation 14:10).[23]

We will return to the problem of religious violence in chapters 5 and 6, but the key point at this stage is the way in which the problem of evil is engendered by the amplification of religious abductions and nurtured by sacerdotal theologians (and philosophers) who keep the focus on deduction and induction. When bad things happen to religious people, they naturally default to the sort of abductive inferences that hold their groups together: shared imaginative engagement with axiologically relevant supernatural agents. Most members of Adamic traditions do not need to use *modus ponens* to deduce GOD's knowledge of their situation from the premise of divine omniscience. Divine power in situ is not inductively inferred from the analysis of previous empirical observations of GOD. Even if they signal their commitment to a particular Supranatural Agent theodicy, they are more likely to infer "supernatural agency" automatically (and abductively) in ambiguous and existentially intense situations. They feel little need to defend their religious ideas logically or evidentially—or even pastorally—because they are the result of abductions that are generated and supported by the concealed and compulsive forces of theogonic reproduction.

Philosophical reflection on the findings of the biocultural study of religion suggests that it is precisely *religious hypotheses* of a certain sort— Supranatural Agent abductions within Supranatural Coalitions—that are the *origin* of the problem of evil. This brings us back to Nietzsche. Can we move "beyond" good and evil? Questions of origination and *destination* are bound together. Where "ought" we to go from here? How is it even possible to evaluate answers to this question? Here we are, evaluating and being evaluated in and across our various coalitions, seeking goods and trying to avoid evils. It feels frightening, perhaps even nauseating, to consider the possibility of moving "beyond good and evil." Such a move would seem, well, immoral. We cannot ignore the fact that bad things happen to us all; indeed, we ourselves are often the agents of happenings that others (and we ourselves) judge as bad. To evaluate things as good or bad is part of the human condition.

But does axiological engagement require an ontological distinction between good and *evil*? This sort of evaluation can obscure the fact that those who are competing with us are living organisms, just as we are.

Nietzsche pointed out that any living thing "will want to grow, spread, grab, win dominance—not out of any morality or immorality, but because it is *alive.*" Refraining from injuring others and placing one's will on par with others is "in a crude sense" the basis for good manners. This often works well enough, he concedes, if certain economic and other conditions are in place. As a "fundamental principle of society," however, it is the negation of life itself:

> Life itself is *essentially* a process of appropriating, injuring, overpowering the alien and the weaker, oppressing, being harsh, imposing your own form... "Exploitation" does not belong to a corrupted or imperfect, primitive society: it belongs to the *essence* of being alive as a fundamental organic function... although this is an innovation at the level of theory—at the level of reality, it is the *primal fact* of all history. Let us be honest with ourselves to this extent at least![24]

Nietzsche often seemed frustrated at how difficult it was for people to be honest with themselves about the will to power, and how willingly they allowed themselves to be disempowered by "slave morality."

We now have a better understanding of the role of competition, cooperation, and commitment in human evolution. They are all wrapped up within our genetic and cultural heritage. The sanctification of religious in-groups can promote altruistic behaviors, but it also strengthens (and shrouds) the sanctioning of violence against out-groups. Unveiling the mechanisms of theogonic reproduction might facilitate the sort of honest self-reflection for which Nietzsche called, leading to other, more intentional, strategies for living together well. Such intentional reflection will need to focus even more attentively on the *abductive* structure of religious inferences about the axiological relevance of supernatural agent coalitions.

(Phylo)genetic Fallacies

The preoccupation with deductive and inductive arguments among theologians and philosophers bound to the Christian religion is not limited to the "problem of evil." The same sorts of strategies dominate their reactions to challenges that arise from evolutionary scientific hypotheses about the "problem of good." Grounded in empirical research, theoretical developments in the biocultural study of religion provide warrant for the claim that shared imaginative engagement with supernatural agents leads to false retroductive inferences about the actual existence of gods. In other words, they diminish the plausibility of religious hypotheses.

Here too the most common defensive maneuvers among "theistic" philosophers focus on evolutionary science's inability to prove the material falsity of *propositions* about GOD's existence or on its methodological exclusion of spiritual *observations* (religious experience) from its data set. These strategies concentrate on showing how the findings of the biocultural sciences do not necessarily *disprove* or probabilistically *invalidate* belief in the Supranatural Agent of their Coalition.

It *might* be true, the theist can argue, that I—and the people in my GROUP—are really detecting disembodied intentional forces of the sort depicted in our HOLY TEXT. And that is enough. That is, it is enough to immunize supernatural agent abductions from critique and to preserve the cohesion of the in-group because it diverts attention from reflection on the plausibility of the claim *that* its members have special access to the revelations of and ritual engagement with a person-like, coalition-favoring, infinite, intentional Force. Of course theistic arguments are sometimes offensive as well as defensive. They often also involve the construction of hypotheses about the scientific data itself or alternative interpretations of the nature of GOD and the intelligibility of the created WORLD. For the most part, however, they avoid the basic question of the plausibility of religious hypothesizing *itself.*

A growing number of Christian theists (philosophers, theologians, and even scientists) are acknowledging the theolytic pressure produced by research in the cognitive sciences and other disciplines that contribute to the biocultural study of religion and exploring strategies for responding to these new challenges.[25] In this context, I will limit myself to some of the responses offered by Christian contributors to the volume *The Believing Primate: Scientific, Philosophical and Theological Reflections on the Origin of Religion.* My concern is not with the details of their various lines of reasoning but with the way in which they illustrate the reliance on deductive and inductive modes of inference typical of theistic defenses. Their focus on logical problems like the "genetic" fallacy distracts attention from the psychological and political problems related to what we might the "phylogenetic" fallacy—the failure of religious abductions.

Michael Murray, for example, insists that scientific "explanations" of religious beliefs that demonstrate the way in which they are generated by mental tools selected for by natural selection are "totally irrelevant to the *justification* of the beliefs that spring from them."[26] In and of itself, he points out, the fact that beliefs in gods are generated by cognitive mechanisms provides no reason to think that they are false. As Murray puts it in another chapter coauthored by Andrew Goldberg, accounting for a belief's origin "tells us nothing about its truth. To think otherwise is to commit the notorious '*genetic fallacy.*'"[27] This is an example of dodging the bullet by ducking down to the level of deduction. "*If* the theist is right" that "God created the world" and "configured evolutionary history...*then* our coming to believe that there is supernatural reality is something that leads us to true belief."[28] It is important to notice how this sort of strategy for deflecting challenges that arise based on scientific insights into cognitive mechanisms ignores the role of *coalitional* mechanisms. Murray's strategy would work equally well for defenders of belief in other supernatural agents, including Fang ancestor-ghosts or the Flying Spaghetti Monster.

It can only "work," however, as long as it can sidestep the question why members of different coalitions hold contradictory religious beliefs and distract attention from the implausibility of them all. In his chapter on "Explaining Belief in the Supernatural," Peter van Inwegen observes that naturalistic explanations cannot "*demonstrate* that there are no invisible, intangible agents or that human beings cease to exist when they die." Science cannot show that such beliefs are logically *impossible* or *necessarily* false. Avoiding logical contradiction, van Inwegen acknowledges, "is not all that impressive an epistemological achievement." Indeed, we should point out that it is not logically impossible or necessarily false that the world was created by a Flying Spaghetti Monster—a central claim of the Pastafarians.[29] Any evolutionary naturalistic explanation of a phenomenon, argues van Inwegen, "can be incorporated without *logical* contradiction into a 'larger,' more comprehensive supernaturalistic explanation of that phenomena."[30] As we saw in chapter 3, this sort of incorporation is possible in the context of religious representation because counterintuitive god-conceptions are "half-baked" and can be endlessly interpreted in new ways within the shared imaginative world of the groups that ritually engage them.

Other Christian contributors to this volume utilize a defensive strategy that focuses more strongly on inductive inference. Alvin Plantinga, for example, begins by acknowledging that many good evolutionary scientific theories are incompatible with Christian belief. Even the Christian who has a high view of science, however, should not accept this as a defeater of his or her religious beliefs. Why? Because "the relevant scientific evidence is only a proper subset of the Christian's evidence base."[31] In other words, Christians have *more evidence* than naturalistic scientists because they can make supernaturalistic observations. Here we have a rather obvious example of a *petitio principii* fallacy, presupposing that for which one is supposed to be arguing. It is also important to note that Plantinga's strategy could work just as well for the Fang tribes or for the Pastafarians when defending their beliefs in ancestor-ghosts or the Flying Spaghetti Monster.[32]

Justin Barrett also insists that Christians can appeal to their own special evidence base in order to show how "the cognitive science of religion might prove compatible with orthodox Christian theology." Appealing to the biblical story of Adam and Eve, Barrett suggests that "God equipped people with the prerequisite cognitive equipment to have an appropriate relationship with God." However, now we live in a "sinful, fallen world," so God has "used scriptural and other forms of revelation" to clarify "*who* He is," ultimately becoming "human in the person of Jesus of Nazareth."[33]

I will return to the implausibility of this sort of claim in chapter 6 in the context of a discussion of methodological naturalism (and secularism). At this stage, the important point is that such theological claims are based on *religious* hypotheses, that is to say, on supernatural agent *abductions*. They are obviously the result of reflective analysis but, less obviously, they are engendered by an intuitive synthesis of religious representations imaginatively shared within a particular religious coalition. In their defense of such claims, theists themselves often commit "informal" versions of the genetic fallacy. Insinuating that the cognitive architecture of scientists who generate naturalistic explanations is "sinful" or "fallen" makes it easier for members of a religious in-group to discount them. From a Christian perspective, it makes sense that only redeemed (Christian) minds can generate true claims about GOD. In a similar way, it makes sense to the Fang that out-group members cannot detect their ancestor-ghosts. Pointing to the divine genesis of a HOLY TEXT (such as the creation myths in "Genesis") is another somewhat obvious example of a genetic fallacy: the source of the claim counts as warrant for its truth, at least for those who presuppose its divine origin.

Arguing about axiological engagement by focusing primarily on deductive and inductive inferences will get us nowhere. Theists and atheists will just keep talking past each other. When David Lewis-Williams, for example, challenges the validity of religious knowledge by highlighting the role of deduction and induction in science, and asserts that it is characterized by statements that are intended to be "universally true," by the search for "abstract laws" that govern the way the world works, and by empirical observations "that can be repeated and checked," he makes it too easy for theists to strike back.[34] In fact, scientific claims are not always based on replicable observations nor do they always follow logically from universally accepted premises. They are far more hypothetical and fallible than Lewis-Williams's description implies. Just so, they can be assessed as more or less *plausible* by reflective scholars in different research coalitions who value shared access to the same evidence and welcome empirically constrained conceptual clarifications. The same can be said of philosophers (and theologians) who follow the iconoclastic trajectory.

The supernaturalistic axiological claims of theologians (and philosophers) who follow the sacerdotal trajectory are not false *because* they come from a religious source; they fail as inter-subjective and trans-communal interpretations of ambiguous phenomena because they uncritically rely on fallacious—albeit phylogenetically "natural"—abductive inferences about the gods of particular groups. A more productive way of having the talk about religious reproduction is to shift the conversation to the level of abduction and retroduction.

Which of the following sorts of hypotheses about the conditions for axiological engagement is more plausible? That the proscriptions and prescriptions by which *one* of the Adamic Coalitions has inscribed the socius are in fact authorized by a Supranatural Agent who will also judge all other coalitions according to eternally grounded but only recently revealed moral standards... or that this Coalition is held together by the same temporally evolved hypersensitive mechanisms that condition *all* such sociographically prudish coalescing by engendering shared imaginative engagement with psychologically interesting and politically interested supernatural agents?

Naturally, one's evaluation of the plausibility of these hypotheses will be shaped by a whole host of factors, including the extent to which one's evaluative practices are embedded within a religious or a scientific context. There are no logical rules or statistical methods by which to decide between claims that derive from this sort of abductive or retroductive inference. Arguing "hypothetically" about the (non)existence and (ir)relevance of the gods of particular groups may sound difficult—and even dangerous. Humanity is faced today with a new and complex adaptive task: surviving the intensity of "evil" in the world, which we ourselves have created. Learning to resist supernatural agent abductions will not solve all our problems, but it may be a necessary condition for the development of new creative ways of arguing about axiological engagement in an increasingly pluralistic and globalizing social environment. However, *rational* reflection will not be enough. A great deal will depend on whether we can also develop new healthy ways of dealing with the *emotional* ties that bind us to our religious "families of origin."

Chapter 5

Religious Family Systems

Is one religion better than others? This is the sort of question one might try to avoid in polite company. However polite they may be, sacerdotal theologians committed to and working within a particular Supranatural Agent Coalition find it difficult to escape such questions, especially when they begin to probe into alien traditions. Those within their home tradition—or religious "family of origin"—usually want the theologian to send clear and costly signals that he or she believes their religion is superior to others. In the context of dialogue with those from other religious families, of course, such signaling only intensifies the alienation between in-groups. These are some of the challenges faced by scholars in the subdisciplines of "theology of religion" or "comparative theology," who engage in theoretical reflection on, and sometimes offer practical guidance for, participation in interreligious dialogue.[1] In this chapter I will explore the affective dimension of encounters with religious others in light of "family systems theory."

Probing religious aliens can get one into trouble. It makes everyone nervous. Pressing too hard when dealing with ticklish topics such as the relative value (or truth) of different religions can all too easily lead to terrified or even terrorizing defensive behaviors. Probing the gods who are born(e) by religious aliens can be even trickier, since people can get especially touchy when their (supernatural) offspring are subjected to evaluation by others. Nevertheless, theologians who are interested in comparing and contrasting religious ideas and practices are required to engage in such probation. Most of the scholars involved in theological reflection on interreligious dialogue are members of monotheistic religions, or of one of the large-scale traditions that emerged in South or East Asia during the axial age. The sensitivity of the methods used in the mutual probation that characterizes such dialogue can vary widely. However, most of the literature produced in the "theology of religion" seems to be motivated, at least in part, by the iconoclastic forces—especially sociographic promiscuity. As we will see, however, here too theologians are almost always pulled back by the biocultural gravitational field of the sacerdotal trajectory.

Scholars who contribute to the biocultural study of religion are also interested in probing religious aliens. Whether or not they are personally affiliated with a religion, scientists in disciplines like cultural anthropology and cognitive psychology have to develop appropriately sensitive ethnographic and experimental methods when studying religious behaviors. While the oft-noted etymological observation that the probable Latin root of the term religion suggests "binding" (*religatio*) does not get us very far materially, in this context it can serve a heuristic purpose—drawing our attention to the way in which religiosity provides fiduciary ligatures that can bind us (more or less anxiously) together. Insofar as they unveil the theogonic mechanisms that generate gods within groups, *scientific* probing can feel quite alienating to people who are strongly committed to their religious traditions.

It is not hard to understand why facing religious differences can be so anxiety producing. Most of us were taught (or learned by watching anxious significant others) to beware of strangers, and the religious beliefs, practices, and attitudes of "others" often appear very strange indeed. This anxiety about alterity actually binds families (and other groups) together, enhancing their cohesion and chances of survival. This is a natural result of the evolution of human emotional systems: feelings of apprehension about *them*—others whose very existence challenges our complacent interpretation of the world and our selves—help to hold *us* together. However, such binding of anxiety easily can (and usually does) lead to patterns of behavior and thought that inhibit the development of healthy, differentiated persons who can engage others without automatically reacting in ways that are conditioned by the emotional systems of their "family of origin," whether biological or religious.

Researchers in the biocultural study of religion are not (usually) focused on adjudicating between the truth claims or normative proposals of particular religious coalitions, but on explaining the evolved cognitive and coalitional mechanisms that engender all shared imaginative engagement with axiologically relevant supernatural agents. Theologians, on the other hand, are more interested in following out the theoretical (and practical) implications of anthropomorphically prudish and sociographically promiscuous hypotheses about (and for) axiological engagement. We can easily get into precarious positions when discussing these sorts of issues, and we might be tempted to give up on such probative inquiry. However, this delicate task is as important as it is dangerous. In our increasingly complex, interconnected, and volatile global context, suppressing curiosity and conversations about religious others only makes things worse, binding anxiety in ways that hinder transformative encounters within and across religious (and nonreligious) families of origin.

The somewhat surprising cognitive and coalitional biases discovered by experimental research within the biocultural sciences would be a matter of course if evolution naturally selected traits that helped hold families together in stressful environments. We humans appear to have evolved in such a way that we automatically default toward acceptance of the beliefs held by those around us, the beliefs of those who are most like us, and the beliefs that we have held in the past. We are also disposed to wrongly believe that those around us share our beliefs, to readjust our memories of previous beliefs in light of new experience, and to recall only information that confirms our beliefs. We are also more likely to believe things we desire to be true, things that are easier to understand, things that would heighten our prestige if they were true, and things that we will be punished for not believing. Moreover, once we sincerely commit to a belief, such beliefs can actually be strengthened when we are confronted by attempts to undermine them, especially when we are under stress.[2] All of these biases are intensified in *religious* families.

My god Can Beat Up Your god

Small children, especially boys, sometimes need to believe that their attachment figures are not only wiser and stronger than they are, but wiser and stronger than anyone else's attachment figures. Supernatural agent conceptions are never immaculate; the particular features of a person's gods betray their religious family of origin. In other words, the generation of particular mental conceptions of gods in human minds is shaped by the cultural transmission of ritual engagements within specific human groups. When it comes to sexual reproduction, most biologists are doubtful that ontogeny recapitulates phylogeny. When it comes to religious reproduction, however, there is little doubt that theogony capitulates to ethnogeny. As we have seen, in the history of human evolution, bigger gods were needed to hold together bigger groups. As these bigger groups competed to destroy (or assimilate) one another, it helped to imagine ever more powerful supernatural agents who sanctioned this violent competition.

Members of the Adamic religions often emphasize the loving nature of their Supranatural Agent, but He is also depicted in their HOLY TEXTS as a punitive father and ruthless warrior. Richard Dawkins famously described the God of the Old Testament as "arguably the most unpleasant character in all fiction: jealous and proud of it; a petty, unjust, unforgiving control-freak; a vindictive, bloodthirsty ethnic cleanser; a misogynistic, homophobic, racist, infanticidal, genocidal, filicidal, pestilential, megalomaniacal, sadomasochistic, capriciously malevolent bully."[3] This is not the only way this monotheistic God is depicted, of course, but those familiar with the Hebrew Bible will be able to call to mind stories that justify each of these adjectives. Similar narratives fill the New Testament and the Qur'an. Other adjectives, such as merciful and forgiving, only apply to the attitude and behavior of GOD toward those who remain faithful to the GROUP.

Given our understanding of the psychological and political dynamics of human evolution, this is not that surprising. In light of the theogonic mechanisms, it makes sense that some supernatural agents would be imaginatively engaged as idealized father figures or warriors who care more about their own families and coalitions than other groups. In fact, many sacerdotal theologians explicitly claim that their GOD can (and will) beat up all other gods. This is the default position we ought to expect in light of the evolution of religion. It is more difficult to explain the efforts of reflective theologians *within* those religious traditions who struggle against such anthropomorphically promiscuous and sociographically prudish conceptions. How are we to interpret this surprising fact? Below I will attempt to make sense of this phenomenon in light of findings within the biocultural study of religion in general, and the insights of Bowen family systems theory in particular.

One of the most troublesome questions facing theologians who promote "interreligious" dialogue is whether one religion is superior to others. Are the revelations and rituals of one religion "better?" Is one god—or one group—supreme? On the one hand, few people would call themselves religious "supremacists" without serious qualifications. On the other hand, one of the qualities of serious religious allegiance is evaluating the beliefs and norms of one's own religious coalition as ultimately the best, or *superior* to others in important respects. Even if theologians committed to a religion reject the idea that their god will beat up other gods, they must still deal with the question whether their religious group is in any sense *better* than others. The three most common alternatives for addressing this problem are exclusivism, inclusivism, and pluralism. Although it has been heavily criticized, this tripartite typology remains a popular way of framing the options for theology of religions today.

One of the clearest defenses of this framework is provided by Perry Schmidt-Leukel.[4] He proposes that we begin with the property P: "mediation of a salvific knowledge (or revelation) of ultimate/transcendent reality." Schmid-Leukel then asks: Is P given (or instantiated) among the religions? He notes there are four possible answers: (1) no, (2) yes, but only once, (3), yes, and more than once, but with only one singular maximum, and (4) yes, more than once and with no singular maximum. If one frames the issue in this way, then it becomes clear that there are only a limited number of logical options when trying to determine whether P is a property of religion (figure 5.1).

For most (sacerdotal) theologians of whatever religious tradition, the answer "no" is a nonstarter. In light of the conceptual framework developed in chapter 2, I will suggest this is precisely the best place to start in the development of an iconoclastic—a naturalist *and* secularist—"theology of religion." First, however, let's briefly clarify the differences between the roads more often traveled while discussing religious supremacy.

Exclusivists insist that P is given only once and, not surprisingly, that this quality is instantiated only in their own religious in-group. For them, the main problem is how to convince members of religious out-groups of the truth of this claim. The purpose of probing religious aliens is to discover weaknesses in their doctrinal or ethical systems in order to compel them to accept the supremacy of the exclusivist's own tradition. *Inclusivists* accept that P is given more than once, but assert that their own religion represents the only maximal (supreme) instantiation of this

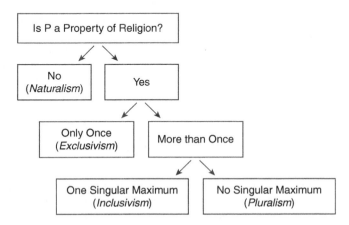

Figure 5.1 Exclusivism, Inclusivism, and Pluralism. Adapted from Schmidt-Leukel, 2005.

property. The problem here is how to discern where, when, and how minimal instantiations occur within other religions. The twentieth-century Roman Catholic theologian Karl Rahner, who argued that some participants of other religions might be "anonymous" Christians, was an inspiration for many of the inclusivist reactions to the rapid growth of pluralist theologies of religion in the 1980s.[5]

Pluralists argue that P is given more than once and that there is no singular maximum instantiation. This does not entail that *all* religions are equal, or even that this property is minimally given in *every* religion. Despite their differences, most of the authors who contributed to *The Myth of Christian Uniqueness*, and later to *The Myth of Religious Superiority*,[6] shared the goal of challenging the notion of religious supremacy. The pluralists were the early champions of the threefold typology, which provided them with a way to distinguish themselves from those who believed their own religion was in some sense the only— or the best—way to experience a transformative relation to ultimate reality. The pluralist is faced with the problem of convincing members of religious coalitions that their traditions are not supreme like they think they are.

The proposals of leading Christian pluralists like John Hick and Paul Knitter have tended to be more anthropomorphically prudish and sociographically promiscuous than those of most other theologians in that tradition. Hick, to whose proposals we will return below, tended to focus on the philosophical arguments for pluralism. Knitter has focused more extensively on the pragmatic effects of exclusivism and inclusivism, which can all too easily reinforce oppressive assumptions about the supremacy of one race, gender, or class. According to Knitter, the problem with claims to religious supremacy is not only that they are false, but also that they contribute to psychological and political dynamics that damage human well-being.[7] I completely agree. However, I will argue that even the pluralist solution still presupposes a religious "myth" that founds the discursive world it shares with inclusivists and exclusivists.

Feeling Religious Difference

In this chapter I hope to contribute to the understanding and ongoing transformation of meetings between religious (and nonreligious) others by attending more closely to the *affective* dimension of cognitive and cultural evolution and the philosophical turn to *alterity* as a generative category for human thought. Most of the focus in academic disciplines such as the theology of religion and comparative theology, as well in the practical exercise of ecumenical and interreligious dialogue, has traditionally been on identifying *similarities* in intellectual *beliefs* (e.g., doctrines) or social *practices* (e.g., rituals). Understanding how and why the relatively iconoclastic lines of flight within pluralistic theologies of religion have always been pulled back by the integrated forces of the sacerdotal trajectory, however, requires more careful attention to the *emotional* dynamics that shape the *differentiation* of religious fields.

It is important to acknowledge that a growing number of Christian theologians of religion have begun focusing more attentively on the concept of difference in their treatment of religious "others."[8] The philosophical (and theological) privileging of sameness over difference goes back to ancient Greece; both Plato and Aristotle favored the category of "the same" in their epistemology, ethics, and metaphysics. One of the most striking characteristics of late modern academic discourse, however, is the valorization of the category of "the other." One finds a growing chorus of voices calling for a higher appreciation of difference—as a constitutive reality and as a regulative category—within the academic study of, as well as in practical responses to, religious pluralism.[9] In fact, the very construction of the notion of a plural-*ism* that focuses on identifying an essential, universal core that is common to all religions has been criticized as an importation of Western modernist values into the encounter with religious others. Mark Heim, for example, has challenged the common "pluralistic" idea that all religions must have the *same* soteriological goal. He argues instead for a real pluralism of religious ends, in which various religions have true (and good) but *different* religious ends. The way forward, he insists, is "to live positively with otherness, not to suggest it is too dangerous to be real."[10]

I agree that tending to difference nonanxiously will be increasingly important for productive and healthy dialogue across (and within) religions, but I do not think that most theologians have recognized how deeply the *affective* forces of the theogonic mechanisms are at work in—and are activated by—the production of sacerdotal theologies of religion. As we will see, the academic study of the role of anxiety among religious others, as well as the actual experience of its binding power in concrete encounters of difference, can activate powerful hidden patterns (patterns that are all the more powerful because they are hidden) of emotional triangulation that covertly shape beliefs about and actions across religious boundaries. It is indeed important to call attention to what religious others say about what they *believe*, and to the ways in which they *act*. But if we fail to attend to what they (and we) *feel*, we are likely to continue binding anxiety over doctrinal or practical issues rather than discovering new possibilities for the transformation of religious emotional systems.

At this stage, however, I want to emphasize the fact that all three of the usual suspects in the theology of religion share an affirmative answer to Schmidt-Leukel's question whether P (mediation of a salvific knowledge—or revelation—of an ultimate reality) is instantiated in religion. Each of these approaches traces the conditions for axiological engagement to a transcendent reality in relation to which some human persons are eternally transformed. However differently this qualitative relation may be narrated, it founds the "world" of interreligious social discourse. From what are some excluded? In what are many included? To what is there a plurality of ways? The answer is eschatological participation in a supernatural coalition, however exclusive or inclusive it might be conceived. Exclusivists, inclusivists, *and* pluralists accept the appropriateness of (some) formulation of P and its instantiation in (at least one) religion. In other words, they all presuppose the existence of a transcendent or ultimate reality, transformative knowledge of which has been made possible by revelation (in some sense). The social rules and conceptual tools of mutual religious probing among theologians (at least in the West) are more regulated than they might appear.

The "mythical" function of the image of supremely mediated religious transcendence in this discourse has not been adequately acknowledged, even by pluralists. The power of this founding "myth" to structure the debates among theologians of religion is due, in part, to the fact that it escapes probation itself because it is hidden, so to speak, before the foundation of the interreligious world of discourse. By calling the instantiation of Schmidt-Leukel's P a "myth," I mean to do more than claim it is "false." I mean to say that it a world-founding narrative that surreptitiously structures theological encounters with religious difference. Exclusivists, inclusivists, and pluralists typically accept the idea that the human experience of valuing and being valued is originated by, ordered through, and oriented toward a transcendent being above (or beyond) the natural world.

For Christian theologians, between whom most of the conversation occurs, ultimate reality is usually conceived as a Supranatural Agent—and salvation as participation in an ultimate Coalition. Theological debates in the West about the *one* true or supreme religion have been shaped by the theoretical dominance of *mono*-theism in general and Christianity in particular, which was reinforced by the *mono*-polistic dominance of "Constantian" programs during the Middle Ages and "Colonialist" programs throughout the modern period. Insofar as it accepts the idea that there is one ultimate reality, one supreme source of normativity, above or beyond (yet somehow intentionally engaged with) the natural world, even pluralism remains under the influence of the myth of religious transcendence. The very idea of ultimate reality seems to imply identity or *unity*: How can there be more than one "ultimate"? Despite the differences in their answers, most Christian theologians of religion would accept the appropriateness of the question: Which natural agents and coalitions will (or can) participate in the GROUP promised eternal protection by GOD?

It is somewhat obvious that engaging religious difference challenges us to reflect on our ways of thinking and acting. What is less obvious is the role of (and the impact on) our *feeling* within such engagements. It is important to pay attention to the emotional forces that bind people together and inform their boundaries as we propose interpretations of (and strategies for dealing with) those who come from another—or are outside of any—religious family of origin. As we will see below, the way in which people bind anxiety within their most familiar emotional systems automatically (and usually covertly) blocks their capacity for open and authentic encounters with the un-familiar. Our experiences of *feeling* for and with *others* are shaped (more or less intensely) by both fear and desire, by our *longing for* and by our *dread of* being bound to one another. We fear being suffocated or absorbed by needy others, but we also fear being isolated or abandoned by significant others whom we hope will fulfill our needs. We desire independence from the painfully overwhelming demands of others, but our overwhelming desire for pleasurable intimacy demands our dependence on others.

These feelings are intensified when a Supranatural Agent is imaginatively added into the mix, binding people together in relation to the infinitely Unfamiliar. Unfortunately, this religious bundling too often ties *us* together by encouraging bad feelings about *them*: un-familiar finite others. The remainder of this chapter provides an analysis of the way in which emotional bonds shape encounters of religious difference. I will approach this ambiguous phenomenon from the point of view of a particular biocultural theory of human functioning— Bowen's family systems theory. Like all scientific models, this theory has its limitations and will need to be appropriated critically and complemented with considerations from other theories.[11] Nevertheless, for the purposes of this project, it makes sense to begin with Bowen's hypotheses, whose analytical, predictive, and therapeutic power have been empirically tested and theoretically refined over several decades.[12] Analyzing interreligious dialogue in light of family systems theory can help us unveil another dimension of the theogonic mechanisms that operate beneath or behind our *ideas* about and *actions* toward religious others.

Emotional Systems

The observation that religious groups are somewhat like families is nothing new. What Bowen's theory provides, however, is a conceptual framework that can help us see how some dysfunctional behavior within (and across) supernatural coalitions is surreptitiously shaped by the same sort of "emotional systems" that characterize natural coalitions of genetic relatives. It may also help us discover new therapeutic strategies for developing healthier modes of engaging across (and beyond) religious "families." Bowen's theoretical and therapeutic models were oriented toward helping individuals to understand the power of evolved biological forces that bind anxiety in family groups and to facilitate their differentiation from those anxiety-intensifying forces. Bowen himself did not deal in any detail with religious phenomena. However, insofar as religions are made up of humans, insights into the patterns of binding chronic anxiety within *biological* families across generations can shed light on the dynamics of interpersonal and cultural engagement within *religious* families of origin.

What is an "emotional system?" This broad concept refers to naturally occurring systems that are present in complex forms of animal life, enabling organisms to receive, integrate, and respond to information. As a form of *systems* thinking, Bowen theory views the functional processes within individual organisms and the functional processes among organisms as intrinsically interrelated. The emotional systems of and between individuals are intertwined. Bowen's conception of an *emotional* system is derived from Darwinian evolutionary theory; it refers to forces that are operative in all animal behavior. Unlike some other social scientific theorists, he does not use this adjective to indicate conscious sentimental states. In the parlance of the theory, "emotion" does not refer to what is *felt*, but to life forces that normally function automatically and outside our awareness. Bowen also postulates a "feeling system" that registers superficial aspects of the emotional system that are brought into cognitive awareness. We "feel" shame, guilt, anger, jealousy, etc., but the "emotional" system operates, so to speak, below such awareness.[13]

All biological organisms exist within tensional systems characterized by counterbalancing forces: distance and closeness, withdrawal and approach, or repulsion and attraction.[14] These tensions, which are automatically guided to some extent by pre-reflective response mechanisms, are part of human beings' phylogenetic evolutionary inheritance. The dialectical dynamics of human fear and desire described briefly above are particularly complex examples of the way in which these life forces may come to structure the shared life of organisms. When applied to human emotional systems, Bowen prefers the terms *individuality* and *togetherness* forces. We are drawn to each other but we also need our own space.

These counterbalancing "emotional" forces are guided by those parts of the autonomic nervous system that evolved prior to the emergence of the cerebral cortex and prefrontal lobes of the human brain. All of our "higher" level cognitive functioning is still shaped by the same sort of prereflective *emotional fields* that bind all complex organisms together. During periods of calm, the two forces of individuality and togetherness balance each other. When people become anxious, however, the togetherness pressure tends to take over. "During high anxiety periods, human beings strive for *oneness* through efforts to think and act alike. It is ironic that this striving for *sameness* increases the likelihood that a group will become fragmented into sub-groups. We-they factions are a product of the pressure for oneness and the intolerance of *differences* associated with it." [15]

Our fear of difference is engendered by the naturally evolved togetherness forces that operate automatically within the emotional fields that bind human individuals into groups (especially families). This aspect of the theory is similar to Bowlby's concept of the "attachment behavioral system" that activates the search for proximity and the provision of care between infants and their primary attachment figures. Bowen emphasizes the effect of emotional stress in the binding together of larger familial groupings. "As anxiety increases, people experience a greater need for emotional contact and closeness and, in reaction to similar pressure from others, a greater need for distance and emotional insulation." The more people's responses to others are controlled by this emotional anxiety, "the *less tolerant* they are of one another and the more they are irritated by *differences*. They are less able to permit each other to be what they are." [16] As we will see below, healthy functioning over time requires a "differentiation" of the self that enables individuals to avoid "fusion" within the "triangular" binding of chronic anxiety within an emotional system.

Bowen argues that the capacity for differentiation is made possible by the evolution of the human "intellectual" system. The cognitive abilities of *Homo sapiens* enable them to think *about* their emotional systems. Most people, however, live their lives relatively unaware of how intensely their intellectual systems are controlled by (fused with) their emotional systems. It is difficult to see, much less admit, how much of our activity (and thought) is controlled by the triangulated emotional systems in which we feel our way in the world. The more our intellectual and emotional systems are "fused" the more our lives are governed by automatic emotional reactivity, regardless of how independent we "think" we are in our intellectual engagements with others. The greater the fusion, the more vulnerable we are to physical, emotional, and social illness, and the less able we are to control our lives and choose how to react to difference.

The most important emotional system treated in Bowen theory is the "family of origin," a phrase that can refer both to the nuclear family within which a person was raised (typically, parents and siblings) and to the extended family (which includes nongenetic, matrimonially linked kin). In other words, it indicates the familial network—"extended" in both space and time—to which a person is bound (or "triangulated") and in which the boundaries of her sense of self and community emerge. Like most versions of family systems theory, Bowen theory has tended to focus on the typical family patterns of Western society. Our interest, however, is not in the contextually limited applications and exemplifications of the theory, but in its broader (or deeper) analysis of the emotional systems that are at work binding anxiety in all human social formations, including religious organizations of all kinds and at all levels.

A great deal of the behavior within human families is somewhat automatic, instinctually driven by "emotional" responses to stimuli—especially anxiety. This is true of other animal groups as well. Imagine, for example, a herd of cows or a flock of birds. The sudden anxiety of one animal rapidly spreads and infects the whole group, leading to almost simultaneous stampede or frenzied flight. Anxiety also flows from person to person in human families, evoking automatic behaviors and thought processes. The life forces of the emotional system are like the electromagnetic field or gravity, in the sense that one cannot see them, but can feel their effects. Like gravity, we hardly notice the force of the emotional system, unless and until it hurts too much to ignore.

This applies to religious "families of origin" too. We try to control and manage religious plurality intellectually or behaviorally, failing to recognize how deeply the involuntary *emotional* binding of our anxiety guides our behavior toward—and our thoughts about—familiar and un-familiar religious others. Toward the end of his career, Bowen proposed that emotional systems were also at work at the level of "societal process,"[17] but the implications of this suggestion for understanding the dynamics of encountering religious difference across social and cultural boundaries have not been carefully explored. Focusing on the extent to which underlying phylogenetically inherited emotional systems shape the dynamics of our meetings with members of other religious (or nonreligious) families of origin may help us find new ways of facilitating "the talk" about religious reproduction. The theogonic mechanisms help to create a communal space in which people do not have to think about the conditions for axiological engagement, reinforcing the binding normativity that is automatically generated by emotional systems. However, this "normal" bondage is not always as healthy as it seems.

Triangulating Anxiety

Before turning more explicitly to *religious* families of origin, let me back up and clarify two more key concepts within Bowen theory that are particularly relevant for understanding how anxiety is bound (and released) in human emotional systems: triangles and differentiation. First, it is important to make a distinction between *acute* anxiety, which is created by fear of what *is* happening, and *chronic* anxiety, which is fueled by fear of what *may* happen. All animals react "anxiously" when they perceive signs of immediate danger; this is basic to survival. Members of the species *Homo sapiens*, however, react anxiously not just in the indicative but also in the subjunctive mood. This intensive experience of temporality is a result of our extensive cognitive capacities for memory and anticipation. This added complexity has also led to new functional capacities, such as the ability to bind anxiety by *triangulating* it within an emotional system and the ability to *differentiate* a self over (and in) time.

Triangles are like the "molecules" of a human emotional system; they are always in movement, shifting, detaching from, or interlocking with other triangles. A two-person emotional system is inherently unstable and naturally tends toward triangulation. A relatively calm triangle will have a comfortable twosome and a third significant to both. When anxiety increases in the system, each "side" will automatically aim to shift or bind the anxiety in various ways. For example, one member (or both) of the original pair may try to triangulate the third person in order to spread out the anxiety. When frustrated by a spouse, for example, a wife may complain to her mother about her husband, or a father may be more easily angered by a child. Sometimes the significant "third" within a triangle will attempt to form a new, tighter relationship with one member of the comfortable twosome, acting out in ways that draw attention to his or her side of the triangle. The dynamics of "triangling" (and "detriangling") are complex, especially as they operate within extended families. In this context, I limit myself to describing some of the common triangular patterns that operate within nuclear family emotional systems.

Within such systems, triangles easily become "fixed" so that the emotional reaction of one member automatically results in predicable behavior in the others. Each "side" of a familial triangle usually has a specific role, or functional position, such as generator, amplifier, or dampener. The members of the triangle become "fused" with one another, so that a shift in the emotional state of one immediately affects the others. Each has his or her own way of trying to alleviate anxiety quickly by moving it around the triangle. It may appear that the "generator" (e.g., an aggravating child) is the problem, when in fact it is the instinctive and adaptive attempts of the "amplifier" (e.g., an angry mother) and the "dampener" (e.g., an appeasing father) to bind the flow of their own chronic anxiety that is activating the generator.[18] Such adaptations may contain the anxiety temporarily, but that is exactly the problem: the anxiety simply moves around the triangle reinforcing emotional reactivity. Over time this binding of anxiety increasingly consumes the available energy of the family members and often results in symptoms within one or more of those fused in the system.

Bowen theory identifies three basic patterns of triangulating anxiety in family emotional systems: conflict, dysfunction, and projection. These configurations of emotional functioning are often all operative at once, although typically one is dominant. In other words, anxiety is automatically bound in some combination of "conflict between the mates, disproportionate adaptation by one mate to preserve harmony, or focus of parental anxiety on a child."[19] The more *fused* the emotional system, the more the sides are trapped in these *automatic* forms of reactivity that attempt to compartmentalize anxiety, and the more likely symptoms are to appear. Because it is infectious as it flows through the system, anxiety "in" one person can lead to a symptom "in" another person.[20] Triangular patterns are transmitted across generations, both from parent to child (two generations), and through multiple generations as individuals bring their own emotional triangling positions automatically into the formation of new nuclear family emotional systems.

The "spousal conflict" pattern may initially appear to be the most problematic. Ironically, however, clinical experience and empirical research indicate that this way of triangulating is the least likely to result in symptoms (psychological or physical) among members of the emotional system. Unless abuse is involved, the balance between the emotional distance and emotional contact (fighting and making up) of the conflicting couple binds most of the anxiety, and the children are relatively less triangled, free to live their own lives.[21] Nevertheless, they are still partially triangled, and when anxiety increases due to some external stressor, the triangling intensifies and the members of the spousal twosome can act in ways that bind a child to their own "side" or problematize a child in order to reestablish spousal solidarity.

In the "spousal dysfunction" pattern, one spouse behaves in ways that are meant to appease the other, who reciprocally accepts (or demands) appeasement. This often results in an emotional system in which the overfunctioning of one and the underfunctioning of the other are mutually reinforcing. One spouse "borrows" the functioning of the other, and the other spouse (more or less happily) "lends" it. Superficially it may appear that the "richer" lending spouse is functioning well and the "poor" borrowing spouse is functioning badly, but in fact the resources of both "selves" are chronically depleted by this process. The "self" of the lender may appear stronger, but her behavior may be just as controlled by fusion to the emotional system as the borrower's. Often significant thirds (usually children) are automatically triangulated by one or both of the dysfunctional spouses, in an attempt to form a new comfortable twosome in order to manipulate or exclude the other spouse. This is instinctively motivated by a desire to alleviate spousal anxiety but, tragically, it simply reinforces the binding power of the emotional system by keeping the anxiety moving in familiar triangular tracks. Under intense stress or over long periods of time, this pattern typically leads to more significant symptoms in one or more family members.

The deleterious effects of the "projection" pattern are sometimes the hardest to see, because it can appear like one family member is being "helped" by one or both of the other sides of a triangle. For example, parents (or other powerful people, such as siblings or grandparents, in a larger complex of interconnected triangles) might try to reduce the anxiety bound in their own twosome by focusing on a "defect" in a child (or some other third within the family triangulation), identifying him or her as the "problem." The latter may be defined as "pitiful" and wholly dependent on the benevolent attention of the former. Highly fused individuals sometimes manage their own anxiety by putting and keeping a "needy" other in a place where he or she relies upon them. Bowen called such behavior "overcompassion" or "overhelpfulness."

This reinforces the *apparent* strength of the "solving" caretaker(s), and provides *apparent* caregiving for the one with a "problem," but in fact all sides of the triangle are controlled by the automatic emotional reactivity that constitutes the system. The "care" is actually reinforcing the inability of each of the selves to choose how to behave. This process is so prevalent (in families and in society) that Bowen wonders whether "more hurtfulness to others is done in the service of pious helpfulness than in the name of malevolent intent."[22] Might the same be said for the "care" of the gods? At this stage, the key point is that anxious attempts to "fix" others within our own families of origin (religious or otherwise) can actually make things worse. So can insisting on getting our own way or trying to appease everyone. When our beliefs and behaviors are covertly driven by such triangular patterns, they simply intensify the emotional forces (theogonic or otherwise) that bind our anxiety ever more tightly. Happily, there is something we can do—or think—to alter the *way* we feel.

Differentiation of Self

Modifying and reducing chronic anxiety, rather than just moving it around triangles, requires what Bowen calls *differentiation of self.* Family systems theory views individual selves as mutually entangled within groups, and groups as the mutual entanglement of selves, and so "differentiation" (like "fusion") refers to a process that happens both within and between persons. The "major secret" disclosed by the theory, suggests Bowen, is that "an emotional system responds to emotional stimuli. If any member can control his emotional response, it interrupts the chain reaction."[23] Conversely, the interruption of the chain challenges the reactivity of all the members of the emotional system. This means that differentiating a self automatically alters the system, and a more differentiated system automatically alters the selves within it. During the process of differentiation the functioning of the self becomes less "fused" to the relatively involuntary triangling patterns that characterized the family of origin, and the emotional system itself binds less chronic anxiety, which frees the selves within it for healthier and more intentional functioning.

It might seem that the easiest way to "differentiate" is simply to detach from the system, that is, to create emotional distance between one's self and the (anxiety producing) members of one's family of origin. Although such a strategy, whether executed through geographical or psychological separation, can make a person appear to be independent, that person may still be controlled by the togetherness forces of the emotional system. If we simply move away without dealing with our emotional reactivity, we take the system with us and will replicate the patterns of triangular anxiety-binding in all of our new relationships, including those with religious others. Bowen calls this failed strategy "emotional cutoff."[24] Cutting off from one's family of origin fails because if a person is vulnerable to being activated when in emotional contact with familial triangles, then he is vulnerable to the same activation by togetherness forces in any and all other emotionally intense contexts. Under stress, the old patterns automatically emerge. Differentiation only works if one maintains *emotional contact* with one's family of origin.

The distinctive characteristic of a well-differentiated person is the capacity to distinguish between emotional and intellectual processes within herself and in her relations with others.[25] Differentiating the self from the automatic triangulation of its family system can help a person remain calm in emotionally charged relationships, and to choose how to engage with both familiar and unfamiliar others. A poorly differentiated person is more deeply enmeshed or fused within emotional systems, immediately reacting in ways that follow the typical patterns of moving around anxiety that operated in his family of origin. Most of his energy is exhausted in this triangular emotional binding (regardless of his functional position in the triangle), and he is less able to control his actions or thoughts. Bowen also distinguished between *basic* and *functional* differentiation, and between a *solid*- and a *pseudo*-self.[26] A person may appear to be differentiated when distant (emotionally or physically) from his family of origin; his pseudo-self might function quite well in everyday life. Under extreme stress, however, his basic level of differentiation and the emotional reactivity (or neutrality) of his solid-self are revealed.

The basic differentiation of one solid-self within a set of family triangles affects the whole system because it disrupts the normal flow of anxiety. When one person tolerates the anxiety and takes responsibility for him or herself, rather than continuing to triangulate in one of the ways described above, the other members of the emotional system will intensify their own triangling efforts in order to return the system to its habitual functioning. The togetherness forces shift into overdrive. If the differentiating person can resist these forces and maintain a higher level of intellectual functioning—while staying in emotional contact—the effect will be a chain reaction that can enable others to see, and alter, their own role in the binding of anxiety. This "detriangling" process increases the capacity of the individual self and of the system for adapting when external factors—such as encounters with radical religious otherness—produce acute anxiety. This can have a therapeutic effect not only on family emotional systems, but also on wider political and social systems.[27]

How does one go about differentiating a self in a way that can make the whole system more healthily differentiated? Bowen offered several practical suggestions for authentically differentiating a self, both within a therapeutic context and on one's own.[28] We can summarize them in terms of three interrelated processes or tasks. First, one can work on developing the capacity to recognize the automatic functioning of the emotional system within one's own family, and especially one's own role within it, and practice not following the usual triangulation strategies. Observing and resisting automaticity, however, is only possible if one remains in emotional contact with those who activate the triangling. Healthy differentiation of self, and the detriangling of emotional systems, begins by attending to the way in which one's *own* behaviors and thoughts are regulated by the system. Learning to be less "emotionally reactive" in the differentiation process does not mean repressing or ignoring one's feelings; in fact, one becomes more intensely aware of feelings, but they do not automatically determine the way one acts or thinks.

Second, Bowen encourages the development of person-to-person relations with members of one's family of origin (nuclear or extended). The "highroad" to increasing one's basic level of differentiation is "changing oneself *while in relationship* to the past."[29] Staying in emotional contact with one side of a significant familial triangle while attempting to differentiate a self is difficult because togetherness forces will exert pressure on all sides to alleviate anxiety by moving it around in the old ways that have worked (however painful they might be) to bind the family together. "The togetherness opposition to individuation, or differentiation, is so predictable that differentiation *does not occur without opposition* from the togetherness forces."[30] The goal here is to stay in conversation with one person at a time without triangling, that is, without habitually attempting to control, appease, or change the subject in order to keep the anxiety moving in a familiar flow. Actively engaging dormant triangles in one's family of origin can help one to see more clearly one's own (and others') patterns of emotional reactivity and to resist the urge to triangle in stressful relationships with significant others.

Third, one can practice detriangling the self while in emotionally intense *new* contexts. This strategy involves intentionally placing oneself in relation to people from other families of origin and observing one's own reaction to alien togetherness forces. Here too, the task is to stay in emotional contact without immediately counterattacking or defending the self, appeasing the other, or picking a new topic, in other words, without giving in to the usual triangling strategies. This requires remaining neutral "emotionally" while staying active "intellectually." If individuals can resist the temptation to alleviate anxiety through emotional or physical distance (cutoff), and make ongoing intellectual decisions to tolerate the anxiety that naturally arises when one resists the triangling power of the evolved togetherness forces, then, over time, chronic anxiety and emotional reactivity can be reduced across family systems. To what extent might this apply to encounters between *religious* others?

Fusion in Religious Families of Origin

All families have issues, and most of us have issues with our families. This is equally true of religious coalitions. People not only take their old triangles to school, play, and work, they also bring them into temple, church, or mosque. We are tempted to think that it is the particular issues that we have with doctrinal formulations or moral regulations, for example, which cause the anxiety in religious families of origin. If only we could resolve those issues, we think, then the anxiety would go away. On the contrary, it is the underlying emotional triangular binding of anxiety that generates (or at least exacerbates) our counterproductive and even destructive ways of dealing with issues—both inside and outside the boundaries of a religious family. The natural, intuitive response to anxiety is to give in to the togetherness forces and to fall into familiar triangling habits in order to hold (some of) the group together, especially during encounters with religious others. A blinding obsession with what we think is "the issue"—for example, the correct belief or the appropriate practice—keeps us from seeing the automatic reactivity that is driving the emotional triangulation of anxiety, fueling our conflicting, appeasing, or projecting thoughts and behaviors.

All religious families have distinctive features that reflect their particular historical context but, insofar as they are composed of bioculturally evolved human organisms, they are also characterized by nested hierarchies of psychologically (and politically) interlocking emotional triangles. Anxiety also flows through and is bound up within the emotional systems that subtend and support the reproduction of gods in groups. Religious anxiety may sometimes have to do with existential concerns about being bound to the *eternal*, but it is functionally bound up in emotional triangles just like all other *chronic* anxiety. We might refer to smaller, more intimate bindings (such as devotional groups, congregations, temples, mosques, or ashrams) as "nuclear" religious families, and larger, more complicated bindings (such as Christian denominations, or larger groupings such as the Adamic traditions) as "extended" religious families. My purpose here, however, is not to develop such a classification, but to point out the underlying emotional systems that are at work wherever there is shared imaginative engagement with axiologically relevant supernatural agents. Due to limited space, and for reasons that should be obvious from the previous section, I will utilize examples from my own religious family of origin (evangelical Christianity).

Sometimes atheists seem to assume that if people would just listen to rational arguments they would automatically let go of their gods. However, this does not take seriously enough an important empirical fact about religious life: the gods are imaginatively triangled within the existentially binding emotional systems that operate "beneath" most intellectual reflection about religious representations. Simply attacking people's beliefs or alarming them by pointing out the consequences of their behaviors will only intensify their anxiety, reinforcing the triangling patterns that hold their religious selves and groups together. Once the gods are imaginatively engaged in a social group, it should be no surprise that they are depicted as conflicting, appeasing, or projecting—as they so often are in religious myths and popular religious discourse. Triangulating gods within a religious family of origin strengthens the cohesion of the group, but it also increases the *fusion* of the emotional system. Believing that a god is on (or against) "our side" intensifies the anxious need to cut off lines of difference, to triangle "others" into (or force them out of) the boundaries of a religious coalition.

Triangulating the gods only intensifies emotional reactivity and hinders the differentiation of selves capable of engaging nonanxiously across boundaries of religious (and nonreligious) difference. These emotional processes are perhaps more evident in cults (for those of us not in them), but the need to be surrounded by those who believe *the same* things and act in *the same* ways is operative within all religious families. In fact, it is operative in all groups—including atheist coalitions. The question is whether the togetherness forces bind individuals in groups in ways that lead to unreflective conformity of belief and behavior. When emotional systems function behind the veil, as it were, intuitive default mechanisms automatically shift anxiety around in familiar triangles, which diminishes the capacity for differentiated intellectual reflection on "the issues."

If our anxiety about religious aliens is managed by emotional (or physical) distance, any crossing of familiar boundaries will only be the encounter of pseudo-selves. We may even think (and feel) we are differentiated in our functioning. As long as we are able to keep our triangles moving, alleviating anxiety relatively quickly through our automated emotional reactivity, we are able to hold our selves together—in groups. Forming more solid-selves and increasing basic levels of healthy differentiation, however, will require that we learn to tolerate anxiety about reflective argumentation regarding supernatural agent coalitions while remaining in emotional contact—without fusing or cutting off. The triangulating strategies of conflict, appeasement, and projection are all attempts to change or control the others in the emotional system. Increasing basic differentiation (as well as reducing chronic anxiety in the "family") requires changing and controlling one's *self*. Differentiating a solid-self begins with learning to observe the emotional system and one's own reactivity within it.

Within religious families, "conflictual" triangulation often involves an automatic and rigid defensiveness about one's beliefs, which can easily lead to offensive attacks on those who disagree. We might call this an *assimilating* strategy, attempting to control others by forcing them into conformity. In the broader history of my extended religious family of origin, this has taken an extreme form (at the level of broader societal process) in what we might call the *Constantinian* approach to ecumenism and the *Colonialist* approach to missions, both of which attempt to make everyone *the same*. Assimilation usually operates in more subtle ways. In my narrower family of origin, North American evangelicalism, "statements of faith" have been used to identify the "issues" around which chronic anxiety is bound and to protect the boundaries of religious communities. Ironically, this has led to increased splintering, to the proliferation of religious "gated" communities, each with their own binding doctrinal statement that determines who gets in, and who gets kicked out. Individuals whose religious triangulation habits follow the assimilation pattern typically respond to the acute pain caused by reflective challenges to their beliefs by automatically—and dogmatically—defending them at all costs.

The dysfunctionally "appeasing" mode of triangular anxiety-binding is just as obsessed with sameness as the "conflicting" mode. Instead of pushing for maximal sameness, however, it attempts to find minimal sameness as quickly as possible. We might call this an *attenuating* strategy: keep or restore the peace at any price. Sometimes, however, the cost of achieving functional harmony so hastily is higher than we realize. Ecumenical and interreligious dialogue that hurriedly moves beyond (or covers over) the differences, and focuses primarily on the issues about which representatives of the religious families can more easily agree, can obscure the deeper operation of the emotional systems that are automatically driving much (if not most) of the participants' reactivity. A person who immediately responds to challenges to his beliefs by attenuating, becoming quiet, or backing down to keep everyone calm may appear more differentiated. Insofar as such responses are based on emotional reactivity, however, they only reinforce the binding of anxiety, which will continue to flow through and around the system.

If Bowen theory is right about the effects of triangulation within emotional systems, then we actually make things *worse* when we put all our effort into creating one big, happy religious family rather than differentiating selves. Anxiously attempting to hold the system together, or at least binding some parts of it together by holding other parts of it apart, only *intensifies* the fusion. To find common ground, conferences involving the hierarchical elite and professional theologians of sacerdotal coalitions usually end up focusing on similarities between the different ritual practices of subcoalitions within the GROUP or abstract doctrines about the nature and revelation of GOD. However, such dialogue has relatively little effect on the daily lives of the members of those religious groups who, quite naturally, are more interested in supernatural agents like demons, dead saints, or divine saviors. Does this mean we should discourage intellectual reflection about the differences between monotheistic coalitions? No, but it does mean we may need to question the plausibility (and feasibility) of trying to keep the peace by managing the boundaries of coalitions that are held together by shared imaginative engagement with supernatural agents.

What about the triangular pattern Bowen called "projection," which attempts to relieve anxiety by shifting the focus onto an issue or person who is identified as "the problem?" In religious families, this strategy of *accommodating* (in the sense of altering the system to make room for an *other*) works well for binding together those who perceive themselves as providing "the solution." Like the other two strategies, this approach is still obsessed with sameness, but its attempts to secure the identity of the group are oriented toward keeping "the others" in their place. As we saw above, however, Bowen argues that the damage done by this mode of triangling can be far worse than the other two. Those identified as problematic may be outside or inside the community; either way, they are defined as requiring special attention. Often, this attention is based on differences in race, class, gender, or some other boundary marker.

In the recent history of my North American evangelical family of origin, for example, a great deal of energy has been focused on keeping certain types of people in their place; women in the family but outside the ministry, some minorities and "the poor" dependent on the benevolence of the family but out of sight, and homosexuals at the margin or just outside the family. Figuring out how to accommodate all of these problematic "others" distracts attention from the automatic emotional reactivity of the white, affluent, heterosexual males whose "solutions"— on either side of the issues—bind anxiety ever more tightly in this sort of Supranatural Agent Coalition.

Domesticating Infinity—the Triangulation of GOD

As we noted in previous chapters, theology evolved in the wake of the axial age as the need for bigger gods in bigger groups led to the conception of an infinite intentional Force that conditioned any and all axiological engagement whatsoever. The major monotheistic coalitions, each in its own way, struggled to domesticate GOD within its own religious Family.

Despite—or, perhaps, because of—its inconceivability, the concept of a Supranatural Agent worked relatively well when it came to sanctifying a doctrinal coalition and sanctioning the violence necessary to draw and secure the boundaries of a HOLY LAND. When one "nuclear" religious family (such Roman Catholicism, Lutheranism, or even Anabaptism) within a larger "extended" monotheistic Family (such as Christianity) dominates a particular society, its members have little need to think about the plausibility of their religious conceptions. After the Reformation, the Thirty Years' War and other events that further diversified the societal landscape of Europe and West Asia, the differences between religious families became increasingly difficult to ignore. Which religious GROUP has the right idea of GOD and the GOD-given right to rule?

"Comparative theology" evolved in the nineteenth century, in the wake of the expansive European colonization of other cultures across the globe, which led to encounters with even more alien religions, and brought back waves of "foreigners" to European (and North American) shores. This expanding eco-sociological niche required sacerdotal theologians to adapt, to develop better explanations of the relation between Christianity's Supranatural Agent and the supernatural agents of these other coalitions. What role does GOD play within a religious Family as it meets un-familiar religions with alien gods? Like many other religious conceptions, the idea of GOD designates an axiologically relevant counterintuitive PERSON. It makes sense that finite god-conceptions would be intuitively triangulated within the emotional systems of human persons, natural agents who imaginatively engage supernatural agents. But how could an infinite GOD be triangulated? A triangle is formed when two fixed points are delineated in relation to a third fixed point, or when two lines in flight are closed off by another line. Either way, the points or lines are de-fined in their relation to one another.

As we have seen, however, infinity cannot be domesticated. Triangulation cannot capture "the infinite." Infinity resists de-finition, refuses closure, and rejects boundaries. This is true in religiosity as well as geometry. To be a finite thing (or process) is to be bounded by that which is other, to be defined over against that which that thing is not. One cannot define absolute in-finity simply as not-finite, for then it would be merely one thing (the infinite) over against an other (the finite). In other words, the metaphysically infinite cannot be triangulated. Religious emotional systems, however, are composed of anxious human selves, who are always tempted to triangle anything they cannot control. The sacerdotal forces go into overdrive, struggling to domesticate an imagined infinite Intentionality within the psychological and political triangles of the religious Family, while simultaneously insisting on the logical impossibility and doxological inappropriateness of any domestication of the almighty Father, Creator of all finite things.

Christian scholars who engage in comparative theology, or in the theology of religion, are often more resistant to the theogonic mechanisms than other monotheistic theologians. When the task is dialoguing with religious others about ultimate reality, following the iconoclastic forces of sociographic promiscuity and anthropomorphic prudery seems to make more sense. Nevertheless, most scholars in these subfields of theology typically end up giving in to the forces of the sacerdotal trajectory, appealing to the infinite mystery of the nature of a disembodied (or contingently embodied) Force that is in some sense intentionally related to all human groups.

This sort of ambivalent (non)domestication of infinity can be illustrated in the work of Christian theologian of religion Keith Ward. In *Images of Eternity,* Ward reviews five of the world's major religions and identifies a feature that he believes they all share: the "dual-aspect" doctrine of God. This doctrine emerges out of what he calls an "iconic vision" in which the infinite is discerned in and through the finite.[31] Ward limits himself to Hinduism, Buddhism, Judaism, Christianity, and Islam—religious traditions that originated in South Asia and West Asia. He does not treat the East Asian traditions of Confucianism or Daoism, which have far less person-like and coalition-favoring conceptions of *ultimate* reality (although the quotidian life of their faithful adherents is saturated with rituals engaging proximate supernatural forces). A fuller analysis of the differences these between these East Asian religions and the five traditions treated by Ward would also require attention to the distinctive roles played by supernatural agents in the revelation of sacred texts.[32]

In this context, however, I want to focus on Ward's description of a "dialectic" that he finds in the writings of major theologians within the religions of South and West Asian origin. This dialectic attempts to maintain *both* that the infinite (or unconditioned) cannot be described in relation to the finite using any categories whatsoever (even "existence") *and* that the infinite can be described as mediated in and through finite "icons" or images authorized by revelation. For example, the Hindu doctrine of non-duality (*advaita*), as expressed in the work of Sankara and Ramanuja, teaches that we must not think of niriguna Brahman (Brahman "without qualities") and the world of appearance as two separate things. In some forms of Buddhism, *nirvana* is understood as beyond being and non-being; it is not defined simply as non-being over against being, nor as another state of being toward which those in *samsara* are oriented. Either of those options would render nirvana finite, at least in the sense that it would be conditioned by its distinction from being per se or from other states of being. Ward illustrates this in the writings of Buddhaghosa and Asvaghosa.

As Ward emphasizes, however, these theologians (in the broad sense of the term) *also* insist that we must speak of a saguna Brahman "with qualities," who relates to the world, or of the compassionate action of the Buddhas in relation to those still on the path to nirvana. Ward points out that one even finds "the infinite" (or unconditioned) described as omnipotent and omniscient in these religions of south Asian origin. On the one hand, leading theologians within these traditions insist that infinite reality cannot be thought—or even experienced as an "existing" thing. On the other hand, they *also* develop a "sense that the world of finite things is able to express an infinite reality beyond and yet infusing it." Although in variable ways and to different extents, they have an "*iconic* vision" with which they can "see things as pointing beyond themselves, as sacramental of a *supreme* reality and value, as visible images of eternity."[33]

Ward observes that a similar dialectic can be found among leading theologians in the three major religious traditions that trace their roots to West Asia. The more strict monotheism of Judaism, Christianity, and Islam shapes the way they deal with the tension in this dialectic. Ward illustrates the "dual-aspect" doctrine of God in the writings of the medieval theologians Maimonides, Thomas Aquinas, and Al-Ghazzali. Despite their differences all three utilize the categories of Aristotelian philosophy, such as potentiality and actuality, matter and form, to try to render intelligible their understanding of the relation between finite creation and the Infinite Creator. On the one hand, God is without attributes and is unrelated to the world. On the other hand, God has all perfections and is the primal cause and providential ruler of the world. God is unknowable yet somehow also revealed in the Torah (Maimonides), is immutable and impassible, and yet somehow united with the suffering nature of Jesus (Thomas), or is beyond all characterization and yet somehow characterized as the most gracious and most merciful (Al-Ghazzali).

All of this is patently "paradoxical," and Ward notes the obvious "intelligibility gap between believers and unbelievers."[34] However, he argues that the "iconic vision" of the world only makes sense if one lives within a particular revelatory tradition, adopting a form of life "which brings out the true nature and goal of human existence in a world in which that goal is hidden and obscured by all the ambiguities of self-will."[35] From the point of view of our analysis so far, there are at least two difficulties with this line of reasoning. First, the problematic dualism between the finite and the infinite, which theologians across religious traditions agree cannot be intelligibly solved, is in each of the cases above simply transferred *into* the infinite, giving it "two aspects." This shifts the problem without solving it. There can be no "solution," as most of these theologians admit (or event insist), for the reasons we have already identified: "the infinite" cannot be conceived as a determinate intentional reality in relation to the whole of "the finite." So, why would one try to shift the ambiguous duality beyond the veil and into the infinite itself? For one thing, it makes it somewhat easier to domesticate GOD within the minds and cultures of a religious Family.

The iconically imagined intentionality of an ultimately valuable and infinite PERSON can be fused within an emotional system—mysteriously hidden and so endlessly useful for religious leaders who triangle GOD in ways that strengthen their "side" within the GROUP. But why would one accept the idea of "two aspects" in the first place? Why not acknowledge that within the natural world we experience an intense and ineffable limitlessness (the first aspect) and that the idea of a sacramentally mediated supreme reality (the second aspect) is simply the result of naturally evolved hyperactive mechanisms for detecting agents and protecting coalitions? This brings us to a second difficulty. In all of these traditional theological formulations, the need for an "iconic vision" presupposes a prior (uncriticized) supernatural *abduction*: the conjecture that a disembodied and unconditioned Force has somehow intentionally manifested itself to (or in) the conditioned, natural world. Such abductions are only made, as Ward himself notes, by those who are *already* situated within a shared imaginative world saturated by the religious ritual and revelation of a particular Coalition.

The dual-aspect doctrine of GOD is only forced upon a theologian if she already believes that infinity and intentionality must somehow be held together, that the existential condition for finite axiological engagement must have some human-like and coalition-favoring attributes. However "open-minded" and "inclusive" such an ultimate reality might be, we are still dealing with a *religious* conception that is anthropomorphically promiscuous and sociographically prudish. Such images (icons) of axiologically relevant Supranatural Agency are intuitively adopted into religious families and automatically intensify the binding of anxiety among intentional human agents. When GOD is drawn into the triangulating strategies of assimilation, attenuation, and accommodating within human coalitions, anxiety is bound to infinity and becomes unbearable—psychologically and politically.

The Tragedy of Sacerdotal Theologies of Religion

The interreligious dialogue among sacerdotal theologians about competing conceptions of a supreme Reality is tragic in at least three senses. First, as we have noted in earlier chapters, comparing and contrasting the gods of different groups all too easily leads to the sort of tragedy with which we are all too familiar: hostile acts of terror—physical or emotional—carried out against religious "others." This tragic behavior, illustrated almost daily in world headlines, is most often associated with extreme *exclusivists*, who engage religious others only to change or destroy them. Of course, most of those who embrace the theory of exclusivism in their theology of religions are not committed to the destruction of others in this (natural) world. It is not uncommon, however, for even the most peace-loving exclusivists to insist that those who are not part of their coalition face a (supernatural) world of hellish violence or annihilation unless—or purgation until—they see things from *their* Supranatural Agent's point of view. This "surprising fact" is indeed tragic, but from the perspective of theogonic reproduction theory it is a "matter of course"; the tendency to believe in punishing gods appears to have been naturally selected precisely because it promotes cooperative, committed, and relatively peace-loving behavior *within in-groups*.

Second, scholarly debates over religious supremacy also illustrate what Pascal Boyer called "the tragedy of the theologian." As we saw in chapters 2 and 3, no matter how hard theologians try to promote the idea of an infinite intentional Force, religious practitioners will default rather quickly to detecting finite supernatural agents and protecting local supernatural coalitions. The maximally counterintuitive ideas codified and policed by religious leaders may be memorized and repeated, but as soon as people begin to reason about pragmatic issues that affect the fortunes of their kith and kin, they naturally tend to return to the kind of inferential and preferential strategies that helped our early ancestors survive. As though bearing GOD were not difficult enough, many *inclusivist* theologians of religion want the members of their own coalitions to consider the possibility that their GROUP may not have cornered the market on salvific axiological engagement. Reflecting on this kind of "theologically correct" idea requires the capacity to resist the evolved default toward sociographic prudery, which makes such conceptions very difficult to bear.

We can illustrate this sort of "tragedy" by pointing briefly to the efforts of two leading inclusivists currently working in the field. Francis X. Clooney, S. J., has brought his own Roman Catholic tradition into deep comparative dialogue with some of the Vedantic traditions within Hinduism. Instead of starting with a theory of religion (a strategy he attributes to the pluralists), he begins with a more inductive reading of individual texts. Clooney calls his approach an "including theology," but explicitly sees his efforts as "confessional," and "a kind of Christian witness."[36] He insists that comparative theology (a phrase he prefers to "theology of religion") should not be "primarily about which religion is the true one, but about learning across religious borders in a way that discloses the truth of my faith, in the light of their faith."[37] The problem, however, is that it is precisely *which religion is the true one* that concerns the practicing Roman Catholic (as well as the practicing Hindu). If some other supernatural agent coalition *truly* mediates access to a supremely attractive eschatological future, why would she continue engaging in the same costly ritual signaling of commitment to her own in-group?

Mark Heim, one of the leading Protestant scholars in this field, provides us with another example. In his first major methodological analysis of the theology of religions, *Salvations: Truth and Difference in Religion*, he argued that neither exclusivism nor pluralism (in their classical forms) allows a balance between real openness to other religions and a commitment to practicing one's own.[38] Heim insisted that any attempt to move "beyond inclusivism" would not be faithful to the historical concreteness of real religions, which *do* see themselves as supreme in some sense. In *The Depth of Riches: A Trinitarian Theology of Religious Ends*, Heim set out a fuller constructive proposal, arguing there are a variety of real (and good) eschatological consummations. Once one has reached the "summit" of one's own religious tradition (e.g., heaven), however, from that perspective the other summits of the other religions will appear "lower."[39]

From a Christian point of view, argues Heim, one can still affirm a kind of trinitarian exclusivism; only Christians achieve communion with the triune God. From their perspective, other achievements seem to be of a "lesser good." Those from other traditions will make similar judgments about the supremacy of *their* religious ends. Despite all this, Heim still presupposes *one* Creator, who providentially offers salvation to all, drawing any positive response, "however limited, toward the *fullest* providential good."[40] For our purposes, the more important point is that such a proposal will not be very compelling to a layperson committed to pursuing her own summit; it asks her to accept a complex theory of religious difference that challenges what she currently believes and, *ex hypothesi*, will always believe to be true—that her religious "end" really is the highest. Tragically, for the inclusivist, such maximally counterintuitive theories are not likely to gain any traction or reduce anxiety about religious aliens among regular believers.

Pluralists must also deal with the "tragedy" of being a (sacerdotal) theologian, but in this context we can use this type of theology of religions to illustrate a third sense in which debates over religious supremacy are tragic. The Greeks not only gave us some of our most well-known theogonic myths, they also invented the tragedy as a theatrical form. In this sense a *tragedy* is an aesthetic presentation of human suffering, a display of the weakness and limitations of the human condition, and an offering of sensual engagement with the terrors of reality that is also intended to bring pleasure to the audience. Especially in the tragedies of Euripides and Aeschylus, this often involved the use of a *deus ex machina*, that is, an actor playing the role of a god lowered onto stage in a box whose arrival surprisingly and mysteriously provided the key turn in the plot.

It seems fitting to use this "tragic" metaphor to describe the most typical sort of approach taken by pluralist theologians of religion. John Hick's classic proposal in this field, *An Interpretation of Religion,* is motivated in part by the observation that human suffering is often intensified by competing claims about religious supremacy. Adopting a Kantian distinction between noumena and phenomena, he argues that "the Real" (which may also be called Ultimate Reality, the Transcendent, etc.) cannot be experienced "in itself." However, its universal presence can be "humanly experienced" in the various (phenomenal) forms made possible by the "conceptual-linguistic systems and spiritual practices" of the religions.[41] One can see the similarity to Ward's notion of an "iconic vision." On the one hand, Hick is well aware of the philosophical problems with thinking of the divine in terms of personal agency, and the preference among theologians across religious traditions for what he calls the metaphysical *impersonae* of the Real.

On the other hand, because human beings *need* to think and experience the Real as personal, he also insists that religious language about supernatural agency can be considered "literally true" of divine *personae*.[42] What I referred to above as the "myth" of religious transcendence is still foundational for Hick's pluralist model. The various religious coalitions are still interpreted as mediating "soteriological alignment with the Real," and "about to the same extent" although to different "groups of human beings."[43] By affirming a "cosmic optimism" that "proclaims the real possibility, which can even begin to be realized here and now, of a *limitlessly better* state,"[44] Hick introduces a *deus ex machina* that is apparently intended to give us pleasurable relief in the midst of a display of religious anxiety about finitude.

Still, could one not argue that pluralism is worth fighting for? Elsewhere, Hick makes clear that his hypotheses are meant to resist "absolutized Christian patriarchalism."[45] At the very least, such approaches might offer more hope in helping us to avoid the tragic violence that too often flares up around exclusivist claims to religious supremacy. Isn't pluralism better than nothing? Well, it depends, of course, on what one means by "better" and whether "nothing" is really our only other option. As we saw above, psychological experiments in a variety of contexts have shown that raising mortality salience—for example, reflecting on one's own death or one's possible eternal separation from loved ones—*automatically* increases negative reactions to out-groups and aggression against worldview-threatening others, as well as the tendency to detect finite supernatural agents of the sort that hold together small-scale coalitions.[46]

This means, tragically, that when religious pluralists approach "the talk" about the plurality of gods in groups by focusing on the (more or less pleasurable) experience of human beings vis-à-vis an alleged transcendent Reality after death, they are actually *activating* the theogonic forces that drive human cognition toward over-detecting disembodied intentional forces whose potentially punitive presence leads to the over-protecting of human coalitions. The three senses in which sacerdotal theologies of religion are tragic are interrelated. As long as they include supernaturalistic ideas (such as Schmidt-Leukel's "P"), such proposals will *intensify* the anxious reactions that human beings naturally have when presented with their own finitude. Answering "yes" to Schmid-Leukel's question discussed above (figure 5.1), and taking any one of the three usual routes (exclusivism, inclusivism, or pluralism) in the theology of religion only makes things worse even though—or precisely because—it *hides* the binding of anxiety in religious emotional systems by offering appeasing religious "solutions."

Reframing the discussion in light of the distinction between the sacerdotal and iconoclastic trajectories opens up a different way of thinking about the options for developing hypotheses within the theology of religion (figure 5.2). The sacerdotal trajectory generates hypotheses that reproduce shared imaginative engagement with supernatural agents, reinforcing the intuitive mechanisms that bind anxiety in in-groups by engendering abductive inferences about punishing gods. This outcome might please exclusivists (and some inclusivists), but it is precisely what most pluralists are trying to avoid.

The iconoclastic trajectory, on the other hand, leads toward theolytic retroductive hypotheses about the conditions for axiological engagement. It engenders reflective resistance to the "iconic vision" of axial age religions, which presupposes ritual engagement with the revelation of a supremely valuable reality beyond the natural world. An

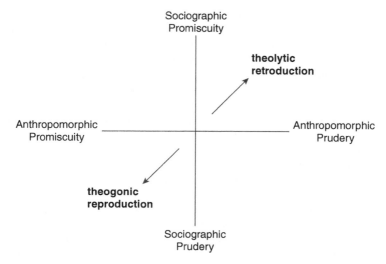

Figure 5.2   Hypotheses in the "Theology of Religion"

iconoclastic theology of religion works at dissolving the promiscuous god-suppositions triangulated within prudish religious groups. In a sense that I will describe in more detail in chapter 6, it is both naturalist and secularist—and *atheist*. At this stage, however, I want to focus on the sort of intensification that is activated when one begins to contest the evolved theogonic forces and experiment with more anthropomorphically prudish and sociographically promiscuous ways of thinking, acting, and feeling about evaluative interactions within and across religious (and nonreligious) families.

Differentiation and Iconoclastic Intensification

The easiest way to respond to the togetherness forces that are always at work in the emotional systems that subtend religious (and other human) groups is either to acquiesce to the triangulating dynamics within them or to cut off from them. Neither of these options deals with the chronic anxiety that is bound up within religious families. Attempts to placate, control, or "fix" others in (or outside of) one's family of origin only reinforce the triangulating fusion. Attempts to keep calm and carry on by avoiding contact with the family are also evidence of fusion—of the

extent to which emotional stability depends on managing the togetherness forces that still bind one to unbearable absent others. Differentiation,
on the other hand, involves dealing with *one's self*: learning to avoid automatic emotional reactivity *while* maintaining contact with emotionally
significant members of "the family." Such efforts do not depend on the
alteration of (or affirmation from) the other sides of one's triangular
network.

In contexts shaped by the West Asian monotheistic Families, both
sacerdotal and iconoclastic theologies of religion must deal with the
relation between infinity and intentionality. This is true even for atheists who want to have "the talk" about religious reproduction in the academic and public spheres. It may seem strange to suggest that infinity is
an appropriate and even important topic for discussion in these spheres.
One thing we all share as human beings, however, is the finitude of our
axiological engagement. Are there ways of talking about our experiences
of being-limited without binding anxiety in religious in-groups? Can
we overcome the debilitating fear of religious strangers and promote
healthy intentionality within and across boundaries of religious and
nonreligious difference? What steps can we take to circumvent a clash
of religious civilizations and to facilitate the dissolution of the painful knots of emotional triangulation that tie "us" together by holding
"them" apart?

Our analysis up to this point suggests two sorts of strategy for dealing with these problems: differentiating selves and detriangulating gods.
From Bowen's theory we can derive a set of *psychological* strategies for
dissolving anxiety within the emotional systems of religious families.
First, we can practice observing the emotional systems that subtend our
own family of origin—and especially our own role in the triangulation
of anxiety. Only by learning to recognize and reflect on our own emotional reactivity can we begin to alter it. A first step, then, is differentiating a self within the emotional systems in which we are currently fused,
working on improving our capacity to tolerate the anxiety that arises
from encounters with members of our own religious family of origin.
Second, we can develop person-to-person relationships with members of
that family, maintaining emotional contact while resisting the togetherness forces that all too easily lure us into binding anxiety by triangulating others into (or out of) the dynamics of the relationship. A third
psychological strategy involves engaging proactively in encounters with
religious aliens, those outside our extended religious (or nonreligious)
family of origin. Here too it is important to be vigilant against the temptation to assimilate, attenuate, or accommodate the other into (or out of)
an emotional system that feels all too familiar.

As Bowen points out, this is hard work. "One of the most arduous tasks in raising one's basic level of differentiation is recognizing how profoundly anxiety and emotional reactivity influence one's own thoughts, feelings, and actions and the thoughts, feelings, and actions of others."[47] This is as true for those raised as atheists as it is for those deeply entangled within a religious coalition. After all, atheists are people too—and bind anxiety just as naturally as theists do. However, they are less likely to triangulate or be triangulated by disembodied intentional forces. Refusing to participate in supernatural triangles may not automatically dissolve all the fusion within a coalition, but at least it limits the potential triangulation to actually existing natural agents. Furthermore, the research we have been exploring based on Bowen theory and other theories within the bio-*cultural* study of religion suggests that executing this sort of psychological strategy is in fact likely to have *political* effects, transforming the broader emotional fields within which selves are bound together in groups.

In addition to a psychological (and political) strategy for differentiating selves, we can also propose a *theological* strategy—detriangulating the gods. In the Adamic traditions, this means dissolving GOD-conceptions as well as ideas about limited supernatural agents like angels, jinn, or saintly ancestor-ghosts. Dealing with the chronic anxiety bound up in supposedly eternal monotheistic GROUPS will require attending to the way in which an ultimate divine Force is imaginatively triangulated within the emotional systems that subtend the relations among its proximate human forces. Learning how to face our anxiety about being-limited existentially (as well as functionally) without attempting to triangle "the infinite" may also help us learn how to let go of some of our anxiety about finite religious others.

The iconoclastic trajectory opens up a different route for theological reflection on the relationship between religious Families of origin. In fact, this route has been (partially) taken by many intellectuals, activists, and mystics in the monotheistic traditions, but they have almost always been pulled back by the powerful theogonic togetherness forces of the sacerdotal trajectory. If one's religious Family is Judaism, Christianity, or Islam—or even if one simply grew up with one or more of these Families as neighbors—one way to begin is by emphasizing the differentiation-promoting iconoclastic tendencies that are already operative in those Families. The theolytic forces are intensified by reflection on the plausibility of understanding (and the feasibility of organizing) axiological engagement based on Supranatural Agent abductions privileged and patrolled by Supranatural Coalitions. Theological resistance to such emotional triangulation has emerged *within* such Coalitions for a variety of logical, ethical, and aesthetic reasons.

We have already noted a first mode of iconoclastic intensification: *intellectual* reflection on the plausibility of the notion of GOD. This mode is characterized by rational analysis of religious conceptions. One does not have to go very far down this philosophical road before it becomes clear that the idea of infinite intentionality (or intentional infinity) is incoherent. The majority of theologians in the Adamic religions have acknowledged this irresolvable ambiguity at the core of their doctrinal belief systems. For the iconoclastic theologian of religion, this is a good place to start. Instead of immunizing particular conjectures about GOD from critique by appealing to a mysterious "iconic vision," however, she will construct theolytic retroductive hypotheses about axiological engagement that do not rely on ritual or revelation.

What we might call the *activist* mode of intensification is more immediately connected to practical concerns within or across religious Families. This mode is characteristic of theologian-practitioners who are bothered by the way in which particular images (icons) of the infinite intentional Force triangulated within their own Coalitions are utilized by the power elite to suppress dissent and police the boundaries of the GROUP. Criticizing and actively resisting coercive and exclusive practices authorized by those who control the access to rituals and the interpretation of revelation has an iconoclastic, or at least an icon-weakening, effect that challenges sociographic prudery. The problem is that all too often one religious icon (such as a punishing Father) is simply replaced by another (such as an appeasing Friend), and the detection of this new human-like disembodied Agent continues to covertly activate the protection of a new sort of Coalition putatively favored by that Agent.

A third mode of intensification is *mystical*. It is common for those with extensive contemplative experience within a monotheistic tradition to be suspicious about the value of "petitionary prayer" to a divine PERSON who intervenes in the psychological and political concerns of members of a particular GROUP. Mystics typically end up preferring forms of meditation that activate intense experiences that dissolve anxiety about the boundaries of the finite self and the borders of human coalitions. Such individuals are often among those most interested in interreligious dialogue. The problem is not with "mysticism," or the intentional exploration of intense experiences at (and of) the limits of human consciousness, but with the mystifying interpretation of such experiences as *iconically* mediating an infinite disembodied Force that is, after all, in some sense, intentional.

Occasionally intellectuals, often activists, and rarely even mystics will give up on the idea that the god imaginatively engaged within their group is infinite. This may involve a denial of the limitlessness of a divine attribute, such as foreknowledge or predestination. It may involve an explicit affirmation of the essential finitude of god, as in some versions of Christian process theology inspired by A. N. Whitehead. This sort of theological hypothesis dissolves the notion of an infinite intentional Force. Such attempted dissolutions are often met with hostility by religious leaders for whom belief in maximally counterintuitive doctrines is an important costly signal of commitment. In some contexts, however, they are met with indifference, or even with sighs of relief. Minimally counterintuitive ideas about finite gods are easy for most people in the pews to accept. At this point, however, the iconoclastic theologian can point out that when it comes to interpreting ambiguous natural and social phenomena, the Christian guess "finite god," whatever its material peculiarities, is no more cross-culturally plausible than the Fang guess "ancestor-ghost."

While these three modes of intensification within a monotheistic religious Family partially challenge the theogonic forces of the sacerdotal trajectory, they certainly do not go far enough for the atheist iconoclastic theologian who wants to follow out the logic (and practice and aesthetic) of the theolytic forces. As I have emphasized, following this trajectory will not automatically solve all our problems, and may well intensify acute anxieties as the togetherness forces begin to rage. However, the differentiation of atheist selves may also contribute to the development of productive modes of probative axiological engagement that do not triangulate gods within groups.

Chapter 6

Letting gods Go: Naturalism and Secularism

Many parents find it difficult to let their children go. In extreme cases, parental selves are so fused with their progeny that they cannot live without them under their roof, or at least under their control. Many children in late adolescence also find it difficult to let go of their parents and live on their own—a difficulty often faced again in the late senescence of the parents. Insofar as the gods are imaginatively triangulated within our religious families of origin, it is difficult to let them go as well. Some gods, like ancestor-ghosts and GOD, are conceptualized as progenitors. As we have seen, however, all supernatural agent conceptions are descendant from cognitive and coalitional mechanisms, the offspring and not the ancestors of humanity. The gods are born—and we have borne them. Once the identities of selves and groups become entangled with shared imaginative engagement with gods, bound up in ongoing attempts to rightly interpret their revelations and correctly practice their rituals, it is hard to imagine surviving without them.

Religious togetherness forces played an important role in holding together the mental and social worlds of our actual *Homo sapiens* ancestors in Upper Paleolithic environments. We are the descendants of individuals whose anthropomorphic promiscuity and sociographic prudery ran wild, enabling them to cooperate within and stay committed to their coalitions as they competed with other hominid groups. Whatever else it may reproduce, however, the unreflective functioning of these hypersensitive, evolved theogonic mechanisms generates fallacious abductions about causality in the natural world and hostility toward out-groups in the social world. This was not such a big problem for hunter-gatherers living in small-scale societies in sparsely populated areas. Today, however, a growing number of us live as digital nomads, hunting and gathering information to help us survive and thrive in an ever more densely populated globalizing socius. In this increasingly interconnected environment, the bogus ecological and belligerent sociological conjectures of some affect us all.

Is it time to let the gods go? Answering this question is beyond the scope of this book; indeed, it is beyond the scope of any book. This is not only because of the complexity of the question but also because the answer will depend on the particular environment in which it is asked and the special interests of those asking it. Behavioral ecologists of religion typically ask concrete questions like: Are *these* behaviors engendered by shared imaginative engagement with supernatural agents maladaptive in *this* environment.[1] Approaching the question more broadly, at the level of the global habitat shared—and the evolved tendencies inherited—by all contemporary humans, will require the ongoing collection of data and extensive multidisciplinary integration of the relevant theories within the biocultural study of religion. Alongside such efforts it will be important to go on reflecting critically and creatively on the feasibility of our abductive methodologies and the plausibility of our metaphysical retroductions.

In this chapter, I limit myself to some (admittedly abstract) reflections on the potential consequences of scientific *naturalist* and pragmatic *secularist* hypothesizing in the contemporary global environment. Can we learn to live on our own, probing and producing hypotheses about the conditions for axiological engagement without triangulating supernatural agents into our coalitions? *Methodological* naturalists and secularists have already answered this question in the affirmative. Nevertheless, many scholars within the biocultural sciences and many politicians within pluralistic contexts hesitate to follow through on the *atheistic* retroductive inference: it is time to let the gods go *metaphysically*. The first half of this chapter explores and challenges this reticence to embrace an affirmative atheism. The second half examines some of the most common psychological and political objections to engendering atheist conceptions in cognition and culture, none of which adequately attends to the reciprocal reinforcement of theogonic mechanisms, whose integration intensifies codependence on gods and conflict among groups.

I will argue that the beliefs and behaviors that reproduce naturalism and secularism are also reciprocally reinforcing. Integrating the theolytic forces of these modes of hypothesizing can further clarify the consequences of religious intercourse and lead to the construction of even more productive postpartum theological conjectures about the conditions for (and alteration of) axiological engagement. Integrative atheism might also help us reflect more clearly on—and deal more adequately with—other evolved cognitive and coalitional biases that surreptitiously shape our evaluation of intuitive behaviors that increase our chances of passing on our *own* genes and cultures while blinding us to their wider environmental impact. But let us not get ahead of ourselves. Setting aside for a moment the question of its advisability, is liberating human intentionality from supernatural agent coalitions even possible?

Must gods Be Born(e)?

Is the bearing of gods necessary? At the individual level, the answer is clearly "no." Some people do indeed let go of their gods. In fact, some children are raised as atheists and have never had to bear them in the first place. Disbelief in gods and GOD is growing rapidly. Counting the world's nonbelievers through surveys is difficult because people have different attitudes toward terms like "atheism" and "religion," and governments have different policies toward enforcing or tolerating their existence. Acknowledging these and other methodological complexities, Phil Zuckerman has argued that an analysis of global data suggests that there were at least 500 million and perhaps as many as 750 million "non-believers in God" in 2007. As he points out, this makes it the fourth largest group after Christianity, Islam, and Hinduism. More recent census data suggest that nonbelief continues to multiply, especially in the minds and subcultures of Western youth.[2] There are surely many reasons for this spread of disbelief within the human population, but I will argue that it is due, in part, to the fact that naturalism and secularism "work" in an expanding number of environments. In such milieux, fewer people need gods to make sense of the world or to hold their groups together.

The rapid proliferation of nonbelief has led to what we might call the biocultural study of *non*-religion. The phenomena of atheism, agnosticism, irreligion, and nonreligion are increasingly popular topics of research in a variety of academic disciplines.[3] Atheists were once considered aberrations of nature and subversive to society. In many contexts today, however, it is relatively easy to be an atheist. Based on their own research and a wider review of the literature, Ara Norenzayan and Will Gervais identify four different pathways to disbelief. First, because hyperactive "mentalizing" is associated with personifying tendencies, the detection of gods will not come as intuitively to relatively "mind-blind" individuals. Second, individuals in contexts characterized by existential security are often indifferent to the idea of supernatural beliefs and practices. Norenzayan and Gervais call this "apatheism." A third pathway is "inCREDulous" atheism. Individuals in societies where secular institutions take on the prosocial functions of religion are often not as exposed to the sort of credible displays of belief (CREDs) that engender faith in supernatural agents. Finally, some people think their way to atheism, engaging in analytic reflection that overrides religious intuitions.[4]

If gods are not born(e) by every individual in all social environments, one might wonder whether atheist conceptions could spread more widely in the population globally and eventually eradicate the need for shared imaginative engagement with axiologically relevant supernatural agents. Many scholars in the biocultural study of (non)-religion are doubtful. Pascal Boyer suggests that the evolutionary mechanisms that have led to "religion" are so deeply ingrained that they will probably always have to be somehow accommodated even within future secular civilizations, although the health and survival of the latter will require active resistance to theocratic societies that are "versions of Hell on earth."[5] Jesse Bering is even more pessimistic. The religious illusions that "keep us hobbled in fear" are not likely to fade away any time soon; nature, he thinks, "has played too good a trick on us."[6] Robert McCauley envisions a less antagonistic relation between science and religion although—or, in part, because—the latter appears inexorably adaptive. "Science poses no threat to the persistence of popular religion, because, with respect to both cognitive and social arrangements, science is costly, difficult, and rare whereas religion is cheap, easy, and *inevitable*."[7]

Some biocultural scientists are more optimistic about the possibility that atheist conceptions could continue to multiply and fill the earth. David Lewis-Williams argues that the hallucinatory visions of the Apostle Paul or Hildegard of Bingen were taken seriously in the ancient and medieval worlds because no one knew that they were the result of electrochemical stimulations in the brain caused by epilepsy or migraines. He is hopeful that, no matter how much "God's empire strikes back,"[8] the steady growth of scientific knowledge will continue to eclipse belief in supernatural beings that intervene in the world. Ilkka Pyysiäinen concludes that "folk psychology" is probably here to stay, but "religion— as far as we can distinguish it from nonreligion—does not have to be part of it." Instead of attacking an "imagined totality" called "religion," however, he advocates the use of "reflective thinking and the best scientific evidence to continuously reevaluate all kinds of cherished beliefs." If religion as we know it eventually withers away, argues Pyysiäinen, "this will be a by-product of other changes—just as religion once emerged as a by-product."[9] Other philosophers and historians of religion express even more optimism about a future in which naturalism and secularism replace "religion."[10]

What about the future of "theology?" A great deal depends on whether the iconoclastic trajectory that emerged out of disciplined reflection on the existential conditions for axiological engagement in the wake of the West Asian axial age can be liberated from the forces of the sacerdotal trajectory that have managed for over two millennia to dominate and domesticate it within monotheistic religion. As we have seen, the idea of GOD is inconceivable. Yet, religious leaders and scholars bound up within these coalitions have continually tried to force—while at the same time forbidding—its conception within the imaginative worlds of their GROUP. Most sacerdotal theologians acknowledge that the idea of an infinite intentional Force *cannot* be borne. Tragically bound up within the pious triangulation of a Supernatural Coalition, however, they struggle to fill believers' minds with ideas about the imagined attributes of an infinitely holy GOD while simultaneously reminding them that because His holiness is infinite they *must not* conceive a finite image of Him in their minds.

The ongoing futile attempts to insert this unimaginable concept into the religious imagination of the Adamic traditions are at least partially responsible for the rise of naturalism and secularism. An *infinite* Supernatural Agent who is supposedly *always* watching you unblinkingly is not really "interested"—just a bit creepy. An *eternal* Supernatural Agent who has supposedly *already* determined and judged what you are going to do is not "interesting" —just a bit depressing. Even if it actually existed, there would really be no point in worrying about this sort of an Agent. Since worrying about punishing disembodied intentional forces is what makes religious conceptions "work," holding together cooperative and committed selves in groups, then GOD has no relevance for daily life. One might as well get on with figuring out how the world works and refiguring the socius without Him. If we can get along fine without worrying about GOD, then perhaps we can get along without finite gods as well.

In fact, naturalist scientists and secularist politicians do in fact get along without them—*methodologically*. But why are so many scholars in the academic sphere and policy-makers in the public sphere still resistant to letting the gods go *metaphysically*? Of course, part of the answer may well be the veiled functioning of theogonic mechanisms. I leave this sort of soul-searching to the individuals embodied and embedded in the emotional systems that subtend their disciplinary and cultural "families of origin." In this context, I limit myself to an exploration of some of the factors that influence our default evaluations of the theoretical plausibility of theolytic retroductions and of the pragmatic feasibility of engendering atheist conceptions in cognition and culture.

Methodological Naturalism and Anthropomorphic Prudery

Like "religion," the word "naturalism" has a wide semantic range. Owen Flanagan, for example, identifies 15 different ways in which the term can be used. As he notes, however, all of these definitions seem to have something in common: the dispensability of "supernaturalism."[11] Observing that the vast majority of contemporary philosophers have embraced naturalism, Flanagan focuses his attention on defending it against the increasingly infrequent critique that it does not provide an adequate basis for—or guidance in—ethics. One cannot jump from "is" (nature) to "ought" (morality), argues the critic, and so there must be something beyond nature to ground normativity. The early modern dualistic metaphysics and epistemology presupposed by this sort of objection has lost its hold on most philosophers, and many proposals for "naturalizing" ethics in light of late modern holist categories and Darwinian evolution have appeared in recent years.[12] Moreover, as we saw in chapter 4, research in evolutionary moral psychology has demonstrated that *natural* processes "selected" for altruistic behavior long before notions of supernaturally authorized norms were conceived in human minds.

Evaluations of the plausibility of such naturalistic hypotheses are dependent, of course, on the extent to which anthropomorphic promiscuity is contested when making conjectures about the conditions for axiological engagement. Scientists, at least while they are doing science, are anthropomorphic prudes. They resist the tendency to guess "agent" automatically when confronted with ambiguous phenomena. However, most scientists go further and explicitly ban supernatural agents from their educated guesses. In other words, they are *methodological* naturalists when making scientific abductions. The phrase "methodological naturalism" has its own contentious history, but in the context of this multidisciplinary experiment in postpartum theology, I will use it to designate *the exclusion of appeals to the causality of supernatural agents from theoretical interpretations in the academic sphere.* Clearing the field of god-hypotheses, this methodological disposition has made room for powerfully productive and ever more plausible explanations of how the world works.

As we have seen, several scholars within the biocultural study of religion go even further and follow through on the retroductive inference that gods do not exist. In other words, they are *metaphysical* naturalists who explicitly eliminate supernatural agents from their list of "ontological inventory items" (to borrow a phrase from Wesley Wildman).[13] Others, however, hesitate at the edge of a chasm that they believe they cannot (or ought not) cross: the artificial gulf between methodological and metaphysical naturalism. For example, Lee Kirkpatrick assures his readers that he is being careful not to fall into the *"veridicality* trap," that is, not to assume that if a religious belief can be explained in terms of psychological attachment figure relationships, then it must be false. Evolutionary psychology, Kirkpatrick insists, has nothing to say about the correctness or incorrectness of beliefs in gods; decisions on such matters depend on one's "extra-scientific" personal assumptions.[14] Todd Tremlin acknowledges that many religious people will find cognitive research about their god-representations threatening, but comforts them by noting that the "cognitive science of religion does not set out to challenge the *veracity* of religious thought and behavior but, rather, to better understand them."[15]

At one level, this self-limitation makes sense. Scientists can choose to focus their research on the *processes* by which certain kinds of ideas emerge rather than on the truth of the *content* of those ideas. But why should they go out of their way to convince readers, precisely at this point, that they have no interest in the conditions for the actualization of the phenomena they are studying? Psychologist Paul Bloom devotes an entire book to explaining the evolved mechanisms that generate conceptions of "immaterial" entities like a "soul" that can be separated from a "body," mechanisms that so easily mislead children (and the rest of us) into accepting Cartesian dualism. However, he concludes by reassuring religious people that all of this is "logically separate from the question of whether God exists."[16]

As we saw at the end of chapter 4, it would indeed be a *deductive* logical fallacy to deny the truth of a belief *because* of the way in which it was generated or the qualities of the person who has it. But this applies equally to theological *and* psychological claims, and it should not distract us from questioning the plausibility of *any* hypothesis. Like most scientists who study human behaviors, Bloom does not hesitate to assert: "Descartes was mistaken . . . We do not have immaterial souls."[17] He has no difficulty following through on retroductive inferences that lead to the rejection of a "ghost in the machine." Why, then, the reticence to challenge the plausibility of abductions that involve other disembodied intentional forces? Why not reject hypotheses that suppose "ancestor-ghosts" live in the heart of the forest or the "Holy Ghost" lives in the hearts of believers?

Scientists regularly make retroductive conjectures about the conditions for the actualization of the phenomena they study. Contemporary physicists deny the existence of the "lumineferous ether" through which scientists once believed that light moves. Contemporary physicians deny the existence of the four distinct substances or "humors" that scientists once believed flowed through the human body influencing health and temperament. In other words, they reject claims about the supposed existence of causally relevant forces. Why suddenly stop critically reflecting when it comes to the existence of gods? It may not be the task of scientists—*qua* physicists, physicians, psychologists, etc.—to make theological claims about the conditions for axiological engagement. But I see no good reason why they should be prohibited, or inhibit themselves, from engaging in disciplined reflection about those conditions. Like all other hypotheses, of course, their "theological" conjectures would need to be critically assessed from the widest possible variety of perspectives.

One sometimes finds this reluctance to discuss retroductive hypotheses involving god-conceptions even among "religious naturalists" who are quite comfortable reflecting theologically (in the wider sense of the term). In *Religion Is Not about God*, for example, Loyal Rue explicitly affirms *methodological* naturalism, aiming for a general account of religion "without invoking supernatural principles of explanation." He even seems to affirm *metaphysical* naturalism, "the view that nothing transcends Nature—the real is natural and the natural is real." Nevertheless, when it comes to the concrete question of the actual existence of supernatural agents, Rue is evasive: "Perhaps there are gods, perhaps not. I will not pretend to know one way or another." Because God is "inscrutable," he argues, we should not bring such questions into the business of understanding religious phenomenon.

Part of the problem here is Rue's exceptionally broad definition of religions as "narrative traditions" that are formulated and revitalized by "ancillary" intellectual, experiential, ritual, aesthetic, and institutional strategies, a definition that does not take into account the findings of the biocultural sciences about the role of gods in religious groups.[18] For our purposes here, however, the more interesting problem with this sort of evasion, common among so many scientists as well as "religious naturalists," is that leaving space for the gods to roam freely in the human Imaginarium invites its colonization by sociographically prudish coalitions. In other words, the tendency toward out-group antagonism that such strategies are often intended to diminish or dissolve is actually heightened because withholding judgment about the existence of GOD— or dismissing the relevance of such retroductive inferences—helps hold up the veil behind which the furtive and fertile theogonic mechanisms continue reproducing human-like, coalition-favoring supernatural agents.

The same can be said of "religious atheists" like Ronald Dworkin. In *Religion without God*, he defines the religious attitude as one that affirms the meaning of human life and the beauty of the universe, and insists that it does not matter which of "the two camps of religion, godly or godless, you choose to join."[19] As our review of the literature in the biocultural study of religion in the last five chapters has shown, however, it really does matter. First, the hyperprotective coalitional anxiety of those in the "godly" camp will be continually activated by their ongoing hyperdetection of and ritual engagement with supernatural agents. Second, "godless" anthropomorphic prudes are less likely to see themselves as a "camp" in the first place, and are more likely to be characterized by the societal openness and appreciation of science that Dworkin himself explicitly champions.

Avoiding "the talk" about religious reproduction may be motivated by compassion, toleration, or simply a desire to remain neutral. But in this case, inaction is not neutral; a failure to make retroductive inferences about gods increases the chances that people will continue bearing them as they bind themselves ever more tightly into in-groups. As we have seen, the theogonic mechanisms were reciprocally resolved and integrated during the course of human evolution, and they continue to reinforce one another in contemporary minds and cultures. This is why an anthropomorphically prudish *methodology* is not enough, at least if we are also interested in developing pragmatic hypotheses that actually promote nonanxious sociographically promiscuous interaction in pluralistic contexts.

Methodological Secularism and Sociographic Promiscuity

The term "secularism" and the diverse phenomena it has been used to describe have also been the subject of contentious debate in the last few decades. In the late 1950s and 1960s, it was not uncommon to find strong versions of a "secularization thesis" that predicted the eventual evaporation of religion. The devastating critiques of religion by Nietzsche, Marx, and Freud had been taken up by later "masters of suspicion" in philosophy, sociology, and psychology and strengthened by empirical social scientific research throughout the first part of the twentieth century. To some scholars, it seemed inevitable that the rising tide of modernization would finally wash away all vestiges of the sacred, at least from the public sphere. The resurgence of religious fundamentalism and the emergence of New Age forms of spirituality in the 1970s and 1980s, however, led many secular theorists to make an about-face. Observing in 1999 that the world is "as furiously religious as it ever was, and in some places more than ever," sociologist Peter Berger conceded that secularization theory, which he had championed in the 1960s, is "essentially mistaken."[20]

After the events of 9/11, an increasingly popular academic refrain began to swell, announcing the arrival of a postsecular age. Reports of the death of secularization, however, have been greatly exaggerated. In the last decade, new empirical research in a variety of contexts, including Africa, Asia, Australia, South America, and the Middle East, as well as Europe and North America, has led some scholars to modify, clarify, and nuance secularization theory in a variety of ways.[21] Pippa Norris and Ronald Inglehart have argued that if we conceptualize secularization as a *tendency* rather than as an iron rule for predicting the future, it fairly describes what is going on in much of the world.[22] The word "secularism" was coined by George Holyoake in a context dominated by Christianity (nineteenth-century Britain) as part of his call for a formation of society around principles that did not invoke clerical or scriptural authority. Already in this seminal text, one finds a tension between a commitment to create a shared set of principles to which atheists *and* theists can agree and a commitment to an atheist view of the world that rejects the claims of traditional sacerdotal theology.[23]

In this context, my concern is highlighting the reticence among many social and political theorists to bridge the gap between what I will call methodological and metaphysical secularism. Although it has only been partially borne within some cultures, the birth of "secularism" in the nineteenth century has altered the way in which many people assess proposed sociographic prescriptions. *Methodological* secularism calls for *the exclusion of appeals to the authority of supernatural coalitions from normative inscriptions of the public sphere.* Like calls for methodological naturalism, this is increasingly uncontroversial in democratic, pluralistic societies. Practicing members of religious coalitions may be invited to bring in resources from their traditions as part of the discussion, but policy decisions affecting all members of the state or military decisions affecting members of other states are not (supposed to be) *only* or even *primarily* based on appeals to the alleged revelations of the god of a particular group.

In *A Secular Age*, Charles Taylor asks "Why is it so hard to believe in God in (many milieux of) the modern West, while in 1500 it was virtually impossible not to?"[24] My interest here is not in the plausibility of the sociological hypotheses Taylor himself offers as possible explanations for this massive shift in the conditions of belief (and disbelief) over the last few centuries, but in pointing out a tension in his work that is commonly found among *religious* social theorists. On the one hand, Taylor is clearly sociographically promiscuous, a methodological secularist who resists the enforced inscription of the socius based on appeals to particular religious authorities within what he calls our "post-Durkheimian dispensation." On the other hand, he hopefully predicts a future in which more and more people break out of the "immanent frame" and respond to their "sense of fullness" that "corresponds to reality," namely, a "transcendent reality (which for me is the God of Abraham)."[25] At the end of his book, Taylor provides warrant for this optimism by telling the stories of two nineteenth-century white, Western, male scholars (Charles Péguy and Gerard Manley Hopkins) who converted to Roman Catholicism, the GROUP to which Taylor himself belongs.

Given his own explicit affirmation of faith in GOD, it is easy to understand why Taylor urges atheists and humanists to stop fighting against the incorporation of insights drawn from "religious experience" into moral debates about how to actualize the public good. It makes sense that he would want to undermine what we might call *metaphysical* secularism, the explicit elimination of supernatural authorities from the list of ontological inventory items—and therefore from the list of resources available for axiological reconstruction. To put it more positively, metaphysical secularists affirm the supposition that the most feasible pragmatic hypotheses for inscribing the social field in pluralistic contexts will be those that only strategically engage actually existing (or existentially actualizable) immanent axiological conditions. It is no surprise that Christian thinkers like Taylor reject metaphysical secularism. What is surprising, however, is how often *nonreligious* social theorists and political philosophers also hesitate to embrace this retroductive inference.

John Rawls, for example, defends the idea of "public reason," which he takes to be essential to the conception of a "well ordered constitutional democratic society." He proposes that competing "comprehensive doctrines of truth or right," which are an inevitable result of the reasonable pluralism in a "culture of free institutions," be replaced with "an idea of the politically reasonable addressed to citizens as citizens." However, Rawls insists that it is central to the idea of public reason "that it neither *criticizes nor attacks* any comprehensive doctrine, *religious or nonreligious*, except insofar as that doctrine is incompatible with the essentials of public reason and a democratic polity."[26] Religious citizens can bring their "transcendent values" and religious reasons into the public debate as long as they are translated into "politically reasonable" terms and do not override shared political values. Nonreligious citizens, on the other hand, should *not* base their arguments for sociographic prescriptions on criticisms of religious citizens' theological positions.

Both Taylor's and Rawls' proposals have been criticized heavily by their peers, as all pragmatic hypotheses for altering the axiological conditions that organize and orient political debate within a pluralistic social field should be. I want to draw attention to two problems shared by these proposals, problems that are rarely addressed in the literature on secularism. First, neither scholar distinguishes between human coalitions that are held together, at least in part, by shared imaginative engagement with supernatural agents and human coalitions that are not. Although for quite different reasons, both Taylor and Rawls focus on vague characteristics— like having a "sense of fullness" or a "comprehensive doctrine" —that obscure the very real differences between the sociographic preferential systems of religious and nonreligious persons. The former appeal to disembodied intentional forces to authorize social inscriptions and the latter do not. Reflecting on the empirical findings of the biocultural sciences can bring more precision into the parlance that shapes arguments about the value of "religiosity" and "secularity" in the public sphere.

The second problem is more practical. Because of the way in which theogonic mechanisms reciprocally reinforce one another, prohibiting the promotion of metaphysical secularism within pluralistic contexts immunizes anthropomorphically promiscuous detections of supernatural authorities from critique, which in turn activates the very sociographic prudery that most methodological secularists are trying to overcome. As we have seen, persons who are primed to guess *god* become primarily concerned about the survival of their own *in-group* and more hostile toward cultural others. Whether or not they call it "metaphysics," social theorists and public policy-makers regularly make retroductive inferences about the conditions for axiological engagement. Few would hesitate, except perhaps during a visit to the royal family, to reject the existence of the "divine right of kings." There is no supernatural authority behind the crown. Why stop critically reflecting on the actual conditions for engendering the public good at precisely this point? What is good for the regal goose is good for the ecclesial gander.

For a growing number of people, ritual engagement within supernatural agent coalitions plays no function in regulating their lives, no role in their normative evaluations of social others. In fact, the putative presence of gods within competing groups only makes pluralist discourse more difficult. Why not let them go?

Plausibility, Feasibility, and Theolytic Retroduction

Human beings make abductive and retroductive inferences all the time, quickly assessing the nexus of causal conditions and the possible consequences of their actions within their environment. As we saw in chapters 4 and 5, these assessments are influenced by the extent to which people reflect on their existential suppositions and by the extent to which they are fused within the emotional systems that subtend their coalitions. People automatically default to the hypotheses that seem the most plausible and feasible to them, constructing and acting on the sorts of conjectures that enhance their own chances of survival as individuals or the cohesiveness of their groups. Scientists and politicians (theory-analysts and policy-makers in the broadest sense) are people too, but they are people who (we hope) have devoted themselves to more *intentional reflection* on theoretical and pragmatic hypotheses that affect the rest of us. The environments in which the forces of methodological naturalism and methodological secularism guide such reflection are expanding.

For the purposes of this project, it is important to emphasize three features of the dynamics at work in this expansion. First, much like the theogonic mechanisms, the propensities toward anthropomorphic prudery and sociographic promiscuity are reciprocally reinforcing. Methodological naturalism is more productive in secular environments where coalitions committed to supernatural authorities are hindered from forcing scientists to incorporate gods into their causal explanations. Methodological secularism is more easily fostered in environments where scientists are generating knowledge about the natural world that does not depend on the revelations of or ritual engagement with the supernatural agent of a particular group. This generative productivity is diminished when this reciprocity is not adequately acknowledged and intentionally fortified. Witness the religiously motivated attempts to insert creation narratives involving the Supranatural Agent of the Adamic religions into public school scientific curriculum about the origin of the cosmos and humanity in some parts of the United States.

Second, it is important to acknowledge that these mechanisms are in fact theolytic. Whatever be the intentions of those who follow the trajectory generated by the integration of these forces, such naturalist and secularist pursuits have a broader dissolutive effect on the role of god-conceptions in human thought and action. As the plausibility of scientific naturalist interpretations of the physical world becomes increasingly evident, people have less reason to detect their supernatural agents.

As the feasibility of political secularist inscriptions of the social world becomes increasingly evident, people have less reason to protect their supernatural coalitions. Acknowledging the fallibility and correctability of the theolytic hypotheses constructed and enacted in such contexts is an indication not of their weakness but of one of their most important strengths—their susceptibility to being strengthened by critique. The key point here is that even when their metaphysical versions are explicitly avoided, naturalism and secularism still loosen the grip of gods on minds and cultures.

The third point emerges out of reflection on the first two. Because these forces are reciprocally reinforcing and theolytic by nature, their explanatory and productive power is sapped by the failure to embrace and integrate their metaphysical versions. Scientists and politicians committed to fostering their methodological versions are working against themselves by refusing to follow through on the retroductive inference that supernatural agent coalitions do not exist. Obviously, religious groups exist. And their shared imaginative engagement with gods has effects in the real world. But actual intercourse with disembodied intentional entities is not a condition for axiological engagement. Why? Because gods do not exist. One ought not to be frightened off from embracing this claim by those who would wave out the bugaboo of supposedly outmoded binaries like "religion vs. science" or "religious vs. secular." Much depends on our decisions about designations. Some essentialist and colonialist binary usages of these terms may indeed be outmoded, but either the gods of religious groups are actually causal conditions for axiological engagement or they are not.

As the editors of the journal *Religion, Brain & Behavior* emphasized in their introduction to a recent issue devoted to the scientific study of atheism, it is crucial for scholars to be clear about their use of terms.[27] In this context, I am using the term *atheism* to designate *the affirmation of metaphysical naturalism and metaphysical secularism*. The atheist is positively committed to cooperatively producing naturalist–secularist hypotheses "about" the conditions for axiological engagement (figure 6.1). In the sense in which I have been using the terms, atheism is most definitely *theological* although it is clearly not *religious*. Atheism promotes determined attempts to understand the natural world and inscribe the social world without appealing to supernatural agent coalitions. Atheist hypotheses work against the psychological and political codependence upon the gods that is engendered by the theogonic mechanisms.

Atheists, in my sense of the term, do not want to eliminate dialog about religion from the academic or public sphere. Quite the opposite. They want, finally, to have an open conversation about the causes and

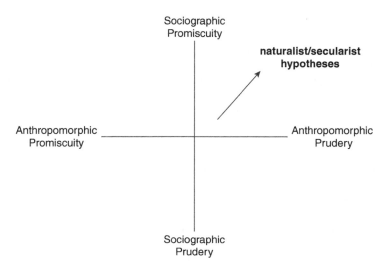

Figure 6.1   Naturalist/Secularist Hypotheses

consequences of its reproduction. People are always constructing (relatively) plausible and feasible retroductive conjectures. Atheists do it too. However, their hypothesizing discloses the way in which "doing it" in religious groups reproduces gods, which only get in the way when it comes to thinking sensibly about an entropic cosmos and acting sensibly in a pluralistic socius. Anthropomorphically prudish and sociographically promiscuous reflection on the processes by which gods are born(e) increases our capacity for adapting *intentionally*. Unveiling theogonic mechanisms does not guarantee that we will find new solutions to our problems, but it may help produce and renew the resolution to deal with them without waiting for the approval (or fearing the punishment) of human-like, coalition-favoring gods.

As we have seen, the urges that lead to the imaginative procreation of supernatural agents contributed to the survival of *Homo sapiens* coalitions in the early ancestral environment. Hypotheses involving gods were intuitively plausible and helped hold together small-scale groups. In our late modern context characterized by ever more densely populated complex literate states, however, letting these procreative urges run wild is no longer feasible. We can no longer afford to romanticize the human search for gods to protect and partner with us; it may once have been a harmless (or even helpful) romantic distraction, but today it is distracting us from the task of developing new strategies for living together in our rapidly changing environment.

Analyzing and altering the conditions for engendering atheist conceptions in minds and groups will not be easy. It will require extensive multidisciplinary research and ongoing multicultural conversations. It will also require psychological and political sensitivity. Alarming people by attacking their beliefs and shaming them for their behaviors will only make things worse, activating and accelerating the very mechanisms the atheist finds problematic. On the other hand, appeasing religious others by enabling their dysfunctional codependence, or treating them as incompetent and needing special care (Bowen's "overcompassion"), can be even more destructive. The goal should not be to force people to *adopt* atheism into their families of origin, but to invite them to *adapt* by nurturing the reflective and innovative capacities they have had all along. We cannot know ahead of time how "the talk" will go or how it will transform the way we treat each other. All we can do is differentiate and delineate our own reasons clearly, calmly, and courageously. The good news is that simply having the conversation can weaken the theogonic forces, especially if the discussion stays at the level of plausibility (and feasibility) and encourages reflection on the affective religious togetherness forces that subtend our intuitive reactions.

In the next four sections, I examine some of the objections to liberating atheist hypotheses that are bound to be raised by some religious—and nonreligious—participants in the conversation as it goes along. Here, I am not interested in objections that appeal to the alleged revelations of supernatural agents ritually engaged by particular coalitions of the sort we explored in chapters 4 and 5. Rather, I will focus on the concerns of those who argue more generally that intuitive belief in (and ritual engagement with) the gods of groups should be left alone because it is epistemically and socially harmless enough—and can even come in handy when trying to facilitate psychological and political health. Such arguments typically fail to account for the extent to which the theogonic mechanisms reinforce one another. Moreover, although these objections are usually raised within complex societies shaped by the West Asian monotheistic Coalitions, they do not contend with the unbearable weight placed upon psyche and polis by the inconceivable Supranatural Agent who allegedly holds them together. Here too postpartum theology can help.

GOD and Other Minds

At the end of chapter 4, I pointed out the way in which the most common tactics among Christian philosophers and theologians for defending faith in GOD and gods against scientific and other atheist challenges are myopically focused on inductive or deductive inferences. This is also true of the sacerdotal strategy examined in this section. In this case, the argument is based on an appeal to the following analogy: just as it is rational to believe in other human minds, although their existence cannot be proven, it is also rational for Christians to believe in GOD (and other relevant gods like angels and demons). On this model, the rationality of religious belief in supernatural agents can be defended by negatively answering one or both of the following questions: Can beliefs in the existence of gods be *disproven* (by deductive inference)? Can claims about special revelatory observations be rendered *improbable* by the empirical analysis of out-group members (by inductive inference)? If not, then the onus for demonstrating irrationality is placed on the nonbeliever. Not surprisingly, this sort of apology for religious rationality is typically marshaled by those who are already bound up within a Supranatural Agent Coalition.

In fact, atheists can never *prove* that supernatural agents do not exist, nor will they have much luck directly challenging the *probability* of observations reported by believers who regularly participate in religious rituals. But this is beside the point. When comparing and contrasting gods and minds, the relevant question is whether it is *plausible* to make the retroductive inference that both are causal conditions in the natural world. Alvin Plantinga devotes most of his book on *God and Other Minds* to demonstrating that the traditional arguments for (and against) God's existence are inconclusive on the question whether "given what we know, it is *impossible* or *unlikely* that God exists."[28] After a long review of the classical deductive and inductive arguments for and against theism, Plantinga concedes that the theist "has no very good answer" to the epistemological question: "How do you know that *p*; what are your reasons for supposing that *p* is true?"

Plantinga insists, however, that the theist does not need an answer. Belief in GOD is in the same "epistemological boat" as belief in other minds. Hence, "if my belief in other minds is rational, so is my belief in God. But *obviously* the former is rational; so, therefore, is the latter." In this context, let us set aside concerns about Plantinga's assumptions about the dualistic relation between the mind and the body, and about the alleged obviousness of the rationality of beliefs in other "minds." For our purposes, the important point to notice is how quickly the whole analogy will fall apart once we set the discussion in the context of abductive and retroductive inferences about plausibility rather than deductive necessity or inductive probability. Plantinga concludes: "Of course there may be other reasons for supposing that although rational belief in other minds does not require an answer to the epistemological question, rational belief in the existence of God does. But it is certainly hard to see what these reasons might be."[29]

In fact, there are several reasons for challenging this supposition, none of which are hard to see in light of the findings of the biocultural study of religion. First, our belief in what we call "other minds" emerges out of actual engagement with other bodily organisms, whose engagement with us involves physical interactions that have clear empirical effects on our bodies and other bodies around us. Second, a belief in another mind is empirically falsifiable. If I am walking at night and see a statue, I might mistake it for a person and think it has a mind. After poking and prodding the statue, I may have good reasons for concluding that my initial belief was false and I will stop attributing intentionality to it. Third, beliefs in other minds are not immune to the "epistemological question." If a person tells me that he has a friend to whom he speaks regularly and who tells him what to do, I might ask to meet the friend. If that person tells me that only he can see or hear this friend, I may very well begin to suspect that this is not a rational belief.

The unveiling of the cognitive and coalitional biases that lead to shared imaginative engagement with axiologically relevant supernatural agents helps us understand why beliefs in gods are immunized from critique in a way that beliefs in other minds are not. I know of only two scientists working in the biocultural disciplines who have embraced arguments of the Plantinga type. In *Why Would Anyone Believe in God?* Justin Barrett explicitly appeals to Plantinga, with whom he shares a religious "family of origin" (Reformed evangelicalism). Barrett emphasizes that "no scientific evidence exists that *proves* other people have minds." He also points out that children learn early that parents do not cease to exist when they leave the room, and that detecting the body of a person on the phone is not a condition for believing that their mind exists.[30] But Barrett does not point out the key weaknesses in these analogies. The child would not have believed in the parents' mentality in the first place if she had not repeatedly encountered their bodies through regular, empirical interactions and mutual investigations. And my belief in the actual existence of an intelligible human on the other end of the phone is grounded in the supposition that the voice belongs to a person who is embodied, a person whom both I and other people could see and touch if she were bodily present.

Matt Rossano also urges readers not to make retroductive inferences about the existence of the gods in whom people say they believe. Religion is all about relationships, he argues, and "You can't tell someone they don't have a relationship that they are convinced they have." His "modest proposal" is that we all agree that the issue of God's existence is irresolvable, and "focus our energies on the consequences of a relationship with God." Instead of asking "Is there something supernatural to relate to?" Rossano wants us to ask: "Are we better off with or without these supernatural relationships."[31] To defend this proposal, he tells the story of three friends: Eddie, Cruiser and Betty-Lou. The young men had been best friends, but recently Cruiser has been hanging out with Betty-Lou. Cruiser is now more careful with his money and does not go out as often with the boys. Eddie is convinced that Betty-Lou is ruining Cruiser's life. However, Eddie is "clueless" about the meaning of "fun with a high-quality woman," a reality that Cruiser himself "only came to understand since his Betty-Lou revelation."[32] The disanalogy between the interaction of these three friends and the debate between an atheist and a theist about the existence of GOD is not difficult to find: Eddie can actually see, hear, and touch Betty-Lou and discuss with her the consequences of her relationship to Cruiser.

In addition to highlighting the intellectual inadequacies of such analogies, it is important to emphasize the practical *social* consequences of the failure to question the actual existence of the gods with whom people imaginatively engage. On the one hand, Plantinga-type arguments might seem relatively harmless, much like the defensive retorts one hears from children when they are questioned about their imaginary friends: "Just because you cannot see or hear them does not mean that they do not exist." In the mouths of adult defenders of competing religious groups, however, such arguments are politically toxic—especially when they reinforce the imaginative boundaries of a GROUP whose members believe their separation from other groups is sanctioned by a GOD. The problem with not ever challenging people about the plausibility of the abductive inferences they are making based on their oversensitive cognitive tendencies to detect agents is that such inferences hyperactivate the *coalitional* tendency to protect their in-groups. Letting anthropomorphic promiscuity run wild not only leads to outlandish interpretations of the natural world, it also fuels the sociographic prudery that drives oppressive inscriptions of the social world.

When those inscriptions are implicitly or explicitly grounded on appeals to the detection of GOD, the infinite intentional Force ambiguously detected in the Adamic religions, the stakes are amplified to eternity. Members of the GROUP find it relatively easy to justify and sanction even the most violent coercive behavior toward defectors and out-group members. Engaging with "other minds" is a native facet of—and a creative factor within—human axiological engagement. Adding "gods" to the mix helped our Upper Paleolithic ancestors survive and populate the planet.

After the birth of GOD, however, we have good reasons to question the feasibility of continuing to organize our lives around our supernatural progeny. But perhaps we are moving too fast. Is it not the case that religion is in some sense "good" for us?

Psychology, Therapy, and "Religion"

There is little doubt that under certain conditions some features of what is commonly called "religion" are health-promoting in many contexts. For example, as we saw in chapter 2, the placebo effects of regular synchronic rituals can actually contribute to physical health. As we saw in chapter 5, being surrounded by people who agree with you can lower stress levels, at least superficially, which can boost the immune system. In this section, however, I am interested in the relation between ritually sustained belief in gods and *psychological* health. Here too there is little doubt that shared imaginative engagement with supernatural agents often plays a role in a person's achievement and maintenance of a sense of psychological well-being. This "surprising fact" would be a "matter of course" if human beings had evolved with the cognitive and coalitional biases we have been exploring.

As we all know, however, imaginative mental interaction with gods can also be emotionally painful and, in extreme cases, promote or exacerbate neurosis—or even psychosis. In chapter 3, we noted some examples of the way in which unhealthy relationships to divine attachment figures are mutually shaped by unhealthy interpersonal relationships with the "other minds" closest to us. In chapter 4, we noted the way in which psychological antagonism toward out-groups can be intensified by the theogonic forces, especially when they are pressed to infinity in the attempt to sanctify a Supranatural Coalition and justify a Supranatural Agent. The effects of "religion" on human minds are ambivalent. This is one reason why clear and empirically tractable definitions are important in our reflective analysis of the phenomena with which the term is usually associated.

Vague references to the therapeutic value of "spirituality" and "faith" can all too easily distract us from the need to talk seriously about the actual mechanisms that lead to—and the consequences that flow from—the reproduction of gods in groups. It is also important to distinguish between psychological stability and the intuitive beliefs that sometimes reinforce it. A devout Christian slave-owner in the antebellum South may have been the very picture of mental health as he thanked GOD for not making him a woman, black, or poor. There are often times when we decide it is worthwhile challenging intuitively held sexist, racist, or classist beliefs that support social oppression, even if a person's psychological well-being is buoyed by those beliefs. Why should intuitive beliefs about gods, beliefs that have increasingly contributed to the intensification of social discrimination for at least the last 60,000 years, be exempt from such challenges?

Therapists who work with adolescent children and senescent parents, for example, know that helping someone let go of "other minds" in relation to whom they have been closely attached and intensely triangulated requires empathy and patience. So it is with facilitating the mental release of images of GOD and other gods. In fact, letting go of old conceptions of GOD and the transformation of old conceptions of the self and others quite often occur simultaneously as part of the therapeutic process. Psychologist James W. Jones highlights and illustrates this process in several of his writings, carefully attending to both the ambiguity of religion and the relevance of theology. In *Contemporary Psychoanalysis and Religion,* Jones describes several cases from his own therapeutic work in which the process of transference slowly contributed to shifts in patients' images of GOD—from a punishing and distant Father, for example, to a nurturing and comforting presence. Building on the categories of self-psychology originally developed by Heinz Kohut, Jones argues for a more positive assessment of the role of religion in therapy.

Jones stresses the significance of a person's *relationship* with God or, to use Kohut's terms, the importance of the function of the divine as an "other representation" within the patient's matrix of "self-objects." Representations of both natural and supernatural others can play a role within this matrix. Jones is not primarily interested in "doctrinal belief or ritual participation," focusing instead on what he calls the *"affective bond with the sacred."* He recognizes the difficulty with making an analogy between the transference relationship of the patient to his therapist and his relationship with God, because the human and the divine are typically envisioned, at least by the patient, as belonging to "different orders of being." Jones insists that this sort of objection might be fatal to his project if he were "attempting to *prove* the existence of God." However, he sets aside questions about "the existence of a divine being" and starts with "the *human experience* of the sacred."[33]

We can understand and appreciate Jones's psychological concerns about therapeutic sensitivity and acknowledge the effectiveness of mediating new, less punitive conceptions of GOD for alleviating acute anxiety. Once again, however, it is important to interrogate the decision to halt abductive and retroductive reflection precisely at this point. How can one (and why would one) *start* with the claim that a person has an experiential relationship with something (the sacred, a divine being, etc.) and then hesitate to make any claims about whether that something exists? This sort of hesitation quickly disappears when psychologists are confronted with extreme cases, as when a delusional psychotic patient believes that the ghost of Adolph Hitler (or Jesus Christ) is giving him instructions for initiating the destruction (or salvation) of the world. No doubt there are other sorts of cases in which it would simply be impossible, or utterly destructive, for individuals to let go of their gods. I am not suggesting that therapists, or others who take responsibility for the nurture of "other minds," press everyone in their care to eliminate all god-representations from their self-object matrix immediately.

However, I am suggesting that many of us could benefit from more careful reflection on the actual consequences of enabling one another's co-dependence on disembodied intentional forces. In his more recent publications, Jones turns his attention to the psychology of religious violence. In *Terror and Transformation: The Ambiguity of Religion in Psychoanalytic Perspective*, he observes the way in which representations of GOD as an omnipotent self-object, an *idealized* parental imago, foster immature dependency and so easily lead to fundamentalism and fanatical violence. In addition to offering psychological strategies, Jones also commends a theological strategy he associates with an "apophatic trajectory" that he finds in many of the world's religions, which can help to "de-idealize" concepts of GOD and provide resources for a "vital religion without idealization."[34] In *Blood That Cries Out from the Earth: The Psychology of Religious Terrorism*, Jones recommends that theologians "find other resources within their traditions to provide devotees with alternative images of God."[35]

Here too we can appreciate and understand Jones's theological concerns about highly personified and idealized representations of a wrathful, punitive GOD and acknowledge the effectiveness of apophaticism in toning down and disarming such dangerous conceptions. In fact, we could interpret this move as an example of what I referred to at the end of chapter 5 as the *mystical* mode of iconoclastic intensification. Tragically, however, the decision not to follow out the retroductive implications of the GOD–dissolving trajectory undermines and even contravenes Jones's attempts to enervate the psychological mechanisms that drive sociographically prudish religious violence. As long as the "mystical" continues to operate within the biocultural gravitational pull of a religious coalition, the GOD-bearing trajectory will continue to domesticate it. The vast majority of a tradition's adherents will automatically default under stress to "theologically incorrect" idealized images of punitive, coalition-favoring gods.

Whether or not the divine self-object images it engenders are cruel or compassionate, or both at the same time, as long as the anthropomorphically promiscuous tendency to detect supernatural agents is encouraged, it will continue to activate anxiety about protecting in-groups and promote antagonism toward out-groups. As we have seen, the theogonic mechanisms reciprocally reinforce one another, even if—or especially when—we are not explicitly attending to their integral interactions. It is true that many of the world's mystics and contemplatives have also worked as "therapists" within their own traditions, trying to foster forms of spirituality that leave behind child-like prayers for satiation and protection. They have invited people to open themselves up to transformative experiences of *infinite intensity* that alleviate anxiety about the boundaries of the psyche and the polis. For this, however, one does not need "religion." Shared imaginative engagement with disembodied *intentional* forces only domesticates such experiences and appropriates them for the adaptive needs of a particular religious coalition.

god and Other Groups

All human groups, like the individuals that comprise them, must adapt in order to survive. But not all groups are held together by the same coalitional mechanisms. Unlike the sort of constitutional democratic society defended by John Rawls, for example, the cohesiveness of religious groups is maintained, at least in part, by ritual interactions based on the alleged revelations of supernatural agents. The question is whether—or to what extent and for how long under what conditions—both religious and nonreligious coalitions can live together within the broader context of a pluralist social field. As we noted above, Rawls is one of many nonreligious political and social theorists who argue that methodological secularism is enough. As long as religious groups are willing to concede that they cannot force other groups to accept their doctrines, and agree to acquiesce formally to "public reason" once the pushing comes to a final shove, nonreligious people should not materially criticize their metaphysical beliefs. Tragically, such policies exacerbate the very crises they are trying to resolve because they fail to account for the reciprocity of theogonic mechanisms.

We can illustrate this problem in the work of Jürgen Habermas who, more than many other scholars in these fields, has responded to the concerns of some of his conscientious theological objectors. Although initially reluctant to enter this "insufficiently reconnoitered terrain," in a series of essays in the 1990s Habermas acknowledged the possibility that it might be appropriate under certain conditions for moral resources drawn from theological discourse within the religious traditions to be brought into wider secular discourse. However, he still insisted that theologians, at least in the public sphere, should maintain a "methodical atheism." If theology were to join philosophy in taking an *"anti-Platonic turn"* and engage in "postmetaphysical thinking," he could think of no reason why it should be excluded from wider discourse—as long as it is methodologically atheistic. In secular space theologians should not appeal to "religious authorship" or insist on meeting religious and nonreligious others on "the bridge of religious experiences that have become literary expressions."[36]

Theologians must translate experiences that have their "home" in the religious sphere into "the language of a scientific expert culture—and from this language retranslate them back into praxis." Habermas recognizes the difficult situation in which many theologians find themselves. On the one hand, they want to engage in "communicative action" and participate in normative debates outside their religious home territory. On the other hand, "from the beginning" the identity of theology has had a "parasitic" status, deriving its function from its attachment to the "dogmatic core" and ritual practices of a religious community. So, the theologian must find a way to represent his or her religious group in the public sphere while avoiding any retroductive inferences for or against the existence of axiologically authoritative supernatural agents. Habermas was not sure what would be left of the Christian "language game" if the notion of a personified divine power was given up.[37] At that point, he left it to religious coalitions and their theologians to figure out.

In his much-discussed 2006 essay "Religion in the Public Sphere," Habermas altered his position in order to overcome what he had come to view as an asymmetric burden placed on the religious citizens of a secular liberal state. Like all citizens, they must still accept that "only secular reasons count" beyond the "institutional threshold" that separates private and informal public life from the legal and executive activities of the state. However, they should not have to bear the "unreasonable *mental and psychological* burden" of splitting their identity into "public and private parts" when they enter public discourse. Habermas now argued that religious citizens should be allowed "to express and justify their convictions in a religious language" even if they are unable to translate them into secular language. In an attempt to balance the burden of participation in the public sphere, Habermas also placed new demands on secular citizens. It is not enough for them to "tolerate" religious people. They must become more self-critical about their "rigid and exclusive secularist self-understanding of modernity," and take religious contributions more seriously. The secular participant in the public sphere should remain agnostic, and refrain "from passing judgment on religious truths" and "from making ontological pronouncements on the constitution of being as such."[38]

In 2007 Habermas articulated his new position in the context of a debate with Roman Catholic philosophers, later published as *An Awareness of What Is Missing: Faith and Reason in a Post-Secular Age*. In that context, he argued that secular reason "may not set itself up as the judge concerning *truths* of faith." In fact, the liberal state "may not demand anything of its religious citizens" that is irreconcilable with a life lived authentically "from faith." Moreover, it must also "*expect*" its secular citizens, in exercising their role as citizens, not to treat religious expressions as simply *irrational*."[39] In my view, the plausibility and feasibility of Habermas's proposals are powerfully called into question by theogonic reproduction theory. In this context, I limit myself to pointing out two ways in which insights derived from the biocultural study of religion and integrated in the last five chapters unveil the limitations of this sort of merely methodologically secular proposal.

First, Habermas's hypotheses about the public sphere are undermined both theoretically and pragmatically by their failure to account for the reciprocally reinforcing dynamics of the evolved *theogonic* mechanisms that engender and reproduce "religion." His well-intentioned proposal is meant to diminish the violent conflict between religious coalitions in pluralistic contexts. However, most of his attention is on religious Coalitions of the sort that emerged in West Asia during the last 2,500 years, the sort of GROUP that virtually all of his theological interlocutors call home. Habermas urges secularists to remember the "shared origin of philosophy and religion in the revolution in worldviews of the Axial Age."[40] Yes, it was in the wake of this crucial period in human history that critical philosophical and theological reflection was born, along with GOD and the Adamic traditions who continue trying to bear Him. However, Habermas's theory does not deal with the much more ancient "pre-historic" integrated biocultural tendencies that drive shared imaginative engagement with supernatural agents.

Sacerdotal theologians can say what they like in the public (or the religious) sphere, but believers' detection of finite person-like, coalition-favoring gods will continue to be activated as long as their interpretation of and interaction with out-groups is shaped by their ongoing ritual participation in a religious in-group. Habermas's arguments are weakened by his failure to account for the intrinsically *theolytic* power of and reciprocal relation between anthropomorphic prudery and sociographic promiscuity. He clearly endorses a naturalistic reading of the cosmos and champions a secular inscription of the socius. By welcoming religious language about gods (and all religious language is about gods, even if indirectly) into the public sphere, while simultaneously forbidding secularists from bringing along their own atheist conceptions, Habermas sets up conditions that will continue to hyperactivate the discursive ambiguity—and exacerbate the conflict—he is working so hard to avoid.

Second, Habermas does not pay adequate attention to the different modes of inference in his recommendations to others about the sorts of argument that are appropriate for them to make in (or about) the public sphere. For example, he insists that secularists should not demand that religious communities renounce "traditional statements concerning the existence of God and a life after death" because the falsehood of such statements "cannot be *deduced* from recent neurological insights into the dependence of all mental operations on brain processes."[41] As we saw in chapter 4, however, religious beliefs are not the result of deduction (or induction) in the first place. They are cognitively constrained and culturally restrained *abductions* about disembodied intentional forces— "guesses" that work well enough (for believers) as long as they are surrounded by and participating in credibility-enhancing displays of costly signaling within their religious in-group.

Habermas urges secularists to accord religious convictions an "epistemic status" that is not "merely irrational."[42] They may not be "merely" irrational but, as we noted in our review of Scott Atran's research in chapter 3, insofar as religious beliefs include "forever half-baked" representations of counterintuitive supernatural ideas that can be endlessly exegeted in open-ended mythico-religious elaborations, they are not susceptible to the normal rules of rational discourse. Moreover, in his zeal for promoting post-metaphysical thinking, Habermas has thrown out the retroductive baby with the onto-theological bathwater. I agree with Habermas that if theology is to play a legitimate role in secular (and academic) discourse it must take an "anti-Platonic" turn and embrace "methodic atheism." But this is not enough. Taking on this role does not rule out—indeed, it requires—the critique and construction of arguments that include *retroductive* inferences about the *existential conditions* for axiological engagement. Although his hypotheses are not "metaphysical" in the classical sense, Habermas himself regularly offers retroductive arguments about the conditions for actualizing a liberal state in which there is less religious conflict.

Beliefs in gods and beliefs in other minds are not equally plausible in most contemporary academic contexts, and proposals for encouraging or discouraging the inclusion of appeals to the authoritative revelations of religious groups in public discourse are not equally feasible in most contemporary pluralistic contexts. Minds and GOD are not in the same epistemological boat. Unlike religious groups, the social crafts and navigational norms of nonreligious groups are not maintained and oriented by imaginatively engaging disembodied intentional forces. As far as we can tell, the latter sort of group did not come into existence until the axial age, around the same time that GOD was born(e). The former sort of group has been around since the Upper Paleolithic and keeps afloat by replicating punitive god-concepts. Behind the veil of superficial dialogue between secular political philosophers and scholarly or priestly representatives of monotheistic GROUPS, the small-scale groups that actually compose the latter go on reproducing conceptions of finite, human-like, coalition-favoring supernatural agents.

If theology is to play a useful role in secular discourse about axiological engagement, it must pry apart and liberate the GOD-dissolving mechanisms from the GOD-bearing mechanisms that are placing an infinitely asymmetric mental and social burden on all of us.

Politics, Peace, and "Religion"

Just as therapists have found that engaging a patient's images of gods (or GOD) can play an important role in psychological healing, so too peacebuilders have found that attending to the special needs of religious groups (or GROUPS) can play an important role in conflict transformation. In fact, the "return of religion" has had a profound impact on academic disciplines that study the dynamics of political interactions as well as on the practical diplomatic and development strategies adopted by negotiators and activists on the ground. Fabio Petito and Pavlos Hatzopoulos, for example, suggest that religion should no longer be treated merely as the "generator of repression" but as the "victim" of an exile from the field of International Relations. Scholars in the latter once thought that religion would have to "vanish for modern international politics to come into being." The global resurgence of religion, however, represents a "return from exile." They argue that now the relations between nations must be reconceptualized through a thick engagement with and exploration of the values within the world's religious traditions.[43]

Religion has also made a comeback in the pragmatic policies of peacebuilders, a growing number of whom explicitly embrace "faith-based" approaches to resolving conflicts and preventing the clash of cultures. Douglas Johnston and Brian Cox, for example, argue that "faith-based diplomats are among the best-equipped" to deal with conflict situations. They can encourage the parties to embrace a "fresh moral vision" that can heal the wounds of the past, engage in the sort of "spiritual conversations" that are important to the wounded parties, and find "spiritual principles" that can establish a common ground between the warring parties.[44] Similarly, David Little and Scott Appleby defend the value of *religious peacebuilding*," wherein religious actors and institutions work toward resolving and transforming deadly conflicts by *"building social relations and political institutions characterized by tolerance and nonviolence."* The success of such activities, they argue, will depend in part upon the efforts of "theologians and ethicists within the religious communities who are probing and strengthening their traditions of nonviolence."[45]

There is little doubt that ignoring or excluding these factors from discussions about resolving global conflicts has done more harm than good—in theory and in practice. Too often, however, celebrations (or remonstrations) of the resurgence of "religion" and its role in promoting peace (or violence) rely on nebulous notions of the phenomena in question. Like their counterparts in theoretical and clinical psychology, most scholars and practitioners in political fields do not adequately attend to the way in which the cohesion of religious groups is protected by the ongoing reproduction of cognitive representations of coalition-favoring disembodied intentional forces. The conversation typically remains at the abstract level of "faith," "moral values," or "spiritual" concerns. Leaving *gods* out of our equations when estimating the cost of involving religious *groups* in attempts to secure peace and prevent further violence leads to serious miscalculations. Because shared imaginative engagement with supernatural agents is what motivates most people's evaluations of and behavior toward members of out-groups, especially under stress, it must be included in any serious analysis of the relationship between politics, peace, and "religion."

In their review of the empirical research supporting terror management theory, Tom Pyszczynski, Sheldon Solomon, and Jeff Greenberg argue that intergroup conflict is due, in large part, to worldviews that provide "self-worth" and promise "death transcendence" by portraying other groups as evil and prescribing their destruction. Such worldviews are easily threatened by the existence of alternative belief systems. For these reasons, they suggest that peace-building must include attempts to help people shift their bases of meaning and self-worth. Moreover, "through whatever methods are possible, we need to reduce the salience of mortality." This makes sense in light of the research we have reviewed in earlier chapters that demonstrates how thinking about death increases aggression toward out-groups.

However, the authors of *In the Wake of 9/11: The Psychology of Terror* go out of their way to insist that the problem is not "religion per se" because human cruelty can also be generated by secular ideologies that offer "symbolic immortality."[46] The problem, they argue, is any worldview that manages the terror of death by making immortality—literal or symbolic—dependent on the destruction of other groups. Like so many other theoretical analysts of conflicts involving religious groups, however, these authors do not acknowledge the extent to which imaginative engagement with disembodied intentional forces within such coalitions *automatically* activates both mortality salience and out-group antagonism.

In his assessment of the global rise of religious violence, Mark Juergensmeyer concludes that the contemporary world still needs "religion," despite the fact it plays a role in motivating terrorism, because it can also help to cure violence by elevating the "moral values of public life."[47] It is important to point out, however, that there are other ways to elevate public values without simultaneously raising the spectre (literally or figuratively) of groups whose coherence depends on ritual interaction with immortality-promising gods. In his critique of the "myth" of religious violence, William Cavanaugh traces the invention of "religion" as part of a "secular" narrative intended to justify the violence of nation-states.[48] Even if Cavanaugh's political hypothesis about the emergence and effects of this narrative over the last four centuries were correct, it would fail to account for the well over forty millennia of social entrainment in *Homo sapiens* groups that has reinforced the phylogenetically inherited tendency to detect punitive supernatural agents that sanction violence against other groups.

At this point, the peace-building practitioner might object that whatever theorists might say, the inclusion of religious actors and institutions in conflict transformation works in practice. But what, exactly, is "working?" When one reads through the narratives of "religious" contributions to peacemaking, there is rarely any reference to gods in the mediation between groups. Faith-based actors may derive inspiration from holy texts and be funded by religious institutions, but their successful interventions are typically characterized by risky interpersonal engagement, advice on restructuring institutions, and the provision of concrete, material aid.[49] On the rare occasions when competing groups share in peacemaking "rituals," this does not usually involve the actual invocation of— or costly signaling of belief in—any of the finite supernatural agents normally engaged by these groups. Without intending to detract from the courageous efforts and admirable effects of many of these intermediaries, we should still stop to ask: Is it really working? Despite occasional, temporary progress in the world's religiously tense hot spots (e.g., Syria, Sudan, Sri Lanka, etc.), the violence flares up again as soon as economic, ecological, or emotional stressors activate either of the reciprocally reinforcing theogonic mechanisms.

Religiously motivated peace-builders can illustrate what I referred to at the end of chapter 5 as the *activist* mode of iconoclastic intensification. Such individuals are typically more resistant than other members of their religious families of origin to coalition-favoring images of GOD and more repulsed by the political pugnacity of monotheistic GROUPS. One of the most influential authors in the field of conflict transformation is John Paul Lederach, a Mennonite scholar-practitioner who has drawn attention to the importance of involving "middle-range" actors within the population, developing integrative frameworks for "empowerment," and fostering "moral imagination."[50] All of this makes good sense. But in what sense is it "religious?" Lederach has helpfully identified some of the significant conditions for altering the modes of axiological engagement between religious groups. However, as long as we fail to notice the way in which our inherited god-bearing tendencies *also* condition out-group antagonism, our activism will only provide cover for their covert operations.

How can we ever hope to facilitate peaceful interaction within and across religious families of origin if we continue to ignore the anxiety-generating triangulation of *gods* that binds their emotional systems together precisely by *activating* the sociographically prudish hostility that alienates them from other groups? Attending to religion will indeed be an important part of the task of developing new productive strategies for dealing with group conflicts in local and global politics (and in our era almost all group conflicts have global and local ramifications).[51] However, we should attend to what *actually* happens in "religion," that is, to the mechanisms that engender the shared imaginative engagement with axiologically relevant supernatural agents that holds in-groups together by holding them apart from out-groups. We should also pay special attention to the role of the conflicts between the Supranatural Coalitions that emerged in the wake of the West Asian axial age and whose conflicting conceptions of how to interpret the revelations and enact the rituals of a Supranatural Agent continue to motivate the sacerdotal filibustering that obstructs and delays the experimental production of naturalist-secularist hypotheses about the conditions for axiological engagement.

This latter sort of hypothesizing is not a panacea for all of our problems. We cannot know ahead of time where our iconoclastic adventures will lead. We will certainly have to face new challenges as we overcome our codependence on supernatural agents and learn to interpret and inscribe our shared worlds without them. But what new opportunities might arise if we let go of the gods? The only way to find out is to empty the conceptual nest of the imagined spiritual progeny at our feet who are constantly tripping us up as we try to find new solutions. Perhaps we should reverse the generational metaphor. What will it take to motivate us to move out from under the roofs of our imagined spiritual progenitors?

Living Together—on Our Own

Can we really live without "religion?" It is equally important to ask whether we can live *with* it and, if so, for how long? During the Upper Paleolithic, the survival benefits of the in-group cohesion that were reinforced by the integration of evolved theogonic mechanisms outweighed the problems associated with the inaccurate interpretations of natural phenomena and the hostile interactions with out-groups that were also generated by these tendencies. But are these hypersensitive cognitive and coalitional biases helping us thrive in our contemporary environments? Perhaps the human race will survive for quite some time as its members share in imaginative engagement with supernatural agents in relatively small-scale groups, more or less hierarchically embedded within larger religious Coalitions, while waiting for a promised immortality. But is this *really living*? Learning to live without the gods would require us to adjust, as we must do when our children move out or we lose our parents (or other attachment figures). However, it would also open up the prospect of discovering how to live on our own—together.

Throughout this book, I have been utilizing a conceptual framework derived from the biocultural study of religion in order to explore the potential value of liberating the iconoclastic from the sacerdotal trajectory of theology. I have argued for the intentional integration of the theolytic mechanisms that meet in the upper right quadrant as a strategy for dissolving the psychological and political anxiety that is intensified by the integration of the theogonic mechanisms in the lower left quadrant. But what about the other quadrants? Might they provide better strategies for critiquing and constructing hypotheses about the conditions for axiological engagement? In my view, neither of these other trajectories is adequate to the theological challenges of our contemporary globalizing, pluralistic environment. They lead to theoretical and pragmatic hypotheses that are either overly prodigal or overly penurious (figure 6.2).

These two trajectories are illustrated in the opposing "theologies" of the groups that come into conflict in the 2009 movie *Avatar*.[52] The film portrays a clash of cultures between the Na'vi, the (mostly) friendly natives of the planet Pandora, and the invading human forces of the RDA mining corporation, the (mostly) nasty humans bent on mining the

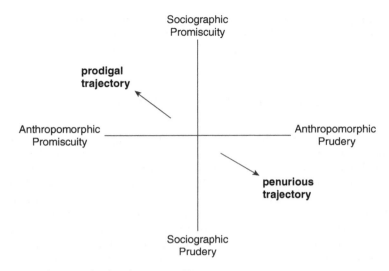

Figure 6.2   Prodigal and Penurious Trajectories

profitable and aptly named "unobtainium" under its surface. The Na'vi are extremely anthropomorphically promiscuous: supernatural agency is detected behind or within everything (plants, animals, mountains, etc.). They are also quite open (at least at first) to other modes of inscribing the socius, enthusiastically sending their children to the school run by the RDA scientists. The corporate leaders of RDA, on the other hand, are anthropomorphic prudes, refusing to acknowledge even the human-like agency of the Na'vi, whom one of them refers to as "blue monkeys." Members of the RDA coalition are also prudish in their sociography, forcing their own norms upon others, with little patience for anything that challenges their capitalist inscriptions. The plot unfolds as the (increasingly) evil capitalists fight the (initially) naïve tree-huggers for control of Pandora.

The doubly promiscuous trajectory in the upper left quadrant is *prodigal* in the sense that it leads to an extravagant expenditure of energy on imaginative engagement with supernatural agents (ubiquitous detection of intentionality) and on profligate pursuit of novel experiences with other groups (inadequate protection of sociality). The doubly prudish trajectory formed in the lower left quadrant is *penurious* in the sense that it leads to stingy refusals to acknowledge members of out-groups (failure to "see" actual, natural intentional agents) and miserly resistance to sharing with and learning from other cultures (stubborn maintenance and expansion of in-group norms). These trajectories guide the "theologies" of the Na'vi and the RDA corporation respectively. Each group has its own (more or less explicit) hypotheses about the conditions for axiological engagement, its own way of conceptualizing that which originates, orders, and orients its value-laden practices.

Like most science fiction, the movie *Avatar* projects a mixture of dystopian anxieties and utopian idealizations grounded in concerns about and aspirations for contemporary human society onto an alien world. As far as we can tell, however, nothing like an axial age had occurred on Pandora; the Na'vi (and other indigenous tribes) are depicted as an odd combination of shamanic small-scale tribes and proto-barbarian clans. RDA is depicted as a stereotypical organizational cog within an industrial-military complex, driven by nothing more than the lust for more profit. The prodigal hypothesizing of the Na'vi is characterized by a relatively loose and open interaction with a pervasive field of supernatural agency held in balance by the mother goddess Eywa who, at least early in the story, is not interested in protecting any particular coalition. The penurious hypothesizing of the RDA, on the other hand, is guided by a strict allegiance to the invisible (but nonintentional) hand that orders the flow of capital-money, and only helps those who help themselves.

The film portrays the planet Pandora as actually infused with minimally counterintuitive agents, like the Tree of Souls—a PLANT that can communicate with the Na'vi, and through which Eywa can interact with all living things on the planet. At the end of the movie (spoiler alert), Jake Sully, a human who has lived among the Na'vi using an "avatar" and changed his allegiance after learning their ways and discovering the destructive intentions of the RDA, tries to convince Eywa, via a neural connection to the Tree of Souls, that the RDA corporation is an evil group that will destroy Pandora and its natural inhabitants. The mother goddess intervenes at the last minute, causing the Pandoran animals to fight against the military forces hired by RDA. As a result of Eywa's divine intervention, RDA is defeated and the Na'vi coalition is saved.

But let's come back to Earth. Our planet is indeed populated by some groups a lot like the RDA and by other groups who resemble the Na'vi. But this is not Pandora. Earth is not populated by supernatural agents. There are no tree-goddesses to save us. It is quite understandable that audiences cheer for the indigenous people as they try to ward off the invaders. We have good reason to be concerned about the behavior of some corporate coalitions within the global capitalist socius, whose (often state-sponsored) policies are leading to the rapid depletion of finite ecological resources. If in fact there were tree-goddesses, or other disembodied intentional forces that could harness the powers of nature, upon which the colonized peoples of the world could call for aid, the prodigal trajectory just might work. But there are not. And it will not.

So, which of the remaining trajectories does it make the most sense to promote as we search for a way to live together (as healthily and peacefully as possible) here on planet Earth? Most of my readers will have been raised in social environments deeply inscribed by the Adamic religious traditions. Given the evolved tendency to detect supernatural agents and protect supernatural coalitions, it is not hard to understand why the sacerdotal trajectory is so tempting. However, for all of the reasons we have been exploring, the attempt to conceive and co-opt a GOD within a religious GROUP has placed a psychological and political burden on humanity that is increasingly difficult to bear. The sacerdotal trajectory helped complex literate states hold together during a difficult period in history, but the exponential growth and global linking of the human population now require us to find new ways of constructing and criticizing theological hypotheses. Neither tree-goddesses nor GOD can save us—from other GROUPS or from ourselves. Perhaps we do not need to be "saved." Perhaps what we need is to get moving, developing god-less theoretical and pragmatic proposals for apprehending and altering the conditions of our axiological engagement.

Chapter 7

Postpartum Theology

The gods are born—and we have borne them. Theoretical insights based on empirical research from dozens of disciplines converge to support the plausibility of the scientific hypothesis that the cross-cultural phenomenon of shared imaginative engagement with axiologically relevant supernatural agents is the result of the integration of evolved *cognitive* mechanisms for detecting and dealing with natural agents and evolved *coalitional* mechanisms for participating in and protecting social groups, mechanisms whose hypersensitivity was reciprocally reinforced and naturally selected despite the normal mistakes that were produced by the former and precisely because of the miserly normativity that was produced by the latter.

What effects will the unveiling of these phylogenetically inherited and culturally manipulated god-bearing dispositions have on our mental and social habits? What will happen if we more intentionally integrate and nurture the god-dissolving forces of naturalism and secularism? We cannot know the answers to this sort of question in advance. All of life is experimental—we have to engage our environment to figure out what we can do. Of course, too much of the wrong kind of experimentation can be just as destructive as no experimentation at all. As long as we live, we keep figuring this out. However, it often helps to reflect with others about our experimental intentions.

Having "the talk" about the causes and consequences of "religion" can foster this sort of reflective intentionality. Discussing the mechanisms of religious reproduction calls for at least as much sensitivity and seriousness as discussing the mechanisms of sexual reproduction. In addition to empathy and earnestness, however, it might not hurt to include a little humor. Sex is kind of funny, when you think about it. Sexual rituals can be quite revealing. We sometimes find it is easy to laugh at the psychological (and political) issues manifested in other people's attitudes and actions as they pursue their copulative strategies. It is more difficult to see the humor in our own sexual beliefs and behaviors. This unevenness in analysis and amusement is also evident when it comes to reflecting on religious revelations and rituals. Our own religious activities seem normal to us, but alien religions are comical (as long as they are not confrontational). Laughing *at* others usually makes things worse, but learning to laugh at *ourselves* can free us to laugh *with* others, which makes life more fun and can be far more productive.

In this book I have proposed that we reconceptualize the discipline of theology as the critique and construction of abductive and retroductive hypotheses about the existential conditions of axiological engagement. In light of a conceptual heuristic derived from the findings of the bio-cultural sciences of religion, I identified four trajectories that theologians might follow in their hypothesizing. The most dominant trajectory by far has been the one that tried to press anthropomorphic promiscuity and sociographic prudery to infinity (and eternity), attempting to bear GOD within the axiological hypotheses of monotheistic GROUPS in the wake of the West Asian axial age. Propelled by the oblique operation of the evolved theogonic mechanisms this sacerdotal trajectory has functioned effectively for centuries in a variety of contexts, colonizing those who follow the prodigal trajectory (which may well have characterized some early hunter-gatherers) and capitalizing on those who follow the penurious trajectory (which may well characterize some modern corporations).

The "death of God" has had surprisingly little effect on the sacerdotal trajectory of theology. Most religious people are not bothered by the idea of the moribundity of an *infinite* disembodied intentional Force because they are regularly participating in rituals and struggling to interpret revelations in ways that activate lively imaginative engagement with (theologically incorrect) *finite* disembodied intentional forces, whose existence and axiological relevance they intuitively find credible. Many reflective theologians have indeed been bothered by the idea, but not enough to follow out the (theoretical and practical) implications of the iconoclastic trajectory. The psychological and political burdens associated with monotheism have seemed worth bearing.

The discovery of the "birth of God," however, along with the increasingly apparent problems with binding humans together in Supranatural Coalitions, may provide new motivation for theologians to explore a more robust integration and implementation of anthropomorphically prudish and sociographically promiscuous strategies. Conversely, the theological production of experimental theolytic hypotheses about the conditions for axiological engagement in our rapidly changing environments might also provide new motivation for fostering naturalist interpretations and secularist inscriptions.

Liberating Atheistic Hypotheses

Methodological naturalists resist appeals to supernatural agents in their scientific descriptions, and methodological secularists resist appeals to supernatural authorities in their normative prescriptions. The vast majority of scientists and politicians in democratic, pluralistic contexts follow these methodologies—*except* when it comes to GOD. They would never dream of appealing to shared engagement with a finite disembodied intentional force (like an angel or a demon) when justifying their activities, and yet many politicians *and* scientists do not think twice about making vague references to an infinite intentional Force that somehow provides the conditions for the orderly organization of society or the orderly investigation of nature. Appealing to GOD in this way may temporarily calm people down by satiating their theogonic urges but, as we saw in chapters 2 and 3, this only provides cover for the hyperactivation of the sort of supernatural agent abductions that intensify anxiety about religious out-groups.

In chapter 6, I proposed the use of the term "atheism" to designate the affirmation of both metaphysical naturalism *and* metaphysical secularism. Following out the *retroductive* implications of the integrated theolytic forces, the postpartum theologian can construct atheist hypotheses about the conditions for axiological engagement that are not bound to the supposition that humans are ultimately dependent on GOD for making sense of their shared natural environments or making sensible choices in their shared social environments. Atheist hypotheses cannot be *proven* to be true, but that is really beside the point. Even debating whether or not they are *probably* true is a red herring. Like all hypotheses, theological conjectures incorporate deductions and inductions but they operate primarily within the inferential modes of abduction and retroduction and must be evaluated in terms of their *plausibility*.

As we noted in chapter 4, *retroductive* hypotheses involve inferences that "lead back to" the existential conditions for the actualization of the ambiguous phenomena interpreted by *abductive* hypotheses, which involve inferences that "lead away from" inductions and deductions and imaginatively (re)conceptualize the phenomena in question. As we noted in chapter 5, a person's evaluation of the plausibility of a theological reconceptualization will be shaped by the extent to which she is fused within the emotional systems of her biological and religious "family of origin"—by the context and purpose of her hermeneutical efforts. In the environments that characterize the academic and the public sphere, adjudicating between reconceptualizations requires arguments that are at least accessible to those who come from other contexts and have other purposes.

Criticizing the role of GOD-conceptions in monotheistic GROUPS by focusing on *logically* impossible worlds, or even on *empirically* improbable worlds, makes it too easy for sacerdotal theologians to deflect atheist challenges by complaining about (and committing) genetic fallacies. Focusing on the intersubjective plausibility and trans-communal feasibility of theoretical and pragmatic hypotheses about axiologically *actualizable* worlds, on the other hand, can foster *reflection* on the extent to which the observation-based inductive inferences incorporated within the well-formed deductive inferences of theological arguments are shaped by phylogenetically inherited and culturally reinforced abductive inferences about the gods of a particular group, whose supposed existence has already been *intuitively* retroductively inferred.

By calling for liberating atheistic hypotheses I am encouraging the *liberation* of the iconoclastic trajectory of theology from the sacerdotal forces that have domesticated it for so long. However, I am also encouraging the experimental production of atheistic hypotheses that are *liberative*, the creation of theoretical and pragmatic proposals that free human intentionality to alter the conditions for axiological engagement after letting go of the gods. What could possibly go wrong? Well, a lot actually. One danger is the formation of new atheist in-groups that bind anxiety within emotional systems that project "the problem" onto religious others whom they identify as a new out-group. Stalin is one of the most oft cited examples. Atheists can indeed be lured into an us versus them mentality that dehumanizes religious people (as weak "sheep") and provides ideological justification for abusing, restraining, or (in the extreme case of dictatorial "shepherds") exterminating them.

Like the other evolved tendencies we have been exploring in this book, *intolerance* would often have been adaptive in early ancestral environments where small groups had to compete for limited resources. However, as the editors of *Religion, Intolerance, and Conflict* argued in their concluding commentary, "the benefits of strong social cohesion that religion engenders may at one time have outweighed the costs entailed by outgroup intolerance and conflict, but this is likely no longer the case."[1] Can atheistic hypotheses really have a liberating effect on human minds and within human cultures? If they want to avoid the tragedies exacerbated by the sacerdotal trajectory, those who commit themselves to iconoclastic theological experimentation should be careful not to become intolerant of religious people as they resist religious intolerance.

It is much easier to see the intolerance of others than it is to see our own. When we cannot tolerate the anxiety generated by staying in conversation with those whose beliefs and behaviors we find intolerable—such as those that lead to racism, sexism, and classism—we all too quickly become intolerant ourselves. Atheists will need to be just as vigilant against this sort of evolved default toward intolerance as their religious interlocutors. However, it is important to take into account the asymmetry of mistrust and hostility that generally obtains between believers and nonbelievers. Researchers in psychology and sociology have long known that anti-atheist prejudice is one of the strongest and most deeply ingrained forms of intolerance. Recent experimental studies, however, suggest that this intolerance is not reciprocal; nonbelievers do not seem to default automatically to suspicion of members of religious in-groups.[2] Ara Norenzayan hypothesizes that this may be because "most atheists do not see themselves as a 'group,' nor do they see themselves as having a 'worldview' in opposition to religious groups."[3]

None of this should be taken to imply that atheism is "the answer" in some essentialist or abstract sense. For the hominid groups that survived during the Upper Paleolithic, religion was an effective (albeit unintentional) solution to the problem of maintaining coalitional cohesion. In some contexts today, such as the few extant hunter-gatherer societies left in the world, it would be pointless and could even be disastrous to promote atheism. In a growing number of contexts, however, "the problem" of cooperation and commitment in large-scale complex literate states is in fact being solved *without* shared imaginative engagement with punitive supernatural agents. Recent psychological experiments indicate that perceptions of the stability of one's government decrease belief in GOD, whereas perceptions of political instability increase the tendency to believe in supernatural agents as controlling forces. In fact, research in a variety of contexts indicates that effective governments can play the same sort of role once played by the gods in promoting prosocial behavior.[4]

As Phil Zuckerman points out, Scandinavia is made up of what may be "the least religious countries in the world, and possibly in the history of the world," and yet they have "remarkably strong, safe, healthy, moral and prosperous societies."[5] Liberating atheistic hypotheses will work differently, if they work at all, in different contexts. Some atheist groups in India, for example, are motivated not only by concerns about "intellectual incompatibility" but also by concerns about the political influence of "godmen" and the social injustice of the caste system.[6] Based on our review of the violent reactionary force generated by the integrated theogonic mechanisms when in-groups feel threatened, and reflection on the appalling failure of some twentieth century god-less experiments, we have good reasons to think that trying to impose atheism will only make things worse. Instead of alienating people by pressuring them to adopt atheist conceptions, it makes more sense to engender them by facilitating reflection on cognitive and cultural adaptations.

There are at least two other good reasons for atheists to be more intentional about attending to *context* in their arguments about axiological engagement. First, ideas about minimally counterintuitive agents (e.g., the angel Moroni or the Flying Spaghetti Monster) may be automatically generated and easily transmitted as a result of evolved cognitive defaults shared by all human beings, but the particular characteristics of the disembodied intentional forces that people actually *believe in* and *commit to* are determined by cultural context. This is why people raised in the Bible Belt in the United States, for example, are more likely to believe in Christ than Krishna. Second, empirical studies have shown that participating in shared imaginative engagement with supernatural agents predicts greater altruism *only* when there are contextual cues that remind people of their religious affiliation or that indicate their charity will be noticed by others. When these cues are absent, the altruistic tendencies of religious and nonreligious people are the same.[7]

These sorts of findings and insights from the biocultural study of religion support the plausibility of the atheist conjecture that axiological engagement is not actually conditioned by the gods and invite the development of more feasible strategies for interpreting and inscribing our shared worlds. Before turning to a final summary of the challenges and opportunities for theology after "the birth of God," I want to point out more explicitly the sense in which a robust integration and implementation of the theolytic forces of the iconoclastic trajectory of theology differs from two other movements within the discipline.

Beyond "Natural Theology"

As we have seen, theology emerged in the wake of the axial age as human populations expanded, clashed, and combined in new complex ways. Whatever else this mode of disciplined reflection accomplished, it clearly played a role in holding together large-scale doctrinal coalitions. As the credibility of appeals to "special" revelations accessible only to members of a specific religious in-group (such as the writings of Holy Scripture or the witness of the Holy Spirit) was increasingly eroded by the rising tide of Renaissance humanism and early modern science, some Christian theologians began to appeal to "general" revelations that were allegedly available to everyone or at least to all men of reason. "Natural theology" was born(e) in the scholarly minds and cultures of seventeenth-century sacerdotal theologians. Similar attempts to defend belief in GOD based on supposedly neutral observations of Nature or dispensations of Reason can be found among patristic and medieval theologians, of course, but the emergence of new philosophical (as well as psychological and political) selection pressures in the socioecological niche of the early modern West required more radical adaptation strategies.

During its infancy and throughout the Enlightenment, natural theology was typically focused on finding self-evident truths that could serve as a universal foundation for logical arguments that proved the existence of an infinite intentional Force. In its original environment, *natural* theology was distinguished from *revealed* theology by its attempt to avoid importing any specifically Christian assumptions into its line of reasoning. Claims about the existence of a GOD resembling the Almighty Creator of the Christian creeds were supposed to appear only in the conclusions, not the premises, of its argumentation. After the foundationalist epistemology presupposed by classical natural theology collapsed under the weight of late modern philosophical critique, this species of attempts to "prove" the existence of a divine Designer (or perfect Being, etc.) nearly went extinct, although one can still find such apologetic arguments in some secluded conservative theological habitats.

Today most Christian theologians who are interested in engaging science constructively, and most scientists who are interested in defending their Christian faith, are more likely to engage in forms of natural theology that *do* acknowledge their contextual bias and explicitly incorporate beliefs derived from the particular religious coalition to which they belong. Such proposals aim to provide a "confessional natural theology" or a "Christian theology of nature." Justin Barrett, for example, argues for the special relevance of the cognitive science of religion in the development of a confessional natural theology nurtured within his Calvinist tradition. He suggests that insights from this field can help adjudicate between competing interpretations of theological topics, such as Calvin's concept of the *sensus divinitatus*. More ambitiously, Barrett also suggests that when scientists identify "children's dispositions toward understanding God," they may actually be "uncovering God-given revelatory mechanisms: wouldn't God design people with early-emerging biases to conceptualize God?"[8]

Barrett is well aware of the problem that even if one accepted this theological hypothesis, one would still need to explain why everyone doesn't grow up to believe in the Christian GOD. The surprising fact that people do not always have fully formed belief in GOD would be a matter of course, argues Barrett, if "a perfectly adequate concept of God does come as part of our biological heritage but that living in a *sinful, fallen world* this concept grows corrupt as we grow." The confessional natural theologian can claim, based on a favored interpretation of an authorized HOLY TEXT (in this case, the creation myths of Genesis) that the diversity of god-concepts we find in the world "is a consequence of human error and not divine design."[9] This sort of theological hypothesis illustrates the adaptive capacity of the sacerdotal trajectory. In order for a religious tradition to survive, much less thrive, it must adapt as its environment changes and protect itself from the invasion of hostile elements that threaten its cohesion or its ability to transmit is doctrinal DNA. The monotheistic traditions that have survived over the centuries are those whose theologians have appealed to the revelation of the Supranatural Agent ritually engaged within their own Supranatural Coalition, especially when talking to each other and to other believers.

The operation of the theogonic mechanisms is easier to spot in "confessional" natural theologies and Christian "theologies of nature," but these integrated forces were already at work in traditional early modern (as well as patristic and medieval) natural theologies that pretended to neutrality and universality. The classical notion of "general" revelation is still an anthropomorphically promiscuous detection of Supranatural Agency. It results from looking at the ambiguous phenomenon of the "whole of creation" and applying the most facile and fecund perceptual strategy, that is, guessing it was caused by a purposive and punitive "Creator." The intentions of the divine Designer imaginatively perceived in this act of abduction are supposed to be plain enough. "For what can be known about God is plain to them, because God has shown it to them. Ever since the creation of the world his eternal power and divine nature, invisible though they are, have been understood and seen through the things he has made. So *they are without excuse.*" St. Paul insists that even if nonbelievers do not have access to special revelation GOD is still justified in punishing them eternally. Those who are covetous, gossip, or disobey their parents, for example, "*know God's decree,* that those who practice such things *deserve to die*" (Romans 1:19–20, 32).[10]

Appeals to religious authorities allegedly backed up by punitive supernatural agents are increasingly rejected and excluded from scientific discussions about the causal nexus of the physical world and from political discussions about the normative regulation of pluralist societies. The conceptual environments within which "natural" theological arguments (of either the classical or the confessional variety) can operate productively are shrinking rapidly. Their main function seems to be holding together religious GROUPS by promoting abductive and retroductive inferences about GOD or other "gods" in the Imaginarium of an Adamic monotheistic tradition. Tragically, this way of binding human beings into coalitions hyperactivates anxiety about religious (and nonreligious) aliens, intensifying conflicts and hindering the sort of creative compromises that might alleviate some of the tension in an increasingly volatile contemporary global environment.

I have been exploring the plausibility and feasibility of a very different sort of adaptive strategy.[11] Surviving and thriving in the rapidly changing niches within which many of us find ourselves may require the construction of even more anthropomorphically prudish *naturalist* theological hypotheses about the conditions for axiological engagement. Such creative efforts can be enhanced by an equally enthusiastic embrace of sociographically promiscuous policies.

Beyond "Secular Theology"

Compared to confessional theological conjectures, which explicitly claim to detect supernatural revelations in the divine Word or through the divine Spirit, most of the hypotheses constructed in classical "natural theology" were relatively anthropomorphically prudish. Even the most prudent, however, still ended up detecting an infinite disembodied intentional Force behind or above the ambiguous phenomena of *Nature*. In this context, I use the phrase "secular theology" to refer to a diverse set of conjectures by theologians with a Christian religious family of origin, all of which reflect on ambiguous phenomena within *Society* and press in the direction of sociographic promiscuity. Like their natural theological counterparts, however, these (more or less bold) explorers of the iconoclastic trajectory are almost always called back by the sacerdotal forces to help fortify the base camp of a religious coalition. For priests or scholars whose vocations are tied to the protection of a GROUP that can be identified by its distinctive ritual practices, theological adventures into "the world" (*saeculum*) are permitted only as long as they do not threaten the cohesion of "the church" (*ecclesia*).

As the implicit hegemonic control of Christianity over Western minds waned over the centuries, so did its explicit hegemonic control over Western cultures. This created a new selection pressure on theology and the coalitions it served. While theologians bound to extremely conservative religious in-groups have been tempted toward sectarianism, more liberal theologians have more often followed a different strategy: intentionally engaging the "secular" in an attempt to find solutions to shared problems. This sort of motivation seems to be behind the (2007) launch of *The International Journal of Public Theology*, whose mission is to foster discussion "of the growing need for theology to interact with public issues of contemporary society."[12] There was a time when Christian theologians could dictate public policies in accordance with the issues they found important, a situation in which some Muslim theologians still find themselves. In most Western contexts, however, Christian theologians *need* to interact with public issues that are important to non-Christians. Why? There are certainly reasons internal to the self-understanding of this GROUP, but this necessity is also conditioned by the competitive pressures of the capitalist marketplace of ideas in which multiple hypotheses vie for attention and approval.

Like "public theology," the phrase "political theology" has a wide semantic range. It can refer to proposals that call for a total restructuring of the (earthly) polis utilizing sacerdotal theological images of a supposed (heavenly) ideal. In *Political Theology*, the book that reintroduced the phrase into the modern discussion, Carl Schmitt argued that "all significant concepts of the modern theory of the state are secularized theological concepts."[13] The second edition of this book was published in German in 1934, one year after he joined the Nazi party. Schmitt's project was the installation of a new kind of "total state," based on antiliberal political intuitions drawn in part from resources in his own Roman Catholic tradition.[14] The idea that all secular social theory, even when it takes up an agonistic relation to religion, is rooted in and inescapably dependent upon (Christian) theology was taken up by Anglican theologian John Milbank, who developed it in his own way in *Theology and Social Theory*.

Milbank is quite clear about the irresolvable tension between secular reason, which requires "methodological atheism," and the faith-based claims of what he calls "Radical Orthodoxy." He explicitly proposes a "supernatural pragmatics," a political theory/practice that is "open, through its creative surrender, to the *supernatural*." Milbank insists that the only alternative to the violence of nihilism is the "*absolute* Christian vision of ontological peace."[15] In the Epilogue to *A Secular Age*, which we discussed briefly in chapter 6, Charles Taylor wrote that "the Radical Orthodox are right that we need some Plato-type understanding of what we are *made for*."[16] For Milbank, however, not just any Neo-Platonic conception of transcendence will do. In a volume honoring Taylor, Milbank praises his work and calls for a "more festive Christianity" that could "reestablish a new and now global Christendom," in which the *ecclesia* stakes its claim to be "the true site of a general will based on a charitable and just distribution."[17] For the postpartum theologian, on the other hand, there is no final solution—secular *or* ecclesial—to the challenges of axiological engagement. All we can do, and this is precisely what we *can* do, is to keep experimenting in the social fields in which we live and move and have our valuing.

Most theologians who use the phrase "political theology" to designate their engagement with the secular world are much less sociographically prudish than Schmitt or Milbank. Still, it is quite common to find the phrase referring explicitly to a *Christian* theology that is attentive to wider political concerns. In the volume on *Political Theology* edited by Peter Scott and William T. Cavanaugh, for example, all of the contributors are Christian theologians (except for two short responsive essays by a Muslim and a Jew at the end). The task of political theology is described in the Introduction as "the analysis and criticism of political arrangements (including cultural-psychological, social, and economic aspects) *from the perspective of differing interpretations of God's ways with the world.*"[18] Such theological hypotheses about axiological engagement still suppose that the GOD of one (or all?) of the monotheistic GROUPS is having (or eschatologically will have) his way with the world.

The essays in *Political Theologies: Public Religions in a Post-Secular World*, edited by Hent de Vries and Lawrence E. Sullivan, are far more sociographically promiscuous. The contributors come from diverse religious (and nonreligious) families of origin and are typically concerned with broader questions about the continuing presence and force of "religion," and especially "public religions," in discussions that have pragmatic legal and economic ramifications in pluralist societies. For the most part, they welcome and participate in the renewal of "theologico-political" inquiry in the public sphere. From the point of view of our analysis of the reciprocally reinforcing theogonic mechanisms, the problem with most of these proposals is that they operate with all too vague conceptions of "religion." Noting the difficulties in defining this contentious term, the editors are careful to include "cultural and cultic objects... individual and collective dispositions... words, things, gestures, and powers" among the phenomena commonly associated with the religion.[19]

Like so many discussions of the relation between the "secular" and the "religious," however, there is no mention whatsoever of the shared belief in and imaginative engagement with the sort of punitive disembodied intentional forces that actually shape the political concerns of religious in-groups.

Unfortunately, this lacuna is also evident in the work of theologians who explicitly embrace the phrase *secular theology* to describe their projects. The "death of God" movement in Christian theology, which emerged in the 1960s with quite promiscuous sociographic intentions, is perhaps the most well-known example. In his Introduction to a volume he edited on *Secular Theology: American Radical Theological Thought*, Clayton Crockett briefly traces the development of this movement from its major early proponents (such as Altizer, Vahanian, and Cox), most of whom were inspired by Paul Tillich's opening up of theology to secular culture, to some of the "postmodern" theologians who began to engage contemporary continental philosophy in new ways in the 1980s (such as Taylor, Winquist, and Raschke).[20]

Despite their radical intentions, some of these proposals for doing theology after the "death of God" still exhibit anthropomorphic promiscuity, at the very least detecting some sort of intentional Presence to which humans can respond. Based on our analysis of the reciprocity of the theogonic mechanisms, it should be no surprise to find that these proposals also contain a somewhat more prudish focus on Christian symbolic inscriptions. In Carl Raschke's contribution to that volume, for example, he argues that deconstructing Christianity leads us into a radical theological space "of the 'saying to' and the 'hearing from' the Presence that presences in time and in history from the peak of Sinai to the mount of Zion."[21] This sort of language may indeed be "symbolic," in a Tillichian or some other sense, but it all too easily activates the evolved cognitive god-detections that reinforce the very anxiety about out-group coalitions that such proposals are trying to dissolve.

In his own constructive work, Crockett is in many ways even more radical than most of his predecessors in the "death of God" movement. He explicitly embraces materialism and rejects any idea of responding to a transcendent Presence. Crockett also calls for more pragmatic theological engagements that actually alter the ecologically damaging practices stimulated by "capitalist nihilism." He follows the iconoclastic trajectory much farther than most theologians, and at times it appears that he will escape the gravitational pull of the sacerdotal forces completely. At certain points, however, his approach still appears tied, albeit tentatively, to a Christian understanding of the death of God. "Logic is always theo-logical, but this logic of theos is always already disposed and broken, because in theological terms God is dead. But this death is precisely what enables *resurrection* and life, because it makes possible an event." Crockett wants to move beyond allegiance to a "determinate form of Christianity," but continues to insist that "the Crucifixion and resurrection of Jesus of Nazareth" is indeed a "genuine event" with potentialities for theological thinking.[22] The task of radical theology, he argues, is "to think the event," which he believes "demands the theological vision of a new St. Paul."[23]

Like most discussions of St. Paul in recent continental philosophy, little or no attention is given to the apostle's overriding concerns in his epistles: to convince his readers that a punitive supernatural agent (Christ) is returning soon and to urge them to maintain the purity of their in-groups. Crockett also utilizes broad definitions of religion, such as "orientation in the ultimate sense," or that which gives "expression to the sense of ultimacy and ineluctable mystery and tragic horror from which our experience cannot escape."[24] He goes out of his way to emphasize that he does not oppose religion, although he does oppose "fanaticism and fundamentalism, including the fairy-tale expectations that a God or gods will rescue us from our predicament and punish the evildoers while rewarding the righteous."[25] As we have seen, however, it is precisely this sort of "fairy tale" that has motivated the vast majority of "religious" people in human history, including St. Paul. It seems to me that a more robust engagement with the findings of the biocultural sciences of religion could strengthen Crockett's project, as well as the projects of other theologians who find inspiration in the works of philosophers like Gilles Deleuze for altering the conditions of axiological engagement in the contemporary world.[26]

The construction of and experimentation with theological hypotheses that are metaphysically *secularist*, in the sense developed in chapter 6, may very well incorporate intellectual resources and pragmatic strategies that have been entangled within the monotheistic traditions that emerged in the wake of the West Asian axial age. The transvaluation *of* values must engage some values in the ongoing act of transvaluation, and it makes sense to engage values that have shaped the contexts in which we live and move and have our valuing. As we talk about the role of "religion" in all of this, however, it is important not to become so distracted by abstract philosophical, psychological, and political analysis that we forget to have a concrete conversation about where the gods come from and why we keep them around.

Intensity, Infinity, and Intentionality

For most of the history of the human species, intentional explorations of existential intensity have been bound up within shared imaginative engagement with supernatural agents. For Nietzsche, the discovery of the "death of God" did not close off the possibility of such exploration; indeed, it opened up an infinite expanse for adventurous intensification. His protagonist Zarathustra, in whose mouth he also placed the madman's message, also spoke thus: "Joy wants the eternity of *all* things, *wants deep, wants deep eternity!*"[27] God may have been dead to Nietzsche, but the original postmortem theologian's passionate fascination with eternal depths remained alive and well. It will be important for postpartum theologians who participate in the unveiling of the cognitive and coalitional mechanisms by which the gods are born(e) to maintain their sensitivity to the distinctive intensity of the human longing for deep eternal joy even, or especially, if all imaginable experiences of joy are conditioned only by the chronic depths of nature.

The biocultural scientific discovery of the "birth of God" provides us with a new opportunity to reflect on and experiment with the capacity of human intentionality without worrying about this or any other imagined spiritual progeny. Theology, in the sense in which I have been using the term, still has a role to play in this theoretical exploration and pragmatic alteration of the conditions for axiological engagement. At least in contexts shaped by the West Asian axial age traditions, conjectures about these conditions involve reflection on the relation between intensity, infinity, and intentionality. Most theologians who follow the sacerdotal trajectory make conjectures about an infinite disembodied intentional Force, a Creator whose eternal intentionality conditions all created temporal intensities. They often (even usually) deny the possibility of fully conceiving its infinity or its intentions, both of which are veiled in "mystery," but this Force is still postulated as the condition for human (and all other finite) intentionality.

Postpartum theologians who follow the iconoclastic trajectory, on the other hand, do not depend on Supranatural Agent postulations in their construction of hypotheses about infinity and the intensive conditioning of intentionality. Wesley Wildman, for example, explicitly rejects Supranaturalism (and supernaturalism) in his theological arguments about axiological engagement. In one of his most recent constructive proposals, Wildman argues that "intense experiences" can be interpreted wholly within a naturalist framework as a class of human experiences that draws on species-wide neurological capacities and that, under certain conditions, are potentially valid ways of actually engaging the "valuational depths of nature."[28] Another example is Gilles Deleuze, who argues that what we experience as conscious intentionality is conditioned by the (nonintentional) emission of singularities, the infinite intensities of pure becoming that constitute the folding and unfolding of the metaphysical surface of absolute immanence. These sorts of *constructive* hypothesis are often quite complex and understanding them usually requires a great deal of philosophical patience as well as openness to other disciplines.

As indicated earlier, however, my focus in this context is on the way in which the *critical* task of iconoclastic theology can *complement* the arguments of scholars who interpret the findings of the biocultural study of religion as rendering implausible all hypotheses that appeal to *finite* disembodied intentional forces. Unveiling the evolved god-bearing mechanisms weakens not only their plausibility as explanations of nature but also their feasibility as prescriptions for society. All too often, sacerdotal theologians try to evade this sort of challenge by deflecting attention from the angels, demons, jinn, saints, etc., imaginatively engaged in common piety, and insisting that the *infinite* disembodied intentional Force postulated in Christianity, for example, is immune from atheist critique because it is the ultimate ground that makes possible all proximate empirical evaluations, and not one finite entity among many whose intentional engagement within nature might be measured and evaluated.

The GOD-bearing mechanisms that motivate this sort of sacerdotal deflection can be unveiled by postpartum theologians familiar with the iconoclastic intensifications (intellectual, activist, or mystical) that have emerged within, pressed the boundaries of, and then collapsed back under the pressure of the religious togetherness forces of monotheistic GROUPS. Like their colleagues in scientific and secular contexts, they can integrate and nurture anthropomorphically prudish and sociographically promiscuous dispositions in their own inquiry and practice. Methodological naturalism and methodological secularism have helped clear the fields of academic and public discourse of imagined supernatural agents, which has made room for the creative construction of innovative theoretical and pragmatic hypotheses. Retroductive theological hypotheses that are naturalist *and* secularist (in a robustly "metaphysical" sense) might also help clear those expanding fields of imagined Supranatural Agents whose detection within monotheistic Coalitions has contributed to the intensification of modes of in-group protection that justify intolerance and sanctify violence at the global level.

When fully integrated and activated within the iconoclastic trajectory of theology, the theolytic mechanisms have a GOD-dissolving effect: they lead to the de-personification, de-politicization, and de-commodification of infinity. The personifying and politicizing of imagined *finite* disembodied forces played a significant role in helping early human coalitions hold together during the Upper Paleolithic. Although the objectification of supernatural agents was surely advantageous to some shamans and other spiritual leaders in small-scale societies leading up to and through the Neolithic revolution, the commodification of religious objects really took off with the rise of priestly classes in the civilizational forms that emerged in the millennia leading up to and through the axial age. Despots maintain their power, in large part, by controlling the means of *natural production*. Priests maintain their power, for the most part, by controlling the means of *supernatural reproduction*. As empires and doctrinal coalitions got bigger so did the gods. The birth of an infinite GOD provided the conditions for the emergence of a Universal Religious Empire that could arrogate to itself, based on the supposed authoritative intentions of a Supranatural Agent, absolute control over all means of production and reproduction.

As we have seen, the concept of an "infinite Person" makes no sense. However, this maximally counterintuitive idea makes no sense differently than a minimally counterintuitive idea. It would be more accurate to call it an utterly counterintuitive Idea. As most sacerdotal theologians have freely admitted, it absolutely cannot and must not be conceived. GOD cannot be conceived, not only because of the limitations of the human mind, but also because the Idea itself is intrinsically incoherent. Trying to fuse intentionality and infinity dissolves the meaning of both, leaving no other option but an appeal to "mystery." Forbidding any finite representation of this mysterious Idea can make it all the more appealing to members of in-groups who imagine that only they are "in the know" about the eternal intentions of this inconceivable infinite Force who promises their own everlasting escape from mortality and an everlasting torturous punishment worse than death for members of out-groups (see, e.g., Revelation 9:3–6, Luke 10:13–16, Jude 7–13, 1 Thessalonians 5:1–11).

Many intellectuals, activists, and mystics within the Adamic traditions have worked hard to contest the intuitive celebration of this sort of violent absolute segregation that flows all too easily from the religious Politicization of infinity. As long as the mental and social fields in which the members of their own Coalitions are held together are populated by supernatural agents and a Supranatural Agent (however forbidden representations of Him might be), their efforts will always be undermined by the covert operation of the reciprocally reinforcing theogonic mechanisms. Monotheistic theologians have been able to adapt and facilitate the survival of the GROUPS they serve by appealing to the nonobjectifiability of infinity, which immunizes utterly ambiguous detections of GOD from critique and which, ironically, enables the commodification of this Idea in the religious marketplace. Iconoclastic theology, on the other hand, breaks objectified religious Images—especially those that allegedly represent an infinite intentional Force—and helps to unveil the sacerdotal mechanisms that engendered them in the first place.

The situation of the postpartum theologian is not any more (or less) tragic than that of the scientist operating within one of the fields that make up the biocultural study of religion. Both are involved in critical reflection upon religious conceptions, although they approach the phenomena at different levels of abstraction. Neither is interested in commodifying special knowledge about or access to supernatural agents.

They share an interest in bringing new insights about the mechanisms of religious reproduction into the "marketplace" of ideas. The philosophically (or politically) oriented scientist can point out the implausibility (or infeasibility) of religious hypotheses that attribute causal and axiological relevance to finite supernatural agents. The theologian can complement these god-dissolving arguments by criticizing sacerdotal conjectures about a GOD who cares for a GROUP.

Scientists, policy-makers, and theologians who follow out the trajectory invigorated by the theolytic forces will always need to continue developing constructive and contestable arguments about the conditions for axiological engagement as they reflect critically on the concrete challenges of the ever-changing niches in which they find themselves. No doubt these hypotheses will be a hard sell. Evolved cognitive and coalitional defaults are preset to resist them. Some anti-atheist prejudice seems to be buoyed by the hidden assumptions that people who do not believe in punitive supernatural agents cannot generally be trusted to cooperate or commit and that policies which do not triangulate the gods cannot hold a society together. As we have seen, however, these assumptions are controverted by the empirical evidence. If naturalism and secularism continue to expand, then over time this sort of prejudice is likely to diminish. For many people, however, atheistic conceptions intuitively feel dangerous for another reason. If we let go of our gods, and loosen our grip on our groups, won't we lose our minds?

What Can We Learn from the Madman?

Theological conversations can be intense. We may sometimes feel like screaming and shining lanterns in people's faces, or marching into a church and crooning an atheist hymn. For the sort of reasons that we have been exploring in this book, such strategies are not likely to be very productive. On the other hand, continuing to delay "the talk" about religious reproduction is even less productive. As in discussions about the causes and consequences of sexual reproduction, it will not help to preach at people about their god-bearing urges in ways that make them feel alarmed or ashamed. However, it helps even less (and can hurt even more) if we throw down our lanterns too early and give up trying to reflect critically with others on the conditions for axiological engagement within a pluralistic marketplace of ideas. So, one lesson we can learn from the madman's experience is to watch our tone while staying in emotional contact with religious (or nonreligious) others. Of course there is no "right" tone that works in every situation, but there may be some tones that are particular unhelpful in many situations.

It is not uncommon for contemporary discussions of the ecological implications of our ongoing psychological and political decisions to end with fervent warnings about the future. In *The Political Mind*, George Lakoff traces some of the ways in which cognitive functioning contributes to political decisions that inhibit "progressive" empathy and "nurturant" social conceptions. Holding out hope that politics will change as minds change, the book concludes: "But we'd better hurry up. The ice caps are melting."[29] In *The Empathic Civilization*, Jeremy Rifkin argues that "we are at a decisive moment in the human journey where the race to global empathic consciousness is running up against global entropic collapse." He ends the book by asking: "Can we reach biosphere consciousness and global empathy in time to avert planetary collapse?"[30] In *Collapse: How Societies Choose to Fail or Succeed*, Jared Diamond identifies some of the key factors that have contributed to the decline and eventual disappearance of a variety of social coalitions over the millennia. The last chapter points to 12 distinct but mutually exacerbating "problems of non-sustainability" in today's world society, which he suggests are "like time bombs with fuses of less than 50 years."[31]

I agree with these scholars' assessments of the seriousness of the situation. I also agree that reflecting carefully and acting intentionally will be necessary for achieving any resolution of the problem that includes the reproduction of psychologically healthy human coalitions. However, I think it is important to point out two potential problems with this way of alerting people to the dangerous political and ecological consequences of their habits. Given the careful scientific analysis and empirical evidence backing up these distress signals about the state of our social and natural environments, we might expect more people to pay attention. However, the surprising fact that these global cautionary tales are mostly ignored would be a matter of course if human beings had evolved to respond to mortality salience by further entrenching themselves in immediately relevant local narratives.

Flooding the airwaves (and filling the bookshelves) with ever-intensifying warnings about impending crises may actually be making things worse. If priming people to think about death automatically activates their coalitional tendency to protect their own in-group, then drawing attention to the increased likelihood of catastrophic war or ecological devastation surreptitiously stimulates sociographic prudery, which, tragically, only further increases their likelihood. This does not mean we should simply avoid talking about the future, but it does mean we might want to pay more attention to the way in which our hypotheses about the future activate (or contest) the evolved theogonic tendencies that, one way or another, will have a powerful bearing on the future.

And that brings us to the second problem. Most naturalist and secularist analyses of the factors that contribute to the difficulties facing the global human community do not adequately attend to the role of shared imaginative engagement with *supernatural agents*. Most practical recommendations for remedying the situation do not account for the mental and social consequences of continuing to bear gods, a lacuna that not only weakens their feasibility but also worsens the very problems they are trying to solve by leaving open a gap that is all too easily imaginatively filled by human-like, coalition-favoring disembodied forces. Why worry about entropic collapse, the ice caps melting or other ecological time bombs when the Supranatural Agent one worships has promised to create a new heaven and a new earth—after casting nonbelieving "children of the evil one" into a new hell (e.g., 2 Peter 3:13, Matthew 13:36–43, Revelation 20:7–15)?

All three of the scholars quoted above are clearly worried about the prevalence of conservative and fundamentalist attitudes among religious people, but they treat "religion" as a rather broad set of phenomena that does not necessarily include belief in and ritual interaction with imagined supernatural agents.[32] Their (otherwise admirable) proposals for facilitating civilizational transformation by promoting empathy toward cultural others will unfortunately be sabotaged by the furtive functioning of the anthropomorphically promiscuous detection of gods, which will go on intensifying the very out-group antagonism they are trying to counteract. So, the second lesson we can learn from reflecting on the madman's experience has to do with his message. Announcing the "death of God" or the probable imminent death of (some or all) humans raises mortality salience and automatically strengthens the evolved dispositions toward over-protecting kith and kin and over-detecting ambiguous agents who might help or hinder their survival.

The consequences of continuing to interpret events in the natural world (such as tsunamis or AIDS) as caused by an allegedly just and punitive GOD are no less dangerous than the consequences of continuing to inscribe the social field with rigid moralistic boundaries around a supposedly sanctified GROUP. The theogonic mechanisms of anthropomorphic promiscuity and sociographic prudery are reciprocally reinforcing and so they must be unveiled together, otherwise the one that remains concealed will keep on activating the other. This is why I have suggested a different sort of message: the gods are born—and we have borne them.

In the introductory chapter, I observed that discussing these issues openly might very well lead to a kind of theological postpartum depression, especially among reflective members of sacerdotal coalitions. Naturalists, secularists, and atheists could easily get depressed too. Are we all going to die? Well, yes. That is part of life. Are the gods ever going to leave home? Well, that remains to be seen. Trying to pressure religious families to kick their supernatural agents out of the house and stop ritually reproducing them will only make things worse. How can we bring the new message to the public marketplace and to the churches, as well as to temples, mosques, ashrams, etc., without either completely alienating everyone or simply being dismissed as crazy (or both). Well, I don't know. We'll have to figure this out together.

Let go. This is the sort of proclamation commonly found in the writings (and the sort of practice commonly exemplified in the lives) of a long series of messengers, also considered a bit mad by many of their contemporaries, who have intentionally followed the iconoclastic trajectory over the centuries. We can think, for example, of the nonanxious intentionality manifested in the *wu-wei* of the Daoist, the *anatman* of the Buddhist, and the *adiaphora* of the Stoic. Many of the "madmen" in these and other East, South, and West Asian axial age traditions have invited us to join them in a kind of nonviolent iconoclasm: to loosen our grip on mentally repressive (and socially oppressive) images and to let them fall apart. Anxiously trying to bind the psyche (and the polis) together is not only exhausting, it can also be counterproductive. Restlessly tending to the boundaries by which we maintain our sense of self and control our communities can make us so tense that we cannot enjoy our intentionality. Letting go of the gods might actually help clear our minds for (and open up our groups to) the creative task of constructing more plausible hypotheses and more feasible strategies as we experimentally adapt to and alter our axiological worlds.

Notes

1 THE GODS ARE BORN—AND WE HAVE BORNE THEM

1. Nietzsche (2001, 120).
2. Altizer (1967a, 103, 135). For more examples of early contributions to "Death of God" theology, see Altizer (1967b) and Altizer and Hamilton (1966). Cf. Altizer (2012).
3. See, for example, Caputo and Vattimo (2007).
4. Nietzsche (2001, 131) (Book 3, §151).
5. Feuerbach (1989, Chapter 26).
6. See, for example, McCauley (2013), Pyysiäinen (2011, 2012), Gervais et al. (2011), Wildman (2009), Slingerland (2008), Boyd and Richerson (2005a, 2005b), and Shennan (2002).
7. The literature within and across these fields is far too extensive to summarize here. Throughout this book, I will primarily rely on the endnotes to refer readers to relatively recent publications, many of which include analysis and synthesis of earlier research. Readers interested in exploring additional literature can find bibliographic references and summaries at the website of the Institute for the Bio-cultural Study of Religion: www.ibcsr.org. For collections of essays that include summary contributions by leading scholars in the biocultural study of religion, see Andresen (2001), Pyysiäinen and Anttonen (2002) Bulbulia et al. (2008), Schaller et al. (2010), Geertz and Jensen (2011), Czachesz and Biró (2011), Xygalatas and McCorkle, Jr., (2013), and Dawes and Maclaurin (2013). For an introductory level textbook summary, see Winkelman and Baker (2010).
8. Charles Peirce, for example, argued that an "interpretant" of a sign may be "a feeling...an effort...(or an) intellectual apprehension." (1998, 430). Elsewhere, I have demonstrated how the pragmatic philosophy of Gilles Deleuze liberates thinking, acting, and feeling (Shults, 2014a).
9. See, for example, J. Z. Smith (1982), Asad (1993), Davaney (2000), Taves (2009), and Vásquez (2011).
10. Hawking (1988, 175).

11. Nietzsche (1999, 8). Translation emended, emphases in original.
12. See, for example, Neville (2001).
13. See Jaspers (1953), Arnason et al. (2005), Armstrong (2006), Bellah (2011), and Bellah and Joas (2012).

2 Anthropomorphic Promiscuity and Sociographic Prudery

1. Shults (2011, 2012a, 2012b, 2014a, 2014b, 2014c). Some of the ideas fleshed out in the current project were introduced in these earlier publications.
2. Boyer (2005, 3).
3. Atran and Norenzayan (2004, 713).
4. Bulbulia (2005, 72).
5. Lewis-Williams and Pearce (2005, 26).
6. McCauley (2011, 159).
7. See, for example, Lawson and McCauley (1990), Tweed (2006), Taves (2009), and Riesebrodt (2010).
8. Guthrie (1980, 1993). Guthrie has continued refining his theory over the years. See also, for example, 2002 and 2007.
9. Guthrie (1993, 4).
10. Guthrie (1993, 197).
11. See, for example, Slone (2004, Chapter 4) and Pyysiäinen (2009, Chapter 5).
12. Sperber and Wilson (1995, 48).
13. For an introduction to this research, see Barrett (2004).
14. Kelemen (1999).
15. The first and second phrases were proposed, respectively, by Dennett (1987) and Pyysiäinen (2009). For an overview of empirical research on "mind reading" (ToMM), see Tremlin (2006).
16. Tremlin (2006, 81).
17. Willard and Norenzayan (2013). For a discussion of the bias toward mind-body dualism in children, see Bloom (2004).
18. Durkheim (1965) and Rappaport (1999).
19. See, for example, Gervais and Norenzayan (2012), Purzycki et al. (2012), Bering and Parker (2006), Shariff and Norenzayan (2011), and Atkinson and Bourrat (2011). For literature on relevant ethnographic research and broader theoretical integration of these themes, see the endnote references in the next three subsections of this chapter.
20. Rossano (2010, 102).
21. See, for example, Wigger et al. (2013). Additional literature on this topic is reviewed in Boyer (2010, 32–34).
22. Reddish et al. (2013).
23. Bulbulia (2006). Cf. Sørensen (2007) and Fischer et al. (2013).

24. Sosis (2006). See also Sosis (2000, 2002), Sosis and Alcora (2003), and Sosis and Bressler (2003). For other applications of costly signaling theory to religion, see Bulbulia (2004) and Soler (2012).
25. Greene (2013, 182–183).
26. Norenzayan and Hansen (2006), Granqvist et al. (2012), Barnes and Gibson (2013), H. McGregor et al. (1998), Blogowska et al. (2013), Taubman—Ben-Ari et al. (2002), Mikulincer and Shaver (2001), Pyszczynski et al. (2002), and Vail et al. (2010).
27. See, for example, Burke et al. (2013), Yen and Lin (2012), and Schindler et al. (2012).
28. See, for example, I. McGregor et al. (2010), I. McGregor et al. (2012), and van den Bos et al. (2012).
29. See, for example, Johnson and Reeve (2013).
30. Boyer (2002, 57). Boyer is one of the leading proponents of the "by-product" camp in the biocultural study of religion. Cf. Boyer (2003).
31. See, for example, Boyer (1992, 1994).
32. See, for example, Boyer (1999, 2000).
33. Boyer (2002, 67).
34. See, for example, Hornbeck and Barrett (2013).
35. Boyer (2002, 75). Cf. Boyer (1994b) ("cognitive aspects").
36. Boyer (1994, 34). See also Boyer (1990) and especially 2002b.
37. Atran (2002, 13).
38. Atran (2002, 5).
39. Atran (2002, 66). For additional analysis of the reciprocal relationship between strategies of cognitive classification and cultural construction, see Atran (1990) and Atran and Medin (2008).
40. Atran (2002, 66). Cf. Atran (2006), Atran and Norenzayan (2004), Norenzayan et al. (2006), and Atran and Henrich (2010).
41. Norenzayan and Atran (2004, 165).
42. Ginges et al. (2009).
43. Atran (2010, 33).
44. Atran (2010, 450).
45. Lewis-Williams (1981, 1995, 2002) and Lewis-Williams and Peirce (2004).
46. Lewis-Williams (2002, 96). Emphasis added. Cf. Mithen (1996).
47. Lewis-Williams and Peirce (2005, 69, 285).
48. Lewis-Williams and Peirce (2005, 58). For another treatment of the relation between religion, dreams, and altered states of consciousness, see McNamara (2009).
49. Lewis-Williams (2010, 149, 138).
50. Wildman (2009, 22).
51. Guthrie (1993, 204). Pyysiäinen argues that because we can "have only reflective metarepresentational beliefs about 'Ultimate Reality' as a concept... there is no empirical way to find out whether an Ultimate Reality really exists" (2004, 204). For a discussion of the importance of pragmatic problem solving in cognitive evolution, see Schulkin (2008).
52. Slone (2004).

53. The key experiments that launched this discussion were by Barrett and Keil (1996). See also Barrett (1999) and Barrett with Lanman (2008). In "Dumb gods, petitionary prayer and the cognitive science of religion," Barrett describes how people participating in such experiments automatically make inferences or predictions about supernatural agents that "conform to intuitive expectations people hold about all intentional beings: that they have fallible beliefs, desires that motivate purposeful action, limited attention, limited sensory-perceptual systems for gathering information about the world, a particular physical location in space and time, and so forth" (2002, 95).

54. See, for example, Purzycki (2013).

55. For a fuller analysis of these developments, see Norenzayan (2013).

56. Cf. Mullins et al. (2013) and Assmann (2006, 2010, 2011).

57. Whitehouse (2002, 102). Whitehouse theory of religious modes has been developed and revised in light of extensive cross-cultural anthropological research and psychological experimentation. See, for example, Whitehouse (2000, 2004), Whitehouse with Martin (2004), Whitehouse with Laidlaw (2004), and Whitehouse with McCauley (2005), and with Hodder (2010).

58. Henrich (2009). See also Lanman (2012).

59. See, for example, Norenzayan and Gervais (2013).

60. See, for example, Girard (1977, 1986).

61. Cf. Jay (1992), J. Z. Smith (1987), and Janowitz (2011).

62. See, for example, M. Zuckerman et al. (2013), Shenhav et al. (2012), Caldwell-Harris (2012), Gervais and Norenzayan (2012), Ganzach and Gotlibovski (2013), Razmyar and Reeve (2013), Pennycook et al. (2012), Pennycook et al. (2013), Burris and Petican (2011), and van Elk (2013).

63. See, for example, Shenhav et al. (2012), Legare and Souza (2012), Pyysiäinen (2011), and Geertz and Jensen (2011).

3   THE SCIENTIFIC DISCIPLINE OF THEOLOGY

1. Dawkins (2006, 185).

2. Harris (2010, 167).

3. Dennett (2006, 208, 299).

4. Atran (2002, 49).

5. Lawson and McCauley (1990, 162). Emphasis added.

6. Cf. Shults (2014a).

7. Boyer (2010, Chapter 1).

8. Boyer (2002, 5). Page numbers in the next two paragraphs refer to this book.

9. Boyer (1994, 229, 261).

10. Atran (2010, 434). Cf. Atran and Henrich (2010).

11. Atran (2010, 450).

12. Atran (2002, 156).

13. Atran (2002, 92, 113). Emphasis added in second quotation.
14. Atran (1990, 4).
15. Atran (1990, 264).
16. Atran (1990, 219). Emphases added.
17. Atran (1990, 264, 219). Emphases added.
18. Atran (1990, 250, 264).
19. Atran (1990, 250, 220). Emphasis added.
20. Atran (2002, 290).
21. Lewis-Williams (2010, 117).
22. Lewis-Williams and Pearce (2002, 121, 126. Cf. 2010, 236ff).
23. Lewis-Williams and Pearce (2005, 28).
24. Lewis-Williams (2010, 274). All page numbers in the following paragraphs refer to this book.
25. Lewis-Williams (2010, 48).
26. Lewis-Williams (2010, 86). Emphasis added.
27. Bowlby (1969, 1988). For an overview of therapeutic strategies based on attachment theory, see Wallin (2007). For an object-relations theory approach to the emergence of god-conceptions in children, see Rizutto (1981).
28. See, for example, Mikulincer and Shaver (2007), Rholes and Simpson (2004), and Rom and Mikulincer (2003).
29. Kirkpatrick (2005). Cf. Kirkpatrick (1992), with Shaver (1990), and with Rowatt (2002).
30. Granqvist (2006, 2002, 2003), Granqvist with Hageskull (2001), Granqvist with Ivarsson et al. (2007).
31. For a summary of these pathways, see Kirkpatrick (2005, Chapters 5 and 6) and Granqvist with Mikulincer and Shaver (2010).
32. Kirkpatrick (2005, 156).
33. Ross (2007, 82). Another study (Dickie et al., 2006) found that young men who experienced their mothers as punishing and judgmental were more likely to feel closer to GOD (the latter being typically conceived as a powerful male). The internal modeling of the mother's power was the strongest predictor of a powerful GOD image.
34. Kirkpatrick (2005, 21, 291, 353).
35. Granqvist (2006, 141). Emphasis added.
36. Lawson and McCauley (1990, 176). For a brief overview of key aspects of their theory, see Lawson and McCauley (2002).
37. Lawson and McCauley (1990, 47).
38. Lawson and McCauley (1990, 159).
39. McCauley and Lawson (2002, 43).
40. McCauley and Lawson (2002, 205–206).
41. McCauley and Lawson (2002, 209–210).
42. McCauley (2011, 245–250).
43. Pyysiäinen (2009, 183). Emphasis added. Cf. Pyysiäinen (2012a, 2012b).
44. Pyysiäinen (2004, 161, 171). Emphasis added in last quotation.
45. Pyysiäinen (2004, 76). Emphasis added.
46. Pyysiäinen (2004, 77, 73). Emphasis in last quotation added.

47. Pyysiäinen (2003, 230).
48. Pyysiäinen (2004, 166, 185, 110). Emphasis in last quotation added.
49. See Lieberg (1973).
50. Spinoza is the most obvious early modern example. Late modern examples include Deleuze (2004) and Zizek (2006).
51. For a discussion of the way in which all symbols "break" on "the infinite," see Neville (2006).
52. Shults (2014a). For a review and analysis of other constructive "theological" hypotheses about (what I am calling) the conditions for axiological engagement, see Wildman (2010, Chapter 8).

4 Arguing about Axiological Engagement

1. Peirce (1974, V.189).
2. In her examination of the various ways in which Peirce uses these terms, Phyllis Chiasson (2005, 239) suggests that we might take "retroduction" as an inclusive term for the whole process of discovering and constructing worthy hypotheses, which involves deduction, induction, and abduction. However, my use of the term "retroduction" is closer to the way in which it is described in Danermark et al. (2002, Chapter 4).
3. Nietzsche (1989, 44–45).
4. For an introduction to these sorts of hypotheses, see Sober and Sloan Wilson (1998), Sloan Wilson (2002), E. O. Wilson (2012), de Waal (2013), Hauser (2006), Boehm (2012), Sinnott-Armstrong (2008), Norenzayan and Sharif (2008), Voland and Schiefenhovel (2009), and Bowles and Gintis (2011).
5. For a summary of this research, see Bloom (2013).
6. See, for example, Jensen (2013).
7. Haidt (2007, 2012); Graham and Haidt (2010).
8. Rossano (2010, 176, 60).
9. Rossano (2010, 15).
10. Atran (2002, 173, 156). Emphases added.
11. Pyysiäinen (2003, 182). Emphasis added.
12. Boyer (1994, 147). For Boyer's critique of interpretations of religious ideas as guided primarily either by induction or deduction, see (1994, 75–81, 94–97, 146–48, 220–22, 231–32, and 236–42).
13. Boyer (1994, 218).
14. Boyer (1994, 239; cf. 233).
15. Boyer (1994, 287).
16. Hodge (1981, vol. I, 9–15).
17. Pannenberg (1976, 333). First emphasis added.
18. McCauley (2011, 153–54).
19. McCauley (2011, 228).

20. For an analysis of the role of purity codes in social boundary formation, see Douglas (2002).
21. Teehan (2010, 174).
22. Teehan (2010, 158).
23. Teehan (2010, 139, 172).
24. Nietzsche (2002, 153).
25. See, for example, Peterson (2010), van Slyke (2011), Leech and Visala (2011), Visala (2011).
26. Murray (2009, 169). Emphasis added.
27. Murray and Goldberg (2009, 194). Emphasis added.
28. Murray (2009, 178).
29. See Henderson (2006).
30. van Inwegen (2009, 131, 135). Emphasis added.
31. Plantinga (2009, 167).
32. Some readers might object to my reference to the Flying Spaghetti Monster (FSM). It could be interpreted as a silly distraction in what should be a serious discussion about the rationality of religious beliefs. I disagree. As we have "the talk" about religious reproduction, it is important to ask ourselves what makes us suspicious about the Church of the FSM? Why do we hesitate to take it seriously as a "religion"? The fact that some of its members smile when we point out the counterintuitive nature of their main supernatural agent? The fact that some of its members do not literally believe all of the teachings of the Church of the FSM? How is this different from Christianity?
33. Barrett (2009, 97–98).
34. Lewis-Williams (2010, 32).

5 Religious Family Systems

1. For a discussion of the differences and similarities between what is sometimes called the "new comparative theology" and the "theology of religion," and their common genealogy in the comparative theologies of the nineteenth century, see Nicholson (2009). Some of the themes I develop in this chapter were also discussed in Shults (2010).
2. For summaries and analysis of these sorts of biases see, for example, Boyer (2002), Haselton et al. (2005), Henrich and Henrich (2007), Frey (2009), Hood (2009), Persinger (2009), Atran (2010), Bering (2011), and Shermer (2011).
3. Dawkins (2006, 51).
4. Schmidt-Leukel (2005).
5. The essays in D'Costa *Christian Uniqueness Reconsidered* (1990) were explicit responses to the pluralist proposals in *The Myth of Christian Uniqueness*, edited by Hick and Knitter (1987). In his contribution to the former volume,

D'Costa, a Roman Catholic theologian like Rahner, argued for inclusivism. He later altered his position to a version of exclusivism; cf. D'Costa (2009).

6. Knitter (2005).
7. See, for example, Knitter (1995, 1996).
8. See, for example, Griffin (2005) and Hill Fletcher (2005). For an early example, see Tracy (1990).
9. See, for example, J. Z. Smith (2004), Indinopulos et al. (2006), and Sacks (2002).
10. Heim (1995,154).
11. For example, Bowen's emphasis on "differentiation" can be complemented by John Bowlby's emphasis on "attachment" in order to account for the positive value of affective bonds. See Skowron and Dendry (2004).
12. See, for example, Papero (1990), Jenkins et al. (2005), Skowron et al. (2009), Titelman (1998), and Titleman (2003). For examples of research that applies Bowen's theory to the phenomena of religion and spirituality, see Jankowski and Vaughn (2009), Heiden Rootes et al. (2010), and Jankowski and Sandage (2012).
13. See Bowen (1978, 304–305, 355–356) and Kerr and Bowen (1988, 30–58).
14. Kerr and Bowen (1988, 52).
15. Kerr and Bowen (1988, 121, emphasis added).
16. Kerr and Bowen (1988, 121, emphasis added).
17. Bowen (1978, 414–450); Kerr and Bowen (1988, 141–149).
18. Kerr and Bowen (1988, 142).
19. Kerr and Bowen (1988, 225); cf. Bowen (1978, 377, 433).
20. Kerr and Bowen (1988, 182).
21. Kerr and Bowen (1988, 164).
22. Bowen (1978, 434).
23. Bowen (1978, 217).
24. Bowen (1978, 382); cf. Kerr and Bowen (1988, 276) and Titelman (2003).
25. Cf. Bowen (1978, 303, 363).
26. Kerr and Bowen (1988, 364, 473).
27. See, for example, Ackerman (2003), Skowron (2004), and Friedman (2011).
28. Cf. Kerr and Bowen (1988, 236, 436, 480, 496–499, 502, 540–42).
29. Kerr and Bowen (1988, 276).
30. Bowen (1978 437). Emphasis added
31. Ward (1987).
32. Shults (2012c).
33. Ward (1987, 3). Emphases added.
34. Ward (1987, 161).
35. Ward (1987, 162).
36. Clooney (2001, 27).
37. Clooney (2010, 16).
38. Heim (1995, 222).
39. Heim (2001, 283).
40. Heim (2001, 272). Emphasis added.
41. Hick (2004, xix).

42. Hick (2004, xxxiv).
43. Hick (2004, 375).
44. "The next step beyond dialogue," 3–12 in Knitter (2005), 4. Emphasis added.
45. Hick (1987, 34).
46. See, for example, the literature in note 26 in chapter 2.
47. Kerr and Bowen (1988, 336).

6 LETTING GODS GO: NATURALISM AND SECULARISM

1. See, for example, Sosis and Bulbulia (2011).
2. Zuckerman (2007, 55). For a sociological analysis that reveals some of the reasons for the expansion of disbelief, see Zuckerman (2012).
3. See, for example, Bullivant and Lee (2012), P. Zuckerman (2010), and the target articles by Caldwell-Harris and Johnson in the special issue on the scientific study of atheism in *Religion, Brain & Behavior* 2/1 (February 2012).
4. Norenzayan and Gervais (2013). Cf. Geertz and Markusson (2010).
5. Boyer (2010, 97).
6. Bering (2011, 201).
7. 2011, 251. Emphasis added.
8. 2010, 257.
9. 2009, 187.
10. For example, Robert Carneiro concludes his historical review of the rise and fall of supernaturalism from the Upper Paleolithic to the present with an expression of hope: "The day may yet come when the human race has grown accustomed to its own cosmic solitude and insignificance. And as it continues to explore the universe, it will be satisfied with truth and no longer feel the need to look for solace" (2010, 424). Michael Shermer insists that because religion "has no systematic methods of explanation of the natural world, and no means of conflict resolution on moral issues when members of competing sects hold absolute beliefs that are mutually exclusive," it cannot be the best route for the future of humanity. "Flawed as they may be, science and the secular Enlightenment values expressed in Western democracies are our best hope for survival" (2011, 186–87).
11. Flanagan (2006). For additional analyses of the concept of naturalism, see de Caro and MacArthur (2004).
12. See, for example, Casebeer (2003), Flanagan (2007), and de Caro and MacArthur (2010).
13. Wildman (2009, 24).
14. Kirkpatrick (2005, 353).
15. Tremlin (2006, 199).
16. Bloom (2004, 216).

17. Bloom (2004, xii).
18. Rue (2005, 2–3, 143, 363).
19. Dworkin (2013, 10, 159).
20. Berger (1999, 2).
21. See, for example, Warner (2010), Bruce (2011), Kuru (2009), Asad (2003), Cady and Hurd(2010), Calhoun et al. (2011), P. Zuckerman (2007), and P. Zuckerman (2010, vol. II).
22. Norris and Inglehart (2004).
23. Holyoake (1896).
24. Taylor (2007, 539).
25. Taylor (2007, 487, 768–69).
26. Rawls (1997, 766, emphasis added). For a fuller presentation of this argument, see Rawls (1996, 2001).
27. Wildman, Sosis and McNamara (2012).
28. Plantinga (1990, xv). Emphasis added.
29. Plantinga (1990, 271).
30. Barrett (2004, 96, 99). Emphasis added in first quotation. Barrett also relies on deductive and inductive inference in his reaction to some of the new atheists in Barrett (2007).
31. Rossano (2010, 27).
32. Rossano (2010, 23).
33. Jones (1991, 65, 113). Both emphases in original.
34. Jones (2002, 117).
35. Jones (2008, 159).
36. Habermas (2002, 67, 74–77, emphasis in original).
37. Habermas (2002, 76, 163, 77).
38. Habermas (2008, 130, 138, 140, emphasis in original).
39. Habermas et al. (2010, 16, 21, 22, emphases added).
40. Habermas (2010, 17). Cf. 2010, 82, and 2008, 141.
41. Habermas (2008, 146). Emphasis added.
42. Habermas (2008, 264).
43. Petito and Hatzopoulos (2003, 1, 14–15). For similar arguments, see Thomas (2005) and Fox and Sandler (2004).
44. Johnston and Cox (2003, 18–19).
45. Little and Appleby (2004, 5, emphases in original). See also Appleby (2000).
46. Pyszczynski et al. (2002, 172, 187, 148).
47. Juergensmeyer (2003, 15, 249).
48. Cavanaugh (2009).
49. For examples, see the chapters in Little (2007) and Johnston and Sampson (1994).
50. See, for example, Lederach (1995, 1997, 2005).
51. For examples of assessments of, and proposals for dealing with, the challenges of religious pluralism in light of globalization and democratization, see Banchoff (2007), Banchoff (2008), and Monsma and Soper (2009).
52. Directed by James Cameron, 2009 (20th Century Fox). I treat these trajectories in more detail in Shults (2014c).

7 POSTPARTUM THEOLOGY

1. Clarke, Powell, and Savulescu (2013, 272). For a discussion of the phenomena of intolerance that incorporates many of the insights from what I have been calling the biocultural sciences of religion, see Powell and Clarke, "Religion, Tolerance, and Intolerance: Views from Across the Disciplines," in the same volume.
2. See Gervais et al. (2011a, 2011b), Gervais and Norenzayan (2012), and Gervais (2011).
3. Norenzayan (2013, 83).
4. See, for example, A. C. Kay et al. (2008), Beit-Hallahmi (2010), Saslow et al. (2013), and Norris and Inglehart (2004).
5. Zuckerman (2010, 2, 4).
6. Quack (2012). Compare this with the very different lines drawn in the conflict between some atheists groups and religious coalitions in Great Britain: (Gutkowski, 2012). For other examples of distinctive expressions of atheism in various contexts, see Zuckerman, volume 2.
7. See, for example, Malhotra (2008) and Batson et al. (1993). As Ara Norenzayan puts it, this suggests that "religious situations are more powerful than religious dispositions" (2013, 73).
8. Barrett and Richert (2003). See Barrett's more extensive defense of such an approach in Chapter 7 of his *Cognitive Science, Religion and Theology* (2011).
9. Barrett (2009, 97, emphasis added).
10. New Revised Standard Version. Emphases added.
11. For a fuller discussion of the "niche" metaphor and theological adaptation, see Shults (2012c). Joseph Bracken (2013, at 1002) interpreted some of my comments in that context as a "lament" over the shrinking of the niche in which natural theology can operate. Naturally, such shrinkage could be cause for lamentation among sacerdotal theologians, but my intention was to show how these environmental changes call for a new (iconoclastic) adaptation, the construction of hypotheses that do "*not* include arguments based on the detection and protection of one's favored Supernatural Agent Coalition, but instead explore radically new options for a *robustly natural(ist)* theology" (2012c, 548, emphases added).
12. http://www.brill.com/international-journal-public-theology.
13. Schmitt, *Political Theology*, 1985, 36.
14. For a discussion of Shmidt's relation to Nazism and Roman Catholicism, see Hollerich (2004).
15. Milbank (1990, 249, 434, emphases added).
16. Taylor (2007, 775). Emphasis added.
17. Milbank (2010), 82.
18. Scott and Cavanaugh (2004, 2, emphasis added).
19. de Vries (2006), 2.
20. Crockett (2001).
21. Raschke (2001, 48).

22. Crockett and Robbins (2012, 144, 153).
23. Crockett (2011, 144).
24. Crockett (2011, 15) and with Robbins (2012, 41).
25. Crocket and Robbins (2012, xvi).
26. For an attempt to bring Deleuze's work into dialogue with these sciences, see Shults (2014a).
27. Nietzsche (2006, 263, emphases in original).
28. See Wildman (2011).
29. Lakoff (2009, 271).
30. Rifkin (2009, 42, 616).
31. Diamond (2011, 498).
32. Diamond devotes a chapter to religion in another recent book, *The World Until Yesterday*, and although he acknowledges the centrality of "supernatural explanation" in most religions, he does not see it as a necessary trait of "religion" (2012, 368).

Bibliography

Ackerman, Fran, "Israeli-Palestinian relations: A Bowen theory perspective," 443–475 in Peter Titleman, ed., *Emotional Cutoff: Bowen Family Systems Theory Perspectives* (New York: Haworth Press, 2003).

Altizer, Thomas J. J., *The Gospel of Christian Atheism* (London: Collins, 1967a).

Altizer, Thomas J. J., ed., *Toward a New Christianity: Readings in the Death of God Theology* (New York: Harcourt, Brace & World, 1967b).

Altizer, Thomas J. J., *The Apocalyptic Trinity* (New York: Palgrave Macmillan, 2012).

Altizer, Thomas J. J. and William Hamilton, *Radical Theology and the Death of God* (Middlesex, UK: Penguin, 1966).

Andresen, Jensine, ed., *Religion in Mind: Cognitive Perspectives on Religious Belief, Ritual and Experience* (Cambridge University Press, 2001).

Appleby, Scott, *The Ambivalence of the Sacred: Religion, Violence and Reconciliation* (New York: Rowman & Littlefield, 2000).

Armstrong, Karen, *The Great Transformation* (New York: Knopf, 2006).

Arnason, Johann P., S. N. Eisenstadt and Bjorn Wittrock, eds., *Axial Civilizations and World History* (Leiden: Brill, 2005).

Asad, Talal, *Genealogies of Religion: Discipline and Reasons of Power in Christianity and Islam* (Baltimore, MD: The Johns Hopkins University Press, 1993).

Asad, Talal, *Formations of the Secular* (Stanford, CA: Stanford University Press, 2003).

Assmann, Jan, *Religion and Cultural Memory*, trans. R. Livingstone (Stanford, CA: Stanford University Press, 2006).

Assmann, Jan, *Cultural Memory and Early Civilization: Writing, Remembrance, and the Political Imagination* (Cambridge: Cambridge University Press, 2011).

Assmann, Jan, *The Price of Monotheism*, trans. R. Savage (Stanford, CA: Stanford University Press, 2010).

Atkinson, Quentin D., and Pierrick Bourrat, "Beliefs about God, the afterlife and morality support the role of supernatural policing in human cooperation" *Evolution and Human Behavior* 32 (2011): 41–49.

Atran, Scott, *Cognitive Foundations of Natural History: Toward an Anthropology of Science* (Cambridge; Cambridge University Press, 1990).

Atran, Scott, *In Gods We Trust: The Evolutionary Landscape of Religion* (Oxford: Oxford University Press, 2002).

Atran, Scott, "The cognitive and evolutionary roots of religion," 181–208 in Patrick McNamara, ed., *Where God and Science Meet, Vol. I: Evolution, Genes and the Religious Brain* (London: Praeger, 2006).

Atran, Scott, *Talking to the Enemy: Faith, Brotherhood and the (Un)Making of Terrorists* (New York: HarperCollins, 2010).

Atran, Scott, and Ara Norenzayan, "Religion's evolutionary landscape: Counterintuition, commitment, compassion, communion" *Behavioral and Brain Sciences* 27 (2004): 713–770.

Atran, Scott, and Douglas Medin, *The Native Mind and the Cultural Construction of Nature* (Cambridge: The MIT Press, 2008).

Atran, Scott, and Joseph Henrich, "The evolution of religion: How cognitive by-products, adaptive learning heuristics, ritual displays, and group competition generate deep commitments to prosocial religions" *Biological Theory* 5/1 (2010): 18–30.

Banchoff, Thomas, ed., *Democracy and the New Religious Pluralism* (Oxford: Oxford University Press, 2007).

Banchoff, Thomas, ed., *Religious Pluralism, Globalization, and World Politics* (New York: Oxford University Press, 2008).

Barnes, Kirsten, and Nicholas J. S. Gibson, "Supernatural agency: Individual difference predictors and situational correlates" *The International Journal for the Psychology of Religion* 23 (2013): 42–62.

Barrett, Justin, "Theological correctness: Cognitive constraint and the study of religion" *Method and Theory in the Study of Religion* 11 (1999): 325–339.

Barrett, Justin, "Dumb gods, petitionary prayer and the cognitive science of religion," 93–109 in I. Pyysiainen and P. Anttonen, eds. *Current Approaches in the Cognitive Science of Religion* (New York: Continuum, 2002).

Barrett, Justin, *Why Would Anyone Believe in God?* (New York: AltaMira Press, 2004).

Barrett, Justin, "Is the spell really broken? Bio-psychological explanations of religion and theistic belief" *Theology and Science* 5/1 (2007): 57–72.

Barrett, Justin, "Cognitive science, religion and theology," 76–99 in Jeffrey Schloss and Michael J. Murray, eds., *The Believing Primate* (Oxford: Oxford University Press, 2009).

Barrett, Justin, *Cognitive Science, Religion and Theology: From Human Minds to Divine Minds* (West Conshohocken, PA: Templeton Press, 2011).

Barrett, Justin, and Frank Keil, "Conceptualizing a nonnatural entity: Anthropomorphism in God concepts" *Cognitive Psychology* 31 (1996): 219–247.

Barrett, Justin, and Rebekah Richert, "Anthropomorphism of preparedness? Exploring children's God concepts" *Review of Religious Research* 44/3 (2003): 300–312.

Barrett, Justin, and Jonathan Lanman, "The science of religious beliefs" *Religion* 38 (2008): 109–124.

Batson, C. D., P. Schoenrade and W. L. Ventis, *Religion and the Individual: A Social-Psychological Perspective* (Oxford: Oxford University Press, 1993).

Beit-Hallahmi, Benjamin, "Morality and immorality among the irreligious," 113–148 in Phil Zuckerman, ed., *Atheism and Secularity*, vol. I (Santa Barbara, CA: Praeger, 2010).

Bellah, Robert, *Religion in Human Evolution: From the Paleolithic to the Axial Age* (Cambridge, MA: Harvard University Press, 2011).

Bellah, Robert, and Hans Joas, eds., *The Axial Age and Its Consequences* (Cambridge, MA: Harvard University Press, 2012).

Berger, Peter L., ed., *The Desecularization of the World: Resurgent Religion and World Politics* (Grand Rapids, MI: Eerdmans, 1999).

Bering, Jesse, *The Belief Instinct: The Psychology of Souls, Destiny, and the Meaning of Life* (New York: Norton & Norton, 2011).

Bering, Jesse, and Becky D. Parker, "Children's attributions of intentions to an invisible agent" *Developmental Psychology* 42 (2006): 253–262.

Blogowska, Joanna, Catherine Lambert and Vassilis Saroglou, "Religious prosociality and aggression: It's real" *Journal for the Scientific Study of Religion* 52/3 (2013): 524–536.

Bloom, Paul, *Descartes' Baby: How the Science of Child Development Explains What Makes Us Human* (New York: Basic Books, 2004).

Bloom, Paul, *Just Babies: The Origins of Good and Evil* (New York: Crown, 2013).

Boehm, Christopher, *Moral Origins: The Evolution of Virtue, Altruism and Shame* (New York: Basic Books, 2012).

Bowen, Murray, *Family Therapy in Clinical Practice* (London: Aronson, 1978).

Bowlby, John, *Attachment* (New York: Pimlico, 1969).

Bowlby, John, *A Secure Base: Clinical Applications of Attachment Theory* (New York: Routledge, 1988).

Bowles, Samuel, and Herbert Gintis, *A Cooperative Species: Human Reciprocity and Its Evolution* (Princeton and Oxford: Princeton University Press, 2011).

Boyd, Robert, and Peter J. Richardson, *The Origin and Evolution of Cultures* (Oxford: Oxford University Press, 2005).

Boyd, Robert, and Peter J. Richardson, *Not by Genes Alone: How Culture Transformed Human Evolution* (Chicago, IL: University of Chicago Press, 2005).

Boyer, Pascal, "A reductionistic model of distinct modes of religious transmission," 3–30 in Harvey Whitehouse and Robert N. McCauley, eds., *Mind and Religion* (New York: AltaMira Press, 2005).

Boyer, Pascal, *Tradition as Truth and Communication: A Cognitive Description of Traditional Discourse* (Cambridge: Cambridge University Press, 1990).

Boyer, Pascal, "Explaining religious ideas: Elements of a cognitive approach" *Numen* 39/1 (1992): 27–57.

Boyer, Pascal, *The Naturalness of Religious Ideas: A Cognitive Theory of Religion* (Berkeley: University of California Press, 1994a).

Boyer, Pascal, "Pseudo-natural kinds," 121–141 in Boyer, ed., *Cognitive Aspects of Religious Symbolism* (Cambridge: Cambridge University Press, 1994b).

Boyer, Pascal, "Cognitive tracks of cultural inheritance: How evolved intuitive ontology governs cultural transmission" *American Anthropologist* 100/4 (1999): 876–889.

Boyer, Pascal, "Functional origins of religious concepts: Ontological and strategic selection in evolved minds" *Journal of the Royal Anthropological Institute* (N. S.) 6 (2000a): 195–214.

Boyer, Pascal, *Religion Explained: The Human Instincts That Fashion Gods, Spirits and Ancestors* (London: Vintage, 2002b).

Boyer, Pascal, "Why do gods and spirits matter at all?" 68–92 in I. Pyysiäinen and V. Antonnen, eds., *Current Approaches in the Cognitive Science of Religion* (New York: Continuum, 2002).

Boyer, Pascal, "Religious thought and behavior as by-products of brain function" *Trends in Cognitive Sciences* 7/3 (2003): 119–124.

Boyer, Pascal, *The Fracture of an Illusion: Science and the Dissolution of Religion* (Gottingen: Vandenhoeck & Ruprecht, 2010).

Bracken, Joseph, "Actions and agents: Natural and supernatural reconsidered" *Zygon* 48/4 (2013): 1001–1013.

Bruce, Steve, *Secularization: In Defense of an Unfashionable Theory* (Oxford: Oxford University Press, 2011).

Bulbulia, Joseph, "Religious costs as adaptations that signal altruistic intention" *Evolution and Cognition* 10/1 (2004): 19–42.

Bulbulia, Joseph "Are there any religions? An evolutionary exploration" *Method & Theory in the Study of Religion* 17 (2005): 71–100.

Bulbulia, Joseph, "Nature's medicine: Religiosity as an adaptation for health and cooperation," 87–122 in Patrick McNamara, ed., *Where God and Science Meet, Vol. I: Evolution, Genes and the Religious Brain* (London: Praeger, 2006).

Bulbulia, Joseph, Richard Sosis, Erica Harris, Russell Genet, Cheryl Genet and Karen Wyman, eds., *The Evolution of Religion: Studies, Theories & Critiques* (Santa Margarita, CA: Collins Foundation Press, 2008).

Bullivant, Stephen and Lois Lee, "Interdisciplinary studies of non-religion and secularity: The state of the union" *Journal of Contemporary Religion* 27/1 (2012): 19–27.

Burke, Brian L., Spee Kosloff and Mark J. Landau, "Death goes to the polls: A meta-analysis of mortality salience effects on political attitudes" *Political Psychology* 34/2 (2013): 183–200.

Burris, Christopher T., and Raluca Petican, "Hearts strangely warmed (and cooled): Emotional experience in religious and atheistic individuals" *The International Journal for the Psychology of Religion* 21 (2011): 183–197.

Cady, Linell E., and Elizabeth Shakman Hurd, eds., *Comparative Secularisms in a Global Age* (New York: Palgrave Macmillan, 2010).

Caldwell-Harris, Catherine L., "Understanding atheism/non-belief as an expected individual-differences variable" *Religion, Brain & Behavior* 2/1 (2012): 4–47.

Calhoun, Craig, Mark Jeurgensmeyer and Jonathan van Antwerpen, eds., *Rethinking Secularism* (Oxford: Oxford University Press, 2011).

Caputo, John D., and Gianni Vattimo, *After the Death of God*, ed. J. W. Robbins (New York: Columbia University Press, 2007).

Carneiro, Robert, *The Evolution of the Human Mind: From Supernaturalism to Naturalism* (Clinton Corners, NY: Eliot Werner, 2010).

Casebeer, William, *Natural Ethical Facts: Evolution, Connectionism and Moral Cognition* (Cambridge, MA: MIT Press, 2003).

Cavanaugh, William T., *The Myth of Religious Violence: Secular Ideology and the Roots of Modern Conflict* (Oxford: Oxford University Press, 2009).

Chiasson, Phyllis, "Abduction as an aspect of retroduction" *Semiotica* 153–1/4 (2005): 223–242.

Clarke, Steve, Russell Powell and Julian Savulescu, "Religion, intolerance and conflict: Practical implications for social policy," 266–272 in Clarke, et al., eds., *Religion, Intolerance, and Conflict* (Oxford: Oxford University Press, 2013).

Clooney, Francis X., S. J., *Hindu God, Christian God* (Oxford: Oxford University Press, 2001).

Clooney, Francis X., S. J., *Comparative Theology: Deep Learning across Religious Borders* (West Sussex, UK: Wiley-Blackwell, 2010).

Crockett, Clayton, ed., *Secular Theology: American Radical Theological Thought* (London: Routledge, 2001).

Crockett, Clayton, *Radical Political Theology: Religion and Politics after Liberalism* (New York: Columbia University Press, 2011).

Crockett, Clayton, and Jeffrey W. Robbins, *Religion, Politics and the Earth: The New Materialism* (New York: Palgrave Macmillan, 2012).

Czachesz, István, and Tamás Biró, *Changing Minds: Religion and Cognition through the Ages* (Leuven: Peeters, 2011).

D'Costa, Gavin, ed., *Christian Uniqueness Reconsidered: The Myth of a Pluralistic Theology of Religions* (Maryknoll, NY: Orbis, 1990).

D'Costa, Gavin, *Christianity and World Religions: Disputed Questions in the Theology of Religions* (West Sussex, UK: Wiley-Blackwell, 2009).

Danermark, Berth, Mats Ekstrom, Liselotte Jakobsen and Jan ch. Karlsson, *Explaining Society: Critical Realism in the Social Sciences* (London: Routledge, 2002).

Davaney, Sheila, *Pragmatic Historicism: A Theology for the Twenty-first Century* (Albany: State University of New York Press, 2000).

Dawes, Gregory W., and James Maclaurin, *A New Science of Religion* (New York: Routledge, 2013).

Dawkins, Richard, *The God Delusion* (London: Random House, 2006).

de Caro, Mario, and David MacArthur, eds., *Naturalism in Question* (Cambridge, MA: Harvard University Press, 2004).

de Caro, Mario, and David MacArthur, eds., *Naturalism and Normativity* (New York: Columbia University Press, 2010).

de Vries, Hent, "Introduction," 1–88 in Hent de Vries and Lawrence E. Sullivan, eds., *Political Theologies: Public Religions in a Post-secular World* (New York: Fordham University Press, 2006).

de Waal, Frans, *The Bonobo and the Atheist: In Search of Humanism among the Primates* (New York: Norton & Norton, 2013).

Deleuze, Gilles, *The Logic of Sense*, trans. Mark Lester (New York: Continuum, 2004).

Dennett, Daniel, *The Intentional Stance* (Cambridge: MIT Press, 1987).

Dennett, Daniel, *Breaking the Spell* (New York: Penguin, 2006).

Diamond, Jared, *Collapse: How Societies Choose to Fail or Succeed* (New York: Penguin, 2011).

Diamond, Jared, *The World until Yesterday: What Can We Learn from Traditional Societies?* (New York: Viking, 2012).

Dickie, Jane R., Lindsey V. Ajega, Joy R. Kobylak and Kathryn M. Nixon, "Mother, father, and self: Sources of young adults' God concepts" *Journal for the Scientific Study of Religion* 45/1 (2006): 57–71.

Douglas, Mary, *Purity and Danger* (London: Routledge, 2002).

Durkheim, Emile, *The Elementary Forms of Religious Life*, trans. J. W. Swain (New York: Free Press, 1965).

Dworkin, Ronald, *Religion without God* (Cambridge, MA: Harvard University Press, 2013).

Flanagan, Owen, "Varieties of naturalism," 430–452 in Philip Clayton, ed., *Oxford Handbook of Religion and Science* (Oxford: Oxford University Press, 2006).

Flanagan, Owen, *The Really Hard Problem: Meaning in a Material World* (Cambridge, MA: MIT Press, 2007).

Frey, Ulrich, "Cognitive foundations of religiosity," 229–241 in Voland and Schiefenhovel, eds., *The Biological Evolution of Religious Mind and Behavior* (Heidelberg: Springer, 2009).

Feuerbach, Ludwig, *The Essence of Christianity*, trans. George Eliot (Amherst, NY: Prometheus, 1989 [German 1841]).

Fischer, Ronald, Rohan Callander, Paul Reddish and Joseph Bulbulia, "How do rituals affect cooperation? An experimental field study comparing nine ritual types" *Human Nature* 24 (2013): 115–125.

Fletcher, Jeannine Hill, *Monopoly on Salvation? A Feminist Approach to Religious Pluralism* (New York: Continuum, 2005).

Fox, Jonathan, and Shmuel Sandler, *Bringing Religion into International Relations* (New York: Palgrave Macmillan, 2004).

Friedman, Edwin H., *Generation to Generation: Family Process in Church and Synagogue* (New York: Guildford Press, 2011).

Ganzach, Yoav, and Chemi Gotlibovski, "Intelligence and religiosity: Within families and over time" *Intelligence* 41 (2013): 546–552.

Geertz, Armin W., and Jeppe Sinding Jensen, *Religious Narrative, Cognition and Culture: Image and Word in the Mind of Narrative* (Sheffield, UK: Equinox, 2011).

Geertz, Armin W., and Gudmundur Ingi Markusson, "Religion is natural, atheism is not: On why everybody is both right and wrong" *Religion* 40 (2010): 152–165.

Gervais, Will M., "Finding the faithless: Perceived atheist prevalence reduces anti-atheist prejudice" *Personalithy and Social Psychology Bulletin* 37/4 (2011): 543–556.

Gervais, Will M., Azim F. Shariff and Ara Norenzayan, "Do you believe in atheists? Distrust is central to anti-atheist prejudice" *Journal of Personality and Social Psychology* 101/6 (2011): 1189–1206.

Gervais, Will M., Aiyana K. Willard, Ara Norenzayan and Joseph Henrich, "The cultural transmission of faith: Why innate intuitions are necessary, but insufficient, to explain religious belief" *Religion* 41/3 (2011): 389–410.

Gervais, Will M., and Ara Norenzayan, "Like a camera in the sky? Thinking about God increases public self-awareness and socially desirable responding" *Journal of Experimental Social Psychology* 48 (2012): 298–302.

Gervais, Will M., and Ara Norenzayan, "Analytic thinking promotes religious disbelief" *Science* 336 (2012): 493–496.

Gervais Will M., and Ara Norenzayan, "Reminders of secular authority reduce believer's distrust of atheists" *Psychological Science* 23/5 (2012): 483–491.

Ginges, J., I. Hansen and A. Norenzayan, "Religious and popular support for suicide attacks" *Psychological Science* 20 (2009): 224–230.

Girard, Rene, *Violence and the Sacred*, trans. P. Gregory (Baltimore, MD: Johns Hopkins, 1977).

Girard, Rene, *The Scapegoat*, trans. Y. Freccero (Baltimore, MD: Johns Hopkins, 1986).

Graham, Jesse, and Jonathan Haidt, "Beyond beliefs: Religions bind individuals into moral communities" *Personality and Social Psychology Review* 14/1 (2010): 140–150.

Granqvist, Pehr, "Attachment and religiosity in adolescence: Cross-sectional and longitudinal evaluations" *Personality and Social Psychology Bulletin* 28 (2002): 260–270.

Granqvist, Pehr, "Attachment theory and religious conversions: A review and a resolution of the classical and contemporary paradigm chasm" *Review of Religious Research* 45 (2003): 172–187.

Granqvist, Pehr, "Religion as a by-product of evolved psychology: The case of attachment and implications for brain and religion research, " 105–150 in P. McNamara, ed., *Where God and Science Meet, vol II, The Neurology of Religious Experience* (London: Praeger, 2006).

Granqvist, Pehr, and B. Hageskull, "Seeking security in the new age: On attachment and emotional compensation" *Journal for the Scientific Study of Religion* 40 (2001): 529–547.

Granqvist, Pehr, T. Ivarsson, A. G. Broberg and B. Hagekull, "Examining relations among attachment, religiosity and NewAge spirituality using the Adult Attachment Interview" *Developmental Psychology* 43/3 (2007): 590–601.

Granqvist, Pehr, M. Mikulincer and P. R. Shaver, "Religion as attachment: Normative processes and individual differences" *Personality and Social Psychology Review* 14/1 (2010): 49–59).

Granqvist, Pehr, M. Mikulincer, V. Gewirtz and P. R. Shaver, "Experimental findings of God as an attachment figure: Normative processes and moderating effects of internal working models" *Journal of Personality and Social Psychology* 103/5 (2012): 804–818.

Greene, Joshua, *Moral Tribes: Emotion, Reason, and the Gap between Us and Them* (New York: Penguin Press, 2013).

Griffin, David Ray, *Deep Religious Pluralism* (Louisville, KY: Westminster John Knox, 2005).

Guthrie, Stewart, "A cognitive theory of religion" *Current Anthropology* 21/2 (1980): 181–203.

Guthrie, Stewart, *Faces in the Clouds: A New Theory of Religion* (Oxford: Oxford University Press, 1993).

Guthrie, Stewart, "Animal animism: Evolutionary roots of religious cognition," 38–67 in I. Pyysiäinen and V. Anttonen, eds., *Current Approaches in the Cognitive Science of Religion* (New York: Continuum, 2002).

Guthrie, Stewart, "Anthropology and anthropomorphism in religion," 37–62 in Harvey Whitehouse and James Laidlaw, eds., *Religion, Anthropology and Cognitive Science* (Durham, NC: Carolina Academic Press, 2007).

Gutkowski, Stacey, "The British Secular *habitus* and the War on Terror" *Journal of Contemporary Religion* 27/1 (2012): 87–103.

Habermas, Jürgen, *Religion and Rationality: Essays on Reason, God and Modernity* (Cambridge, MA: MIT Press, 2002).

Habermas, Jürgen, *Between Naturalism and Religion*, trans. C. Cronin (Malden, MA: Polity, 2008).

Habermas, Jürgen, Norbert Brieskorn, Michael Reder, Friedo Ricken and Josef Schmidt, *An Awareness of What Is Missing: Faith and Reason in a Post-secular Age*, trans C. Cronin (Malden, MA: Polity, 2010).

Haidt, Jonathan, "The new synthesis in moral psychology" *Science* 316 (2007): 998–1002.

Haidt, Jonathan, *The Righteous Mind: Why Good People Are Divided by Politics and Religion* (New York: Pantheon, 2012).

Harris, Sam, *The Moral Landscape* (New York: Free Press, 2010).

Haselton, M. G., D. Nettle and P. W. Andrews, "The evolution of cognitive bias," 724–746 in David M. Buss, ed., *The Handbook of Evolutionary Psychology* (Hoboken, NJ: Wiley and Sons, 2005).

Hauser, Marc, *Moral Minds: The Nature of Right and Wrong* (New York: HarperCollins, 2006).

Hawking, Stephen, *A Brief History of Time* (New York: Bantam, 1988).

Heiden Rootes, Katie M., Peter J. Jankowski and Steven J. Sandage, "Bowen family systems theory and spirituality: Exploring the relationship between triangulation and religious questing" *Contemporary Family Therapy* 32 (2010): 89–101.

Heim, Mark, *Salvations: Truth and Difference in Religion* (Maryknoll, NY: Orbis, 1995).

Heim, Mark, *The Depth of Riches: A Trinitarian Theology of Religious Ends* (Grand Rapids, MI: Eerdmans, 2001).

Henderson, Bobby, *The Gospel of the Flying Spaghetti Monster* (New York: Random House, 2006).

Henrich, Joseph, "The evolution of costly displays, cooperation and religion: Credibility enhancing displays and their implications for cultural evolution" *Evolution and Human Behavior* 30 (2009): 244–260.

Henrich, Natalie and Joseph Henrich, *Why Humans Cooperate: A Cultural and Evolutionary Explanation* (Oxford: Oxford University Press, 2007).

Hick, John, "The non-absoluteness of Christianity," 16–36 in Hick and Knitter, eds., *The Myth of Christian Uniqueness* (Maryknoll, NY: Orbis, 1987).

Hick, John, *An Interpretation of Religion: Human Responses to the Transcendent*, second edition (New Haven, CT: Yale University Press, 2004).

Hick, John, "The next step beyond dialogue," 3–12 in Paul Knitter, ed., *The Myth of Religious Superiority* (Maryknoll, NY: Orbis, 2005).

Hick, John, and Paul Knitter, eds. *The Myth of Christian Uniqueness: Toward a Pluralistic Theology of Religions* (Maryknoll, NY: Orbis, 1987).

Hodge, Charles. *Systematic Theology*, three volumes (Grand Rapids, MI: Eerdmans, 1981 [Orig. 1871]).

Hollerich, Michael, "Carl Schmitt," 107–122 in Peter Scott and William T. Cavanaugh, eds., *The Blackwell Companion to Political Theology* (Oxford: Blackwell, 2004).

Holyoake, George J., *English Secularism* (Chicago, IL: Open Court, 1896).

Hood, Bruce M., *The Science of Superstition: How the Developing Brain Creates Supernatural Beliefs* (New York: HarperOne, 2009).

Hornbeck, Ryan G., and Justin L. Barrett, "Refining and testing 'Counterintuitiveness' in virtual reality: Cross-cultural evidence for recall of counterintuitive representations" *The International Journal for the Psychology of Religion* 23 (2013): 15–28.

Indinopulos, Thomas A., Brian C. Wilson and James C. Hanges, eds., *Comparing Religions: Possibilities and Perils?* (Leiden: Brill, 2006).

Jankowski, Peter J., and Marsha Vaughn, "Differentiation of self and spirituality: Empirical explorations" *Counseling and Values* 53 (2009): 82–96.

Jankowski, Peter, and Steven J. Sandage, "Spiritual dwelling and well-being: The mediating role of differentiation of self in a sample of distressed adults" *Mental Health, Religion & Culture* 15/4 (2012): 417–434.

Janowitz, Naomi, "Inventing the scapegoat: Theories of sacrifice and ritual" *Journal of Ritual Studies* 25/1 (2011): 15–24.

Jaspers, Karl, *The Origin and Goal of History* (London: Routledge and Kegan Paul, 1953).

Jay, Nancy, *Throughout Your Generations Forever: Sacrifice, Religion and Paternity* (Chicago, IL: University of Chicago Press, 1992).

Jenkins, Steve M., Walter C. Buboltz, Jr., Jonathan P. Schartz and Patrick Johnson, "Differentiation of self and psychosocial development" *Contemporary Family Therapy* 27/2 (2005): 251–261.

Jensen, Jeppe Sinding, "Normative cognition in culture and religion" *Journal for the Cognitive Science of Religion* 1/1 (2013): 47–70.

Johnson, Dominic D. P., and Zoey Reeve, "The virtues of intolerance: Is religion an adaptation for war?" 67–87 in Clarke, Powelle and Savulescu, eds., *Religion, Intolerance, and Conflict: A Scientific and Conceptual Investigation* (Oxford: Oxford University Press, 2013).

Johnson, Dominic, "What are atheists for? Hypotheses on the functions of non-belief in the evolution of religion" *Religion, Brain & Behavior* 2/1 (2012): 48–99.

Johnston, Douglas, and Cynthia Sampson, eds., *Religion: The Missing Dimension of Statecraft* (Oxford: Oxford University Press, 1994).

Johnston, Douglas, and Brian Cox, "Faith-based diplomacy and preventive engagement," 11–29 in Douglas Johnston, ed., *Faith-Based Diplomacy: Trumping Realpolitik* (Oxford: Oxford University Press, 2003).

Jones, James W., *Contemporary Psychoanalysis and Religion: Transference and Transcendence* (New Haven, CT: Yale University Press, 1991).

Jones, James W., *Terror and Transformation: The Ambiguity of Religion in Psychoanalytic Perspective* (New York: Taylor & Francis, 2002).

Jones, James W., *Blood That Cries out from the Earth: The Psychology of Religious Terrorism* (Oxford: Oxford University Press, 2008).

Juergensmeyer, Mark, *Terror in the Mind of God*, third edition (Berkeley: University of California Press, 2003).

Kay, A.C., D. Guacher, L. Napier, M.J. Callan and K. Laurin "God and the Government: Testing a compensatory control mechanism for the support of external systems" *Journal of Personality and Social Psychology* 95 (2008): 18–35.

Kelemen, Deborah, "Why are rocks pointy? Children's preference for teleological explanations of the natural world" *Developmental Psychology* 35 (1999): 1440–1452.

Kerr, Michael, and Murray Bowen, *Family Evaluation: An Approach Based on Bowen Theory* (New York: W.W. Norton, 1988).

Kirkpatrick, Lee A., *Attachment, Evolution and the Psychology of Religion* (New York: The Guilford Press, 2005).

Kirkpatrick, Lee A., "An attachment-theory approach to the psychology of religion" *The International Journal for the Psychology of Religion* 2 (1992): 3–28.

Kirkpatrick, Lee A., and Phillip R. Shaver, "Attachment theory and religion: Childhood attachments, religious beliefs and conversion" *Journal for the Scientific Study of Religion* 29/3 (1990): 315–334.

Kirkpatrick, Lee A., and Wade C. Rowatt, "Two dimensions of attachment to God an their relation to affect, religiosity and personality constructs" *Journal for the Scientific Study of Religion* 41/4 (2002): 637–651.

Knitter, Paul, ed., *The Myth of Religious Superiority: A Multifaith Exploration* (Maryknoll, NY: Orbis, 2005).

Knitter, Paul, *One Earth, Many Religions* (Maryknoll, NY: Orbis, 1995).

Knitter, Paul, *Jesus and the Other Names: Christian Mission and Global Responsibility* (Maryknoll, NY: Orbis, 1996).

Kuru, Ahmet T., *Secularism and State Policies toward Religion: The United States, France and Turkey* (New York; Cambridge University Press, 2009).

Lakoff, George, *The Political Mind: A Cognitive Scientist's Guide to Your Brain and Its Politics* (New York: Penguin; 2009).

Lanman, Jonathan A, "The importance of religious displays for belief acquisition and secularization" *Journal of Contemporary Religion* 27/1 (2012): 49–65.

Lawson, E. Thomas and Robert N. McCauley, *Rethinking Religion: Connecting Cognition and Culture* (Cambridge: Cambridge University Press, 1990).

Lawson, E. Thomas and Robert N. McCauley, "The cognitive representation of religious ritual form: A theory of participants' competence with religious ritual systems," 153–176 in I. Pyysiäinen and V. Anttonen, eds., *Current Approaches in the Cognitive Science of Religion* (New York: Continuum, 2002).

Lederach, John Paul, *Preparing for Peace: Conflict Transformation across Cultures* (Syracuse, NY: Syracuse University Press, 1995).

Lederach, John Paul, *Building Peace: Sustainable Reconciliation in Divided Societies* (Washington, DC: United States Institute of Peace Press, 1997).

Lederach, John Paul, *The Moral Imagination: The Art and Soul of Building Peace* (Oxford: Oxford University Press, 2005).

Leech, David, and Aku Visala, "The cognitive science of religion: Implications for theism?" *Zygon* 46/1 (2011): 47–64.

Legare, Cristine H., and Andre L. Souza, "Evaluating ritual efficacy: Evidence from the supernatural" *Cognition* 124 (2012): 1–15.

Lieberg, Godo, "Die 'theologia tripertita' in Fosrchung und Bezeugung," 63–115 in Hildegard Temporini, ed., *Augstieg und Niedergang der Römischen Welt*, vol. I.4 (Berlin: Walter de Gruyter, 1973).

Lewis-Williams, David, "The thin red line: Southern San notion and rock paintings of supernatural potency" *The South African Archaeological Bulletin* 36 (1981): 5–13.

Lewis-Williams, David, "Seeing and construing: The making and 'meaning' of a southern African rock art motif" *Cambridge Archaeological Journal* 5/1 (1995): 3–23.

Lewis-Williams, David, *A Cosmos in Stone: Interpreting Religion and Society through Rock Art* (Oxford: AltaMira Press, 2002).

Lewis-Williams, David, *The Mind in the Cave: Consciousness and the Origins of Art* (New York: Thames & Hudson, 2002).

Lewis-Williams, David, *Conceiving God: The Cognitive Origin and Evolution of Religion* (London: Thames & Hudson, 2010).

Lewis-Williams, David, and David Peirce, *San Spirituality: Roots, Expression and Social Consequences* (Oxford: AltaMira Press, 2004).

Lewis-Williams, David, and David Pearce, *Inside the Neolithic Mind* (London: Thames & Hudson, 2005).

Little, David, and Scott Appleby, "A moment of opportunity? The promise of religious peacebuilding in an era of religious and ethnic conflict," 1–23 in Harold Coward and Gordon S. Smith, eds., *Religion and Peacebuilding* (Albany, NY: State University of New York Press, 2004).

Little, David, ed., *Peacemakers in Action: Profiles of Religion in Conflict Resolution* (New York: Cambridge University Press, 2007).

Malhotra, D., "(When) Are religious people nicer? Religious salience and the 'Sunday Effect' on prosocial behavior" *Judgment and Decision Making* 5 (2008): 138–143.

McCauley, Robert N., *Why Religion Is Natural and Science Is Not* (Oxford: Oxford University Press, 2011).

McCauley, Robert N., "Explanatory pluralism and the cognitive science of religion: Why scholars in religious studies should stop worrying about reductionism," 11–32 in Dimitris Xygalatas and William W. McCorkle Jr., eds., *Mental Culture* (Durham, UK: Acumen, 2013).

McCauley, Robert N., and E. Thomas Lawson, *Bringing Ritual to Mind: Psychological Foundations of Cultural Forms* (Cambridge: Cambridge University Press, 2002).

McGregor, Holly A., Jeff Greenberg, Jamie Arndt, Joel Lieberman, Sheldon Solomon, Linda Simon and Tom Pyszczynski, "Terror management and aggression: Evidence that mortality salience motivates aggression against worldview-threatening others" *Journal of Personality and Social Psychology* 74/3 (1998): 590–605.

McGregor, Ian, Mike Prentice and Kyle Nash, "Approaching relief: Compensatory ideals relieve threat-induced anxiety by promoting approach-motivated states" *Social Cognition* 30/6 (2012): 689–714.

McGregro, Ian, Kyle Nash and Mike Prentice, "Reactive approach motivation (RAM) for religion" *Journal of Personality and Social Psychology* 99/1 (2010): 148–161.

McNamara, Patrick, *The Neuroscience of Religious Experience* (Cambridge: Cambridge University Press, 2009).

Mikulincer, Mario, and Phillip R. Shaver, "Attachment theory and intergroup bias: Evidence that priming secure base schema attenuates negative reactions to out-groups" *Journal of Personality and Social Psychology* 81/1 (2001): 97–115.

Mikulincer, Mario, and Phillip R. Shaver, *Attachment in Adulthood: Structure, Dynamics, and Change* (New York: The Guilford Press, 2007).

Milbank, John, "A closer walk on the wild side," 54–82 in Michael Warner, Jonathan Vanantwerpen and Craig Calhoun., eds., *Varieties of Secularism in a Secular Age* (Cambridge, MA: Harvard University Press, 2010).

Milbank, John, *Theology and Social Theory:* (Oxford: Blackwell, 1990).

Mithen, Steven, *The Prehistory of the Mind: The Cognitive Origins of Art, Religion and Science* (New York: Thames and Hudson, 1996).

Monsma, Stephen V., and J. Christopher Soper, eds., *The Challenge of Pluralism: Church and State in Five Democracies*, second edition (Lanham, MD: Rowman & Littlefield, 2009).

Mullins, David A., Harvey Whitehouse and Quentin D. Atkinson, "The role of writing and recordkeeping in the cultural evolution of human cooperation" *Journal of Economic Behavior & Organization* (2013): S141–S151.

Murray, Michael J., "Scientific explanations of religion and the justification of religious belief," 168–178, in Jeffrey Schloss and Michael J. Murray, eds., *The Believing Primate* (Oxford: Oxford University Press, 2009).

Murray, Michael J., and Andrew Goldberg, "Evolutionary accounts of religion: Explaining and explaining away," 179–199 in Jeffrey Schloss and Michael J. Murray, eds., *The Believing Primate* (Oxford: Oxford University Press, 2009).

Neville, Robert C., ed., *Ultimate Realities* (Albany: State University of New York Press, 2001).

Neville, Robert C., *The Truth of Broken Symbols* (Albany: State University of New York Press, 2006).

Nicholson, Hugh, "The reunification of theology and comparison in the new comparative theology" *Journal of the Academic Academy of Religion* 77/3 (2009): 609–646.

Nietzsche, Friedrich, *The Gay Science*, trans. J. Naukhoff (Cambridge: Cambridge University Press, 2001).

Nietzsche, Friedrich, *Thus Spake Zarathustra*, trans. Adrian Del Caro (Cambridge: Cambridge University Press, 2006).

Nietzsche, Friedrich, *The Birth of Tragedy*, trans. R. Speirs (Cambridge: Cambridge University Press, 1999).

Nietzsche, Friedrich, *On the Genealogy of Morals*, trans. W. Kaufmann (New York: Vintage, 1989).

Nietzsche, Friedrich, *Beyond Good and Evil*, trans. Judith Norman (Cambridge: Cambridge University Press, 2002).

Norenzayan, Ara, *Big Gods: How Religion Transformed Cooperation and Conflict* (Princeton, NJ: Princeton University Press, 2013).

Norenzayan, Ara, and Azim F. Sharif, "The origin and evolution of religious prosociality" *Science* 322 (2008), 58–62.

Norenzayan, Ara, and Ian G. Hansen, "Belief in supernatural agents in the face of death" *Personality and Social Psychology Bulletin* 32/2 (2006): 174–187.

Norenzayan, Ara, Scott Atran, Jason Faulkner and Mark Schaller, "Memory and mystery: The cultural selection of minimally counterintuitive narratives" *Cognitive Science* 30 (2006): 531–553.

Norenzayan, Ara, and Will M. Gervais, "The origins of religious disbelief" *Trends in Cognitive Sciences* 17/1 (2013): 20–25.

Norenzayan, Ara, and Scott Atran, "Cognitive and emotional process in the cultural transmission of natural and nonnatural beliefs," 149–169 in M. Schaller and C. S. Crandall, eds., *The Psychological Foundations of Culture* (Mahwah, NJ: Lawrence Erlbaum Publishers, 2004).

Norris, Pippa, and Ronald Inglehart, *Sacred and Secular: Religion and Politics Worldwide* (Cambridge: Cambridge University Press, 2004).

Pannenberg, Wolfhart, *Theology and the Philosophy of Science*, trans. F. McDonagh (Philadelphia, PA: Westminster Press, 1976).

Papero, Daniel V., *Bowen Family Systems Theory* (Boston, MA: Simon & Schuster, 1990).

Peirce, Charles, *The Essential Peirce: Selected Philosophical Writings*, ed. by the Peirce Edition Project, volume 2 (Bloomington: Indiana University Press, 1998).

Peirce, Charles, *Collected Papers*, five volumes (Cambridge: Harvard University Press, 1974).

Pennycook, Gordon, James A. Cheyne, Paul Seli, Derek J. Koehler and Jonathan A. Fugelsang, "Analytic cognitive style predicts religious and paranormal belief" *Cognition* 123 (2012): 335–346.

Pennycook, Gordon, James A. Cheyne, Derek J. Koehler and Jonathan A. Fugelsang, "Belief bias during reasoning among religious believers and skeptics" *Psychonomic Bulletin Review* 20 (2013): 806–811.

Persinger, M. A., "Are our brains structured to avoid refutations of belief in God? An experimental study" *Religion* 39 (2009): 34–42.

Peterson, Gregory R., "Are evolutionary/cognitive theories of religion relevant for philosophy of religion?" *Zygon* 45/3 (2010): 545–557.

Petito, Fabio, and Pavlos Hatzopoulos, eds, *Religion in International Relations: The Return from Exile* (New York: Palgrave Macmillan, 2003).

Plantinga, Alvin, *God and Other Minds* (Ithaca, NY: Cornell University Press, 1990).

Plantinga, Alvin, "Games scientists play," 139–167 in Schloss and Murray, eds., *The Believing Primate* (Oxford: Oxford University Press, 2009).

Powell, Russell, and Steve Clarke, "Religion, tolerance, and intolerance: Views from across the disciplines," 1–35 in Clarke, Powell and Savulescu, eds., *Religion, Intolerance, and Conflict* (Oxford: Oxford University Press, 2013).

Purzycki, Benjamin G., "The minds of gods: A comparative study of supernatural agency" *Cognition* 129 (2013): 163–179.

Purzycki, Benjamin G., Daniel N. Finkel, John Shaver, Nathan Wales, Adam B. Cohen and Richard Sosis, "What does God know? Supernatural agents' access to socially strategic and non-strategic information" *Cognitive Science* 36 (2012): 846–869.

Pyszczynski, Tom, Sheldon Solomon and Jeff Greenberg, *In the Wake of 9/11: The Psychology of Terror* (Washington, DC: American Psychological Association, 2002).

Pyysiäinen, Ilkka, *How Religion Works: Towards a New Cognitive Science of Religion* (Leiden: Brill, 2003).

Pyysiäinen, Ilkka, *Magic, Miracles and Religion: A Scientist's Perspective* (Oxford: AltaMira Press, 2004).

Pyysiäinen, Ilkka, *Supernatural Agents: Why People Believe in Souls, Gods, and Buddhas* (Oxford: Oxford University Press, 2009).

Pyysiäinen, Ilkka, "Reduction and explanatory pluralism in the cognitive science of religion," 15–29 in Czachesz, István and Tamás Bíró, *Changing Minds: Religion and Cognition through the Ages* (Leuven: Peeters, 2011).

Pyysiäinen, Ilkka, "Putting cognition and culture back together again: Religion in mind and society" *Method and Theory in the Study of Religion* 24 (2012): 29–50.

Quack, Johannes, "Organized atheism in India: An overview" *Journal of Contemporary Religion* 27/1 (2012): 67–85.

Rappaport, Roy, *Ritual and Religion in the Making of Humanity* (Cambridge: Cambridge University Press, 1999).

Raschke, Carl A., "A-Dieu to Jacques Derrida: Descartes' ghost, or the Holy Spirit in secular theology," 37–50 in Crockett, ed., *Secular Theology* (London: Routledge, 2001).

Rawls, John, *Political Liberalism* (New York: Columbia University Press, 1996).

Rawls, John, "The idea of public reason revisited" *The University of Chicago Law Review* 64/3 (Summer 1997), 765–807.

Rawls, John, *Justice as Fairness: A Restatement* (Cambridge, MA: Harvard University Press, 2001).

Razmyar, Soroush, and Charlie L. Reeve, "Individual differences in religiosity as a function of cognitive ability and cognitive style" *Intelligence* 41 (2013): 667–673.

Reddish, Paul, Ronald Fischer and Joseph Bulbulia, "Let's dance together: Synchrony, shared intentionality and cooperation" *PLoS ONE 8/8* (August 2013): 1–13.

Riesebrodt, Martin, *The Promise of Salvation: A Theory of Religion*, trans. S. Rendall (Chicago, IL: University of Chicago Press, 2010).

Rholes, W. Steven and Jeffry A. Simpson, *Adult Attachment: Theory, Research, and Clinical Implications* (New York: Guilford Press, 2004).

Rifkin, Jeremy, *The Empathic Civilization: The Race to Global Consciousness in a World in Crisis* (New York: Tarcher/Penguin, 2009).

Rizutto, Anne, *The Birth of the Living God* (Chicago, IL: University of Chicago Press, 1981).

Rom, Eldad, and Mario Mikulincer, "Attachment theory and group processes: The association between attachment style and group-related representations, goals, memories and functioning" *Journal of Personality and Social Psychology* 84/6 (2003) 1220–1235.

Ross, Thomas, "Attachment and religious beliefs—Attachment styles in evangelical Christians" *Journal of Religion and Health* 46/1 (March 2007): 75–84.

Rossano, Matt, *Supernatural Selection: How Religion Evolved* (Oxford: Oxford University Press, 2010).

Rue, Loyal, *Religion Is Not about God* (New Brunswick, NJ: Rutgers University Press, 2005).

Sacks, Jonathan, *The Dignity of Difference: How to Avoid the Clash of Civilizations* (London: Continuum, 2002).

Saslow, L.R., R. Willer, M. Feinberg, P.K. Piff, K. Clark, D. Keltner and S.R. Saturn, "My brother's keeper? Compassion predicts generosity more among less religious individuals" *Social Psychology and Personality Science* 4 (2013): 31–38.

Schaller, Mark, Ara Norenzayan, Steven J. Heine, Toshio Yamagishi and Tatsuya Kameda, eds., *Evolution, Culture and the Human Mind* (New York: Psychology Press, 2010).

Schindler, Simon, Marc-Andre Reinhard and Dagmar Stahlberg, "Mortality salience increases personal relevance of the norm of reciprocity" *Psychological Reports* 111/2 (2012): 563–574.

Schloss, Jeffrey, and Michael J. Murray, eds., *The Believing Primate: Scientific, Philosophical and Theological Reflections on the Origin of Religion* (Oxford: Oxford University Press, 2009).

Schmidt-Leukel, Perry, "Exclusivism, inclusivism, pluralism: The tripolar typology—Clarified and reaffirmed," 13–27 in Paul Knitter, ed., *The Myth of Religious Superiority* (Maryknoll, NY: Orbis, 2005).

Schmitt, Carl, *Political Theology: Four Chapters on the Concept of Sovereignty*, trans. George Schwab (Cambridge, MA: The MIT Press, 1985 [German 1922, 1934]).

Schulkin, Jay, *Cognitive Adaptation: A Pragmatist Perspective* (Cambridge: Cambridge University Press, 2008).

Scott, Peter, and William T. Cavanaugh, eds., *The Blackwell Companion to Political Theology* (Oxford: Blackwell Publishing, 2004).

Shariff, Azim, and Ara Norenzayan, "Mean gods make good people: Different views of God predict cheating behavior" *The International Journal for the Psychology of Religion* 21 (2011): 85–96.

Shenhav, Amitai, David G. Rand and Joshua D. Greene, "Divine intuition: cognitive style influences belief in God" *Journal of Experimental Psychology* 141/3 (2012): 423–428.

Shennan, Stephen, *Genes, Memes and Human History: Darwinian Archaeology and Cultural Evolution* (London: Thames & Hudson, 2002).

Shermer, Michael, *The Believing Brain: From Ghosts and Gods to Politics and Conspiracies—How We Construct Beliefs and Reinforce Them as Truths* (New York: Henry Holt & Co., 2011).

Shults, F. LeRon, "Transforming religious plurality: Anxiety and differentiation in religious families of origin" *Studies in Interreligious Dialogue* 20/2 (2010): 148–169.

Shults, F. LeRon, "Bearing gods in cognition and culture" *Religion, Brain & Behavior* 1/2 (2011): 154–167.

Shults, F. LeRon, "Empathically reading the texts of religious others," 179–195 in Jens Braarvig and Årstein Justnes, eds., *Hellige Skrifter I Verdens-Religionene* (Kristiansand, Norway: Norwegian Academic Press, 2011).

Shults, F. LeRon, "The problem of good (and evil): Arguing about axiological conditions in science and religion," 39–68 in Wildman, Wesley and Patrick McNamara, eds., *Science and the World's Religions, Volume I: Origins and Destinies* (New York: Praeger, 2012a).

Shults, F. LeRon, "Science and religious supremacy: Toward a naturalist theology of religions," 73–100, in Wildman and McNamara, eds., *Science and the World's Religions, Volume III: Religions and Controversies* (New York: Praeger, 2012b);

Shults, F. LeRon, "Wising up: The evolution of natural theology" *Zygon* 47/3 (2012c): 542–548.

Shults, F. LeRon, *Iconoclastic Theology: Gilles Deleuze and the Secretion of Atheism* (Edinburgh: Edinburgh University Press, 2014a).

Shults, F. LeRon, "Excavating theogonies: Anthropomorphic promiscuity and sociographic prudery in the Neolithic and Now," in Ian Hodder, ed., *Vital Matters: Religion in the Neolithic* (Cambridge: Cambridge University Press, 2014b).

Shults, F. LeRon, "Theology after Pandora: The real scandal of the evangelical mind (and culture)" in Derek J. Tidball, Brian S. Harris and Jason S. Sexton, eds., *Essays in Honor of Stanley Grenz* (Eugene, OR: Wipf & Stock, 2014c).

Sinnott-Armstrong, Walter, ed., *Moral Psychology: The Evolution of Morality—Adaptations and Innateness* (Cambridge: MIT Press, 2008).

Skowron, Elizabeth, "Differentiation of self, personal adjustment, problem solving, and ethnic group belonging among persons of color" *Journal of Counseling & Development* 82 (2004): 447–456.

Skowron, Elizabeth, and Anna Dendy, "Differentiation of self and attachment in adulthood: Relational correlates of effortful control" *Contemporary Family Therapy* 26/3 (2004): 337–357.

Skowron, Elizabeth, Krystal L. Stanley and Michael D. Shapiro, "A longitudinal perspective on differentiation of self, interpersonal and psychological well-being in young adulthood" *Contemporary Family Therapy* 31 (2009): 3–18.

Slingerland, Edward, "Who's afraid of reductionism? The study of religion in the age of cognitive science" *Journal of the American Academy of Religion* 76/2 (2008): 375–411.

Slone, D. Jason, *Theological Incorrectness: Why Religious People Believe What They Shouldn't* (Oxford: Oxford University Press, 2004).

Smith, Jonathan Z., *Imagining Religion* (Chicago, IL: University of Chicago Press, 1982).

Smith, Jonathan Z., "The domestication of sacrifice," 191–235 in R. G. Hamerton-Kelly, ed. *Violent Origins: Walter Burkert, Rene Girard, and Jonathan Z. Smith on Ritual Killing and Cultural Formation* (Stanford, CA; Stanford University Press, 1987).

Smith, Jonathan Z., *Relating Religion: Essays on the Study of Religion* (Chicago, IL: University of Chicago Press, 2004).

Sober, Elliot, and David Sloan Wilson, *Unto Others: The Evolution and Psychology of Unselfish Behavior* (Cambridge: Harvard University Press, 1998).

Soler, Monserrat, "Costly signaling, ritual and cooperation: Evidence from Candomble, an Afro-Brazilian religion" *Evolution and Human Behavior* 33 (2012): 346–356.

Sosis, Richard, "Religion and intragroup cooperation: Preliminary results of a comparative analysis of utopian communities" *Cross-Cultural Research* 34/1 (2000): 70–87.

Sosis, Richard, "Why aren't we all Hutterites? Costly signaling theory and religious behavior" *Human Nature* 14/2 (2002): 91–127.

Sosis, Richard, "Religious behaviors, badges and bans: Signaling theory and the evolution of religion," 61–86 in McNamara, ed., *Where God and Science Meet, Vol. I* (London: Praeger, 2006).

Sosis, Richard, and Candace Alcorta, "Signaling, solidarity and the sacred: The evolution of religious behavior" *Evolutionary Anthropology* 12 (2003): 264–274.

Sosis, Richard, and Eric Bressler, "Cooperation and commune longevity: A test of the costly signaling theory of religion" *Cross-Cultural Research* 37/2 (2003): 211–239.

Sosis, Richard, and Joseph Bulbulia, "The behavioral ecology of religion: The benefits and costs of one evolutionary approach" *Religion* 41/3 (2011): 341–362.

Sperber, Dan, and Deirdre Wilson, *Relevance: Communication and Cognition*, second edition (Oxford: Blackwell, 1995).

Sørensen, Jesper, "Acts that work: A cognitive approach to ritual agency" *Method and Theory in the Study of Religion* 19 (2007): 281–300.

Taubman-Ben-Ari, Orit, Liora Findler and Mario Mikulincer, "The effects of mortality salience on relationship striving and beliefs: The moderating role of attachment style" *British Journal of Social Psychology* 41 (2002): 419–441.

Taves, Ann, *Religious Experience Reconsidered* (Princeton, NJ: Princeton University Press, 2009).

Taylor, Charles, *A Secular Age* (Cambridge, MA: Harvard University Press, 2007).

Teehan, John, *In the Name of God: The Evolution of Religious Ethics and Violence* (New York: Wiley & Sons, 2010).

Thomas, Scott M., *The Global Resurgence of Religion and the Transformation of International Relations* (New York: Palgrave Macmillan, 2005).

Titelman, Peter, ed., *Clinical Applications of Bowen Family Systems Theory* (London: Routledge, 1998).

Titelman, Peter, ed., *Emotional Cutoff: Bowen Family Systems Theory Perspectives* (New York: Haworth Press, 2003).

Tracy, David, *Dialogue with the Other: The Inter-religious Dialogue* (Grand Rapids, MI: Eerdmans, 1990).

Tremlin, Todd, *Minds and Gods: The Cognitive Foundations of Religion* (Oxford: Oxford University Press, 2006).

Tweed, Thomas A., *Crossing and Dwelling: A Theory of Religion* (Cambridge, MA: Harvard University Press, 2006).

Vail, Kenneth E., III, Zachary K. Rothschild, Dave R. Weise, Sheldon Solomon, Tom Pyszczynski and Jeff Greeberg, "A terror management analysis of the psychological functions of religion" *Personality and Social Psychology Review* 14/1 (2010): 84–94.

van den Bos, Kees, Josha Buurman and Veerle de Theije, "On shielding from death as an important yet malleable motive of worldview defense: Christian versus Muslim beliefs modulating the self-threat of mortality salience" *Social Cognition* 30/6 (2012): 778–802.

van Elk, Michiel, "Paranormal believers are more prone to illusory agency detection than skeptics" *Consciousness and Cognition* 22 (2013): 1041–1046.

van Inwegen, Peter, "Explaining belief in the supernatural," 128–138 in Schloss and Murray, eds., *The Believing Primate* (Oxford: Oxford University Press, 2009).

van Slyke, James A., *The Cognitive Science of Religion* (Farnum, UK: Ashgate, 2011).

Vásquez, Manuel A., *More Than Belief: A Materialist Theory of Religion* (Oxford: Oxford University Press, 2011).

Visala, Aku, *Naturalism, Theism and the Cognitive Study of Religion* (Farnum, UK: Ashgate, 2011).

Voland, Eckhart, and Wulf Schiefenhovel, eds., *The Biological Evolution of Religious Mind and Behavior* (Heidelberg: Springer, 2009).

Wallin, David J., *Attachment in Psychotherapy* (New York: The Guilford Press, 2007).

Ward, Keith, *Images of Eternity* (Oxford: OneWorld, 1987).

Warner, Rob, *Secularization and Its Discontents* (London: Continuum, 2010).

Whitehouse, Harvey, *Arguments and Icons: Divergent Modes of Religiosity* (Oxford: Oxford University Press, 2000).

Whitehouse, Harvey, "Religious reflexivity and transmissive frequency" *Social Anthropology* 10/1 (2002): 91–103.

Whitehouse, Harvey, *Modes of Religiosity: A Cognitive Theory of Religious Transmission* (New York: AltaMira Press, 2004).

Whitehouse, Harvey, and Luther Martin, eds., *Theorizing Religions Past: Archaeology, History and Cognition* (Oxford: AltaMira Press, 2004).

Whitehouse, Harvey, and James Laidlaw, eds., *Ritual and Memory: Toward a Comparative Anthropology of Religion* (Oxford: AltaMira Press, 2004).

Whitehouse, Harvey, and Robert N. McCauley, eds., *Mind and Religion: Psychological and Cognitive Foundations of Religiosity* (Oxford: AltaMira Press, 2005).

Whitehouse, Harvey, and Ian Hodder, "Modes of religiosity at Catalhoyuk," 122–145 in Ian Hodder, ed., *Religion in the Emergence of Civilization: Catalhoyuk as a Case Study* (Cambridge: Cambridge University Press, 2010).

Wigger, J. Bradley, Katrina Paxson and Lacey Ryan, "What do invisible friends know? Imaginary companions, God, and theory of mind," *The International Journal for the Psychology of Religion* 232/1 (2012): 2–14.

Wildman, Wesley, *Science and Religious Anthropology* (Farnam, UK: Ashgate, 2009).

Wildman, Wesley, *Religious Philosophy as Multidisciplinary Comparative Inquiry* (Albany, NY: State University of New York Press, 2010).

Wildman, Wesley, *Religious and Spiritual Experiences* (Cambridge: Cambridge University Press, 2011).

Wildman, Wesley, Richard Sosis and Patrick McNamara, "The scientific study of atheism" *Religion, Brain & Behavior* 2/1 (February 2102): 1–3.

Willard, Aiyana K., and Ara Norenzayan, "Cognitive biases explain religious belief, paranormal belief, and belief in life's purpose" *Cognition* 129 (2013): 379–391.

Wilson, David Sloan, *Darwin's Cathedral* (Chicago, IL: University of Chicago Press, 2002).

Wilson, E. O., *The Social Conquest of the Earth* (New York: Norton & Norton, 2012).

Winkelman, Michael, and John R. Baker, *Supernatural as Natural: A Biocultural Approach to Religion* (Upper Saddle River, NJ: Pearson Prentice Hall, 2010).

Xygalatas, Dimitris, and William W. McCorkle Jr., eds., *Mental Culture: Classical Social Theory and the Cognitive Science of Religion* (Durham, UK: Acumen, 2013).

Yen, Chih-Long, and Chun-Yu Lin, "The effects of morality salience on escalation of commitment" *International Journal of Psychology* 47/1 (2012): 51–57.

Žižek, Slajov, *The Parallax View* (Cambridge: MIT Press, 2006).

Zuckerman, Miron, Jordan Silberman and Judith A. Hall, "The relation between intelligence and religiosity: A meta-analysis and some proposed explanations" *Personality and Social Psychology Review* 17/4 (2013): 325–354.

Zuckerman, Phil, "Atheism: Contemporary numbers and patterns" 47–65 in Michael Martin, ed., *The Cambridge Companion to Atheism* (Cambridge: Cambridge University Press, 2007).

Zuckerman, Phil, *Society without God: What the Least Religious Nations Can Tell Us about Contentment* (New York: New York University Press, 2008).

Zuckerman, Phil, ed., *Atheism and Secularity*, 2 volumes (Santa Barbara, CA: Praeger, 2010).

Zuckerman, Phil, *Faith No More: Why People Reject Religion* (Oxford: Oxford University Press, 2012).

Index

CPI Antony Rowe
Chippenham, UK
2016-12-27 18:46